The New Testament

The New Testament

An Analytical Approach

Stevan L. Davies

POLEBRIDGE PRESS
Salem, Oregon

Copyright © 2011 by Stevan L. Davies

All rights reserved. Printed in the United States of America. No part of this book may be used or reproduced in any manner whatsoever without written permission except in the case of brief quotations embodied in critical articles and reviews. For information address Polebridge Press, Willamette University, 900 State Street, Salem, OR 97301.

Previously published as *New Testament Fundamentals,* Polebridge Press, 1992.

Cover and interior design by Robaire Ream
Cover art inspired by the Book of Kells

Library of Congress Cataloging-in-Publication Data
Davies, Stevan L., 1948-
The New Testament : an analytical approach / Stevan L. Davies.
   p. cm.
Rev. ed. of: New Testament fundamentals.
Includes bibliographical references and index.
ISBN 978-1-59815-036-0 (alk. paper)
1. Bible. N.T.--Introductions. 2. Bible. N.T.--Textbooks. I. Davies, Stevan L., 1948- New Testament fundamentals. II. Title.
BS2330.3.D38 2011
225.6'1--dc23
                                                                    2011031157

Table of Contents

Chapter 1: Introduction 1

Chapter 2: Judaism and the Roman Empire 19

Chapter 3: Paul's Letters 55

Chapter 4: Gospel Sources 101

Chapter 5: The Gospel of Mark 147

Chapter 6: The Gospel of Matthew 189

Chapter 7: The Gospel of Luke and the
          Acts of the Apostles 231

Chapter 8: The Gospel of John 277

Chapter 9: Apostolic Letters and the
          Revelation to John 315

Analytical Assessment: Tasks and Exercises 357

Appendix: The Gospel of Thomas 367

Index 375

CHAPTER 1

Introduction

OBJECTIVES
- Establish a basic overview of the components of the Bible
- Learn how scholars read the NT *analytically*. i.e. to answer the question, "What happened?" before considering the question, "Is it true?"
- Become acquainted with the tools & resources available for analytical study

Basic Information

All Christian churches use a collection of short books called the Bible as the foundation of their teaching. They believe that the Bible contains revelation from God and may be relied upon as a guide to moral and theological truths. Commonly, in Christian church services, passages from the Bible are read aloud, and the minister of the church delivers a commentary called a sermon, or homily, about the passages. The purpose of a sermon is to point out ways the passages might beneficially be applied to everyday life. The Bible as used in churches is, therefore, not just a collection of written texts but a resource for religious instruction.

The Bible is divided by Christians into two parts. The first part is commonly called the Old Testament and the last part, the New Testament. Each part is made up of separate texts called *books*. The New Testament is written in Greek and is made up of twenty-seven such books. The Old Testament is written in Hebrew; Protestant churches recognize thirty-nine Old Testament books, while the Roman Catholic Church recognizes forty-six. The books about which there is disagreement are called, by Protestants, the *Apocrypha*. Catholics call those books Deutero-Canonical. Protestants recognize the

Apocrypha as historically important although not divinely inspired. Jewish people regard the Old Testament as revelation and use it in their services (particularly the first five books, the Torah); they do not recognize the New Testament as revelation. The term Old Testament can be offensive to Jewish people because it implies the revelations they value are secondary in importance to "new" revelations not contained in their Scriptures. Therefore, in scholarly writing, the term *Hebrew Bible* is now being used as a synonym for Old Testament, as it is used in this textbook.

The Hebrew Bible is important to the New Testament; the authors of the New Testament referenced it repeatedly. They quoted passages from it, constructed arguments based on it, believed they were writing about matters implied in it. They did this because they, like Christian and Jewish people now, believed it to be revelation from God. Throughout this textbook, therefore, we will refer to passages in the Hebrew Bible, and you will be asked to do exercises comparing passages from the Hebrew Bible quoted in the New Testament with the passages as they appear in the Hebrew Bible itself.

The twenty-seven New Testament books can be put into several categories. There are four gospels: Matthew, Mark, Luke, and John. Gospels are accounts of the life of Jesus of Nazareth written in biographical form. The four gospels that appear in the New Testament contain sayings attributed to Jesus, stories of miracles he is said to have performed, a general narrative of his life story at least from the time of his baptism to the time of his burial, and extensive narrative about the last few days of his life. The gospels appear to be biographies, but they are not historical biographies in the twentieth-century sense; they are primarily intended to convey information about the religious meaning and theological significance of Jesus' life. To approach them as books of simple factual history is to miss their authors' intentions entirely.

Three of the gospels—Matthew, Mark and Luke—are very similar in outline and contents, and are sometimes word-for-word identical in Greek; the Gospel of John is quite different.

The Acts of the Apostles (or, Acts) follows the four gospels. Its placement is unfortunate, for it was written by the author of the Gospel of Luke and is a continuation of that gospel. Separated by the Gospel of John, Luke and Acts falsely appear to be two entirely different books. Acts tells of the activities of Jesus' disciples after his crucifixion, focusing first on his disciple Peter and later on Paul. Acts serves as both a history of the early church and a theological interpretation of that history.

After the four gospels and Acts come a series of letters (or, Epistles) attributed to Paul, mainly in order of length, and then a series of short letters attributed to other important figures of the early Christian movement: James, Peter, John, and Jude. Several of them are real letters while others, such as Hebrews and 1 John, are more like essays or sermons.

The last book of the New Testament is Revelation. It is an account of visions seen by a man named John. This is almost certainly not the same man who wrote the Gospel of John or the Letters of John. The visions in Revelation purport to reveal what will happen in the time just before the end of this world and its replacement by the Kingdom of God.

The twenty-seven books of the New Testament are, therefore, of various literary types: interpretive biographies (the gospels), an interpretive history (Acts), letters, essays (Hebrews, 1 John), and a visionary account (Revelation).

Learning the Story

Throughout this book I shall be making recommendations for reading the New Testament. My first recommendation is this: if you want to get a feel for the subject by learning the basic stories and becoming acquainted with the fundamental ideas they contain, read the Gospel of Luke and the Acts of the Apostles. Luke intended to write an interesting and exciting narrative, not a document to be studied line by line, phrase by phrase, so try to read this two-part book straight through from beginning to end. If you feel at a loss concerning the New Testament, if you are not a Christian, or if you are a Christian but do not feel very knowledgeable, then this will enable you to catch up in knowledge of the basic New Testament stories with all but the most well-educated Christian people.

Analytical Study of the New Testament

Analytical study (or, critical study) of the New Testament requires you to adopt a certain kind of approach to the New Testament, one that may be new to you. It does not need to be your only kind of approach; people are quite capable of understanding the same texts from different perspectives. The New Testament may be understood at the same time from a church perspective and an analytical perspective. One must think in different ways in different contexts and circumstances. This textbook is not intended to defend an analytical perspective against a church perspective; it is intended to make the analytical perspective clear so it will be available to any person wishing to use it.

The New Testament as a single entity does not exist. Some believe the New Testament is a single book with various chapters containing essentially the same information. Analytical scholars, on the other hand, regard the New Testament as a collection of diverse letters and pamphlets bound together within a single cover. Looked at in this way, the New Testament is more of a library than a book; therefore, it makes as little sense to ask, for example, "What does the New Testament teach about the Law of Moses?" as to ask "What does the library teach about philosophy?" Each book on the subject in the library will approach philosophy somewhat differently. In the same way, each author in the New Testament approaches the Law of Moses somewhat differently. To study the New Testament is to study a collection of different works by different people who hold different views. There are no hard and fast conclusions from analytical study that say, "This is what the New Testament teaches about X." At best we can conclude, "This is what Matthew or Paul or John teaches about X."

Analytical study of the New Testament is not the study of Jesus. It is, rather, the study of diverse teachings about Jesus: what Matthew taught about Jesus, what Mark taught about Jesus, what Luke taught about Jesus, and so forth. The New Testament records only indirectly what Jesus himself taught. It is quite difficult to distinguish the teachings *about* Jesus from his own teachings, as you shall see as you read this book. While it is not impossible to isolate Jesus' own teachings from the gospel accounts, it is still a highly uncertain endeavor, and no scholarly consensus exists as to what exactly he taught.

The study of the collection of documents called the New Testament focuses on individual documents. Several items in the bibliography found at the end of this chapter discuss the question of Jesus' teachings in considerable detail.

Analytical Study and Christian Theology

Analytical study does not prove or attempt to prove that the New Testament is divinely inspired. Neither does it prove or attempt to prove that the New Testament is *not* divinely inspired. It is neutral. Analytical study is, in great part, the study of the processes through which the New Testament came into being. Analytical study can therefore be said to reveal how revelation came into being; as such, it is a valuable tool for theology.

Analytical scholars are occasionally accused of denying the inspiration of the Scriptures. This misconception places an unnecessary stumbling block in the way of some people. Because this stumbling block can be a serious one, we address it in some detail below.

Some Christians suspect those who use the analytical perspective of failing to approach the New Testament from the perspective of faith. Some may not approach it from the perspective of faith. Some may. But from either point of view, if the New Testament was brought into being through divine inspiration, it is analytical scholarship that seeks to learn how divine inspiration occurred. If the teachings of the New Testament authors contain divine revelation, it is analytical scholarship that seeks to discover clearly and distinctly those teachings in all their diversity. If the New Testament is to be understood on its own basis, within its own context, it is analytical scholarship that seeks most earnestly not to impose contemporary ideas of morality or philosophy or theology on those ancient texts.

The idea of divine inspiration leads logically to the conclusion that the documents of the New Testament teach the truth. It does not, however, lead logically to the conclusion that they teach a particular sort of truth. Therein lies the problem. What sort of truth is in the New Testament? Analytical scholars agree only that the documents of the New Testament express what people of faith in the first century believed to be the truth.

The New Testament books are diverse; differences of opinion are common; different and even contradictory reports of the same event are found; not all the historical statements made are historically accurate; words of people other than Jesus are attributed to Jesus. All these things disturb Christians who presume divine inspiration would not have brought a diverse and sometimes contradictory New Testament into being.

Divine inspiration proceeds as God wished it to proceed. That seems to be an obvious statement, but it has strong implications for the value of analytical study. One should not declare in advance that God dictated revelation directly or that God used eyewitness disciples to write the New Testament. The New Testament texts themselves say nothing of the sort. One must, rather, seek to discover what happened, and, if it turns out to be the case that complex processes of oral tradition, source revision, and personal commentary combined to produce, say, Matthew's gospel, then that was the way God intended it to be. What happened was what God intended to happen; that is the underlying thesis of the idea of divine inspiration. The quest to find out what happened can unify theologians of revelation and analytical scholars.

If a Christian wishes to know what sort of revelation God would bring about, he or she must turn to the New Testament and find out; it is as simple as that. He or she should not decide in advance what kind of revelation God would bring about and then require the New Testament to be in accord with that decision. Some people do this, declaring God would never allow a misstatement of historical fact to occur in inspired books, or that God would never allow contradictions to occur. Such people apply human standards to God; rather than wishing to know what sort of revelation God brought into being, they insist God must have brought into being the kind of revelation they expect. It is almost as if they say, "If I were God this is what I would do," and then react with indignation when they learn God chose to do things another way.

Nearly all denominations of the Protestant and Catholic branches of the Christian church encourage the reading of the New Testament by faithful people. Those who read it are urged to learn from it, find guidance within it, and draw conclusions about God and the Son of God based on it. Nearly all denominations insist freedom of conscience should exist and that the understanding one person achieves cannot be identical to the understanding of another. People of faith may differ, do differ, in what they believe to be the truth about Jesus and his teaching.

Analytical scholarship denies none of this and applies the same principle to the authors of the New Testament. Those authors, too, drew conclusions based on what they knew. Being human, they reached different understandings; divine inspiration is never thought to cancel out the humanity of the inspired authors.

Christians wish the New Testament to be made relevant to contemporary life and for its teachings to be made useful for modern spiritual life. That is not the job of analytical scholarship; that is the job of church ministers. Scholars, as best they possibly can, try to confine their attention to what the texts meant to those who wrote them in the context of their own times and situations. While the analytical study of the New Testament is not based on the assumption the New Testament is divinely inspired, it does not in any way contradict that assumption. Its goal is to understand what the New Testament authors meant to communicate, which is the same exact goal that theologians of the Christian faiths have when they study the New Testament.

The people of faith who wrote the New Testament texts differed in what they believed to be the truth about Jesus and his teachings. The idea of divine inspiration does not logically require them all to understand matters in the same way. Rather, it affirms that divine truth exists in all the various answers they achieved. The idea of truth in diversity is quite acceptable to theology. It underlies the concept of freedom of conscience. What is dubious from a theological perspective is the idea that while Christians today may reach different conclusions, the inspired writers of the New Testament necessarily had to achieve identical conclusions.

"The Lord works in mysterious ways" and only the very arrogant will declare they know how God arranges revelation before they have studied it in all of its diversity. If the New Testament is divinely inspired, as we study it we learn about divine inspiration. If it is not divinely inspired, the New Testament we study still is the most important collection of documents in the history of the Western world.

Outlining New Testament History

The results of modern scholarly investigations are, by and large, in accord with the statements found at the opening of the Gospel of Luke. It is useful, therefore, to use Luke's account in introducing the scholarly approach. In Luke 1:1–4, Luke gives a short account of his method of writing and the sources he used. For readers unfamiliar with how to reference passages in the Bible, please note that citations such as "Luke 1:1–4," are the standard format used by scholars. Luke is the name of the book; 1:1–4 refers to chapter 1 of Luke, verses 1 through 4. A citation reading Galatians 3:2–4, 6 would refer to Paul's letter to the Galatians, chapter 3, verses 2 through 4, and then also verse 6.

Luke's account is, in effect, a brief summary of New Testament history prior to the writing of Luke's gospel. Two translations follow, the first from the New English Bible, the second from the New American Standard Bible:

1. The author to Theophilus: Many writers have undertaken to draw up an account of the events that have happened among us, following the traditions handed down to us by

the original eyewitnesses and servants of the Gospel. And so I in my turn, your Excellency, as one who has gone over the whole course of these events in detail, have decided to write a connected narrative for you, so as to give you authentic knowledge abut the matters of which you have been informed.

2. Inasmuch as many have undertaken to compile an account of the things accomplished among us, just as those who from the beginning were eyewitnesses and servants of the word have handed them down to us, it seemed fitting for me as well, having investigated everything carefully from the beginning, to write it out for you in consecutive order, most excellent Theophilus; so that you might know the exact truth about the things you have been taught.

The Theophilus to whom Luke addresses this letter has a Greek name meaning "lover of God." This probably was the name of an individual, but it could have been a term for any lover of God.

Jesus of Nazareth

The presupposition of Luke's book, as for all New Testament books, is Jesus of Nazareth. Jesus lived, did certain things, and said certain things. A very few of those things were eventually written down. Somehow, some of Jesus' words spoken in the Aramaic language around 30 CE appear in different form in the Greek language about sixty years later in the Gospel of Luke. The process of transmission took place in several stages. Note, incidentally, that I have written CE, meaning "Common Era," rather than AD, meaning *Anno Domini,* "year of our Lord." I will also use BCE, meaning "Before the Common Era," rather than "BC," for "Before Christ." These relatively new abbreviations are becoming standard in scholarship, replacing the earlier church-oriented abbreviations.

Eyewitnesses

Luke mentions eyewitnesses. These people included Jesus' disciples. Like Jesus they spoke Aramaic and most of them were from Galilee. They remembered the sayings they found most important as best they could and repeated them to others. The process of remembering and then repeating what one hears is called *oral tradition,* which is a somewhat technical term for the process of word-of-mouth transmission. A game almost everyone has played involves one person whispering a sentence into the ear of a second; the second then repeats it to a third, the third to a fourth; and after several more repetitions the final person speaks aloud. What the first person said and what the final person says are usually different. In the same way, such changes take place in oral traditions, although the initial saying and the final version are usually recognizably similar. Still, changes take place. Long stories will be made shorter; short sayings may be expanded; details will be altered, especially such seemingly insignificant details as the names of towns and people; explanations will be added to puzzling stories or sayings.

Of the hundreds of thousands of things Jesus said during his life, only a hundred or so sayings remain. Jesus did not decree what people should remember from what he said; the people who heard him made those decisions. This process of choice (what was remembered, what was forgotten) is also part of oral tradition.

Servants of the Gospel

Luke mentions "servants of the gospel," or "servants of the word." The word "gospel" in Greek is *evangelion,* which means "good news." In the New Testament, the "gospel" usually refers to the good news about Jesus. The specific use of "gospel" to mean a biographical book about Jesus came into being after the New Testament period (ca. 30–120 CE).

Servants of the gospel were not eyewitnesses. What they heard came to them second-hand or third-hand or fourth. By Luke's time there were thousands of Christians throughout the Mediterranean world speaking a wide variety of languages.

The most common language throughout the ancient Mediterranean world, the one most often used for business and literary purposes, was Greek. At some point early in the process of oral transmission, some servants of the gospel began to repeat Jesus' sayings in Greek rather than in his own language, Aramaic. This was an enormous change. Not only are Greek and Aramaic different languages, they also originate from entirely different linguistic families. Greek—like Latin, Iranian, Spanish, Sanskrit, and English—is from the Indo-European family of languages; Aramaic—like Syriac, Hebrew, and Arabic—is from the Semitic family of languages. Greek is much closer to English than it is to Aramaic. The Greek language carries the customs and styles of thought found in the philosophy and culture of Greece; Aramaic carries the customs and styles of thought found in the philosophy and culture of Judaism.

It might be argued that the shift from Aramaic oral tradition to Greek oral tradition was the most important conceptual change to take place in the history of the Christian movement. Alas, we have no Aramaic records at all from the first century of Christianity. None. Some scholars make intelligent guesses about the Aramaic originals of the Greek sayings of Jesus, but these remain guesses and are impossible to verify.

Recent archaeological excavations in the city of Sepphoris, which is within easy walking distance of Nazareth, indicate that Sepphoris was a populous growing metropolis and that most of its inhabitants spoke Greek. A local village carpenter almost certainly would have found work there. Accordingly, it is entirely possible that Jesus could speak some Greek as a second language; however, in his speech to peasant Galileans and Judeans he would have used Aramaic, so it remains highly unlikely that the sayings we have of his were originally in Greek.

Connected Narrative

Eyewitnesses retold Jesus' Aramaic sayings to other Aramaic-speaking people, who then told them to people who spoke Greek, who in turn told the sayings in Greek to other Greek-speaking people, some of whom became servants of the gospel. The next logical step would be for someone to begin writing down Jesus' sayings and stories about him. Luke perhaps hints at this stage of development when he states that he will write a "connected narrative" or a narrative "in consecutive order." This implies that before Luke wrote his gospel, there existed written accounts that were disconnected and not in consecutive order. Scholars do believe such accounts existed. In fact, two kinds of disconnected accounts existed. We know that there were lists of some of Jesus' sayings, and lists of some of the miracles attributed to him. Neither kind of list was biographical in the sense of presenting a life story of Jesus or of putting the sayings and miracle stories into a narrative context. Rather, the sayings and miracle stories were written down one after the other and ordered, if at all, by topics.

Although we do not have in our possession ancient copies of the lists of sayings and miracle stories used by the authors of the New Testament, scholars believe these can be recovered by analysis of New Testament documents (see chapter 4, "Gospel Sources"). In 1945, a list of sayings attributed to Jesus was found buried in the desert of Egypt. Called the Gospel of Thomas, it contains many ancient and valuable versions of sayings of Jesus found in the New Testament.

It also includes some sayings that are not found elsewhere, and still other sayings that are attributed to Jesus but which he did not say. The discovery of the Gospel of Thomas has great importance for many reasons, not least of which is that it confirms the existence of disconnected lists, which scholars believe were used in the writing of the New Testament. The Gospel of Thomas presents, through its selection and creation of sayings, the perspective that the Kingdom of God is already present on the earth and people should seek it and find it. Jesus is portrayed as the Wisdom of God on the earth and in heaven. While the Gospel of Thomas does not share specific sayings with the Gospel of John, its perspective is more similar to John's than to any other New Testament text. You will find a brief introduction and discussion of the Gospel of Thomas at the end of this textbook.

Many Writers

"Many writers have undertaken to draw up an account of the events that have happened among us," Luke next writes. This statement points to a fact many people overlook: while the New Testament is a valuable source of information about first-century Christianity and especially about the life of Jesus, for every text it contains, many more have been lost forever. Although he knows the accounts of other previous writers, Luke would not feel the need to provide "Theophilus" with "authentic knowledge" or "the exact truth" unless he found the work of those previous writers to have been inadequate or not authentic enough. Luke carefully took one text, one gospel by one of the writers who preceded him, and rewrote it by eliminating portions, supplementing it substantially, and revising passages that he felt did not adequately convey the truth about Jesus. The text he revised is known to us today as the Gospel of Mark; the text he created is the Gospel of Luke.

The process by which Luke's gospel came into being is similar to the process by which other gospels came into being. While the final author of a gospel should have credit for it, in a broader sense every gospel is the product of many people over many years who worked to choose, remember, refine, revise, translate, collect, interpret, and write down the teachings of and the teachings about Jesus.

The Names of the Gospels

Many people who are beginning to study the New Testament are astonished to discover that Matthew, Mark, Luke, and John had never met Jesus and that Luke, author of Acts, had probably never met Paul. Some people have spent substantial time and effort seeking to prove that the author of the Gospel of John was Jesus' "beloved disciple," that Luke was a physician who traveled with Paul, that Mark was a secretary to Peter, or that Matthew was a disciple of Jesus. But they are forced to base their theories on unreliable data from the second and third centuries, or even later. It is important to realize that nowhere in their gospels do Matthew or Mark or Luke or John claim to have known or traveled with Jesus. Nowhere does Luke claim to have known Paul. Only John appeals to eyewitness testimony, and he does so only to validate specific events mentioned at the very end of his gospel. The idea that the gospel writers were companions of Jesus is common today, but it is an idea found nowhere in the New Testament.

Basic Tools for Research

There are several basic reference tools available for the study of the New Testament. The best way to become familiar with these tools is to select a passage from the New Testament, go to the library, and—using the following kinds of reference books—write a commentary on that passage:

1. *Textbooks on the New Testament.* While generally agreeing on major themes, each textbook will approach the New Testament differently and will help you understand each of the separate New Testament books in a somewhat different way.

2. *Commentaries on the New Testament or on specific books of the New Testament.* These are quite specific studies of texts and usually will comment on and attempt to explain virtually every significant passage, if not every verse, in a given text. Some commentaries seek to take the historical or analytical approach to the New Testament, but many are written from specific denominational standpoints. In using a commentary, you should try to determine the general approach of its author rather than simply to rely upon the author's expertise.

3. *Interlinear translations of the New Testament.* These books take the Greek text and, on every other line, write the equivalent of each Greek word in English. If you become somewhat familiar with the Greek alphabet (which is often given at the beginning of interlinear translations), you will be able to follow the original Greek version more easily than you might think.

4. *Bible dictionaries and encyclopedias.* Each of these provides detailed information about themes, names, places, and so forth. They usually do not have entries for particular verses.

5. *Concordances.* A concordance is a book locating each word in either the whole Bible or the New Testament. They list the passages in which that word occurs, usually with a sentence or a half sentence from those pas-

sages so the reader can see the word's context. The best of them use the original Greek words rather than the words of particular English translations. Sometimes in concordances Greek words are alphabetized by their most common English language equivalents for the convenience of people who haven't studied Greek.

6. *Gospel parallels.* These fascinating scholarly tools are books that place similar passages from different New Testament sources adjacent to one another so that they can be compared easily (see chapter 6, "The Gospel of Matthew"). Using gospel parallels, a reader can see how Matthew and Mark and Luke varied in their construction of similar events and sayings.

End-of-Chapter Exercises

1. What is meant by the term analytical study? In particular, why doesn't an analytical scholar attempt to prove or disprove theological claims?
2. Where have you learned about the Bible prior to reading this book (e.g. church, media, family)? List some advantages and disadvantages of learning from those sources.
3. Much of Christian history was initially maintained in oral traditions. Does your family have any oral traditions (e.g. ancestors' emigration to the United States, wartime experiences, birth of a child)? Describe one from memory. Do you tell it in the same way another family member would? Suggest reasons for any differences.
4. Look at the list of "Basic Tools for Research" on pages 15–17. If you can, go to a library and look at as many of these different tools as possible. Predict some of the different ways you can use these tools to analyze NT texts.

Bibliography

Achtemeier, Paul. *Inspiration and Authority: Nature and Function of Christian Scripture.* Peabody MA: Hendrickson, 1999.

Bock, Darrel, and Buist Fanning. *Interpreting the New Testament Text: An Introduction to the Art and Science of Exegesis.* Wheaton IL: Crossway Books, 2006.

Dunn, J. D. G. *Unity and Diversity in the New Testament.* Philadelphia: Westminster Press, 1977.

Farmer, William R. *Jesus and the Gospel: Tradition, Scripture, and Canon.* Philadelphia: Fortress Press, 1982.

Hann, Robert. *The Bible: A User's Manual.* New York: Paulist Press, 1983.

Hengel, Martin. *The Son of God: The Origin of Christology and the History of Jewish Hellenistic Religion.* Philadelphia: Fortress Press, 1976.

Koester, Helmut. *Introduction to the New Testament.* 2 volumes. Philadelphia: Fortress Press, 1981.

Lohse, Eduard. *The First Christians.* Philadelphia: Fortress Press, 1983.

Miller, Robert. *The Jesus Seminar and Its Critics.* Salem OR: Polebridge Press, 1999.

Osborne, Grant R., and Scot McKnight. *The Face of New Testament Studies: A Survey of Recent Research.* Grand Rapids MI: Baker Academic, 2004.

Robinson, James M., and Helmut Koester. *Trajectories Through Early Christianity.* Philadelphia: Fortress Press, 1971.

Seeley, David. *Deconstructing the New Testament.* Leiden: Brill, 1994.

CHAPTER 2

Judaism and the Roman Empire

OBJECTIVES
- Understand the influence of the Roman Empire and Judaism on the people & events of the NT
- Survey other religions that coexisted with early Christianity and reasons why many gentiles (non-Jews) were eager to adopt the new Christian religion

READ MARK 12:1–44. MAKE A LIST OF EVERY SOCIAL GROUP AND ORGANIZATION MENTIONED OR IMPLIED BEFORE YOU READ THE FOLLOWING PAGES. Doing so will help you realize the relevance of historical knowledge to the interpretation of gospel passages.

Think for a moment about certain obvious facts. The books of the New Testament were written nearly two thousand years ago. Jesus lived and spoke in response to and in reference to the social, economic, religious, and political structures of his own time. These structures were different from those existing today. To understand the New Testament one must therefore understand something of the structures of that ancient time.

People beginning to read the New Testament analytically do not need to know everything about, say, the Pharisees and Sadducees. But certainly when such groups are mentioned, as they frequently are in the gospels, people should have some basic knowledge of their status and their ideas. In the following pages we will discuss particularly the groups and institutions mentioned in Mark 12, for nearly all the most important groups and institutions are mentioned or implied there.

The Roman Empire

Mark 12:13–17 mentions the *Caesar*, the title of the Roman emperor. For much of Jesus' life, the Caesar was Tiberius, who ruled from 14 CE to 37 CE. As an individual the emperor of Rome plays little part in the New Testament, but the empire over which he presided is of great importance. Every person who wrote about or took part in the events narrated in the New Testament lived in the same realm—the Roman Empire. We will consider it first and then turn our attention in more detail to Judaism, a crucial factor for every aspect of the New Testament.

Although Rome had been expanding its territory for several centuries, the birth of the Roman Empire as a fully grown and administratively coherent unit can be dated to the year 27 BCE. In that year the reign of Octavius Augustus Caesar began, a reign that was to continue for the next forty-one years. Augustus Caesar was one of those rare political geniuses capable both of conquering territory and of administering it well. As a result the empire established by Augustus lasted for centuries. During the New Testament period, it was a new empire, and that fact is quite important.

The Roman Empire was not just one more empire, one more conquest of territory; the Roman Empire brought unity to an enormous region containing many different civilizations. By the time Augustus died, the Roman Empire included the areas now occupied by the Netherlands, Spain, France, Belgium, Switzerland, Austria, Italy, the Balkans, Bulgaria, Romania, Greece, Turkey, Syria, Albania, Morocco, Portugal, Lebanon, Israel, Cyprus, Jordan, Egypt, Libya, Tunisia, and Algeria. For decades after the death of Augustus, it expanded, encountering only one opponent capable of holding its own ground—the Parthian Empire in the region now known as Iran. The Roman Empire maintained order through the mixed techniques of warfare, administration, and political control. Apart from occasional border skirmishes, the great majority of the empire's populace lived in peace.

It may be convenient to think of the time before the empire as a time of tribalism. The people of Gaul, Syria, Palestine, Greece, Carthage, and Rome differed in their codes of law, their religions, their languages, their systems of coinage (if any), and the weights and measures they used for commercial purposes. Commerce was difficult in a tribal environment and dangerous in the absence of peace. How many languages must a trader know to sell goods in several regions? How many kinds of coins must a trader carry, how many kinds of law must be obeyed? Who would provide assistance in times of difficulty far from home and family?

During the empire "detribalization" and "urbanization" proceeded at a rapid rate. Ancient local systems of law were terminated in some areas, replaced with Roman law. The Latin language became the language for legal and administrative matters; the Greek language became the language for trade and literature. Roman coins were the legal tender throughout the empire, replacing local coinage. Weights and measures were standardized. Roman engineers built a system of roads and aqueducts throughout the empire, constructing them so skillfully that well-preserved remnants still exist today in many areas of Europe. The government made sustained efforts to eliminate piracy and banditry. A primitive social welfare system was established in Rome and in some other areas. The Roman network of roads allowed authors such as Paul to send letters regularly over hundreds of miles. In the Acts of the Apostles we read that the journeys of the apostles, who were Christian missionaries of the first century, took place easily and relatively safely.

The coming into being of the empire led to the rapid decline of earlier social forms. Widespread travel for purposes of trade (or military service) exposed people to many new influences and new ideas. Truths that seemed certain because one's whole family, whole village, or whole tribe agreed seemed less certain hundreds of miles from home in the environs of a different culture with different assumptions. Old tribal laws gave way to new laws, usually Roman; old forms of social organization supported for centuries by custom began to die out in many regions. Many people moved to cities. The empire's great cities were very pluralistic; their inhabitants had to come to grips with changed circumstances while still retaining aspects of their ancestral cultures.

If you imagine Cuba, Mexico, Columbia, Canada, Brazil, Central America and the United States suddenly became one country under Brazilian law, using Brazilian coinage, administered by Brazilian civil and military authority, establishing Portuguese as the official language, and removing the trade or travel barriers that previously existed between those countries, you may gather some idea of the sort of disorientation that could affect people in the new empire. And yet, despite complaints about heavy taxation, most people were not opposed to the empire. The alternative, they knew, would be a nearly constant state of tribal warfare.

Indeed, the empire brought peace to most and prosperity to many. Stories of the persecution of Christians have led many today to believe the early Christian church and the New Testament texts it produced were opposed to the empire. That is not the case. The four gospels and the letters of Paul were written by people who supported the authority of the empire, eager to explain as best they could that Christians were loyal inhabitants willing to pay taxes and obey authority. Paul was a Roman citizen, a status few Jewish people held, and he was proud of that status.

Like all conquering powers, the Romans imposed taxes on the inhabitants of their empire. Those who had to pay them resented the obligation, especially in areas such as Palestine where many people desired political independence. Palestine, because of the religious nationalism sustaining its Jewish culture and people, was probably the single most rebellious province in the whole empire.

The question asked of Jesus in Mark 12:14–17, "Are we or are we not permitted to pay taxes to the Roman Emperor?" is a clever one, for it is directed at a teacher whose strongest backing came from the people least willing or able to pay such taxes, the peasantry. Jesus' answer, however, is unambiguous: Yes. "Pay Caesar what is due to Caesar." This answer, along with the stories of Jesus dining with and befriending tax collectors, intends to show he was not interested in politically revolutionary activity. The second clause in his answer, "and pay God what is due to God," in the context of a question about taxes, means Jesus also expected his followers to pay the temple taxes required under Jewish law. Such taxes were a religious obligation as well as a civil obligation.

The Jewish People

Mark 12:28–33. This passage in Mark contains the "shema," the single sentence in the Jewish religion that can be said to be a Jewish creed: "Hear O Israel, the Lord our God, the Lord is One." This sentence, and most of the remainder of this short gospel passage, is a fine summary of Judaism, just as Jesus and the rabbi with whom he speaks say they are. And yet, in verse 12:33, we hear something subversive, a denigration of sacrificial animal offerings. The Judaism of Jesus' day, and that of the thousand years previous to it, was focused on the Jerusalem temple where priests daily, and on festival occasions, made animal sacrifices to God as the Torah commanded. The idea that there might be something wrong with this practice, or that it might be somehow inferior to ordinary piety and moral behavior, would have been an unusual idea among the Jews of Jesus' time.

The religion of Judaism is not so much a collection of doctrines and practices as it is a community of people. To be born Jewish is to be Jewish, and then, as now, Jewish people differed on what exactly they understood the requirements of their religion to be. All agreed on the cardinal principal that there is but one true God. The name of God is *Yahweh*, but because the name of God is considered holy, it became customary to refer to God indirectly as *Lord* (*Adonai* in Hebrew, *Kyrios* in Greek). This word was also used, as Lord is in England, to refer to men in leadership positions.

The Lord was believed to have established a covenant with his Jewish people, one dating back to the time of Abraham. A *covenant* is a contractual relationship between two parties: in this case, the Lord and the Jewish people. Their covenant was believed to establish a special relationship. God would protect, increase and discipline the people and provide for them the land of Palestine (the "promised land"); the Jewish people would worship God and be obedient to his commandments.

The principal form of Jewish worship at the time of Jesus took place in Jerusalem at the temple and took the form of the sacrifice of animals and other agricultural produce. This worship was administered by priests who were members of a certain caste, the tribe of Levi, led by men who were descendants of Aaron. No other men in theory were permitted to be priests, and no sacrificial worship was permitted outside of the Jerusalem temple; Judaism was a centralized religion.

The sacrificial form of Jewish religion ended abruptly in the year 70 CE, when the Jerusalem temple was destroyed by soldiers under Roman general Titus. Such sacrificial activities have never occurred again, but during Jesus' time—and for the first generation of the Christian movement after Jesus—the Jerusalem temple continued to be the heart and soul of the Jewish religion. When we hear about Jesus preparing for and presiding over the Passover meal, which came to be called the *Lord's Supper*, or *Communion*, on the day before his crucifixion, his participation in that meal presupposes his attendance at and participation in the ceremonies of Passover sacrifice at the Jerusalem temple.

Mark 12:1–12. This passage tells the story of a clash between a landlord and tenant farmers. The landlord leaves his land to be farmed by people who would receive some of the produce and provide the rest as rent to the landlord. The landlord sends agents to collect the produce due him; the tenants refuse to provide it and attack the agents. This is no imaginary scenario; it reveals something of the real nature of the Palestinian economy in the early first century. Much land, perhaps most of the prime agricultural land, was owned by absentee landlords who did not work the land or live on it but who lived comfortably in major cities. Such landlords ruled over the majority of the Jewish people in Jesus' time. Modern legend has it that nearly all Jews lived in Palestine until driven out by force; in fact, by the beginning of the first century a great many Jews had chosen to live outside Palestine. Major cities such as Alexandria, Egypt; Antioch, Syria; and Rome, Italy, had substantial Jewish minorities. Usually these minorities lived under Jewish Law while the remainder of the city population lived under Roman law or their own customary law. There was frequent conflict between the two segments of the population. Such conflict may have been acceptable to Rome, as it was in Rome's interest to have subject populations fighting among themselves rather than rebelling against the empire.

Jewish traders, merchants, and artisans lived and worked throughout the empire. In every city of moderate size Jewish communities existed. There were Jewish farmers in many regions. As far as we know, most remained loyal to their traditional religion and tried, casually, to keep Jewish Law, paying a small tax to the priesthood for the upkeep of the Jerusalem temple. They felt themselves at home in whatever region they lived. No evidence exists that Jews outside of Palestine desired to settle in Palestine. Jews living outside Palestine were often strongly influenced by the culture surrounding them and were therefore regarded by the Palestinian Jewish leadership with some suspicion.

Jesus' audiences were composed primarily of people in the same social class as the tenant farmers. Poor agricultural workers, shepherds, builders, fishermen, were looked down on as crude, illiterate, ignorant, and (literally) unwashed by the wealthy and educated classes. Tensions between tenant farmers and landlords are easily understandable; those who did all the work and who still lived in poverty resented their legal obligation to provide much of what they produced to the wealthy landowner. They also resented their obligation under Jewish law to tithe, which required them to pay 10 percent of their produce to the priests of the temple in Jerusalem. Their adherence to the stricter requirements of Judaism was seriously doubted by religious leaders, and with good reason: despite the law, tenant farmers especially and small farmers generally tried to avoid tithing. Their untithed food, therefore, was technically "impure,", and strict adherents of Torah Law would not eat it. On top of all this, the farmers had to pay taxes to Rome. One famous saying of Jesus comments on these bleak economic conditions: "The man who has will always be given more; but the man who has not will forfeit even what he has" (Luke 19:26). In more prosaic terms: the rich get richer and the poor get poorer.

Jesus appears to have spoken to the peasants and identified with them; when he spoke to the rich it was usually to tell them to cease being rich and give their wealth to the poor. The poor were Jesus' main supporters. Mark 12:12 indicates Jesus' more wealthy opponents were "afraid of the people" and therefore unwilling to arrest him publicly.

Mark 12:18–25 raises the question of what is or is not allowed in Law. In fact, chapter 12 repeatedly raises questions of Law, both religious and secular. Anyone who wishes to understand the New Testament must understand the role of Law in first-century Judaism. Notice that the word "Law" is capitalized here as a reminder that Jewish Law was not thought to come from courts, congress, or legal officials; Jewish Law was thought to come directly from God. The Law was said to have been given to Moses on Mount Sinai and to have been written down in the Torah, which are the first five books of the Hebrew Scriptures: Genesis, Exodus, Leviticus, Numbers, and Deuteronomy. These five "books of Moses" collectively are called *Torah*, or *Pentateuch*; the word "Torah" means both the books themselves (including the stories contained within them) and the Law contained within the books. We shall often use the term Torah Law rather than Jewish Law, to emphasize that from the Jewish perspective their Law did not come from the officials of their particular ethnic group but from God.

Genesis and Exodus contain narratives with which you are probably familiar: the stories of creation, Adam and Eve, Noah and the flood, Abraham and his covenant with God, Moses leading his people in an Exodus from bondage in Egypt across the Red Sea into the desert, then to Mount Sinai where God's Law was given, and on toward the Promised Land. Leviticus, Numbers, and Deuteronomy are primarily, but not entirely, books of Law. They too contain narrative. Since Torah is both story and Law code, the term can be used quite flexibly. In Galatians 4:21, for example, Paul uses the term as both story and as Law code in the same sentence.

Many Christians assume the Law of Moses (which is another way of saying "Torah") is the same as the Ten Commandments. This is not true. The Law contains the Ten Commandments but also more than six hundred other specific commandments, along with much interpretation and detailed requirements for temple sacrifice and for formal festivals such as Passover. The fact that the Law is concerned with even small details of daily life is crucial to understanding New Testament authors' serious concern with the Law. Christians today may have no interest in that Law (although many Jewish people still seek to follow it carefully), but if they wish to understand Paul and the evangelists they must pay attention to their interests: the Torah Law was of interest to them all as the framework for the entire legal system of the nation of Judea, including civil law, contract law, inheritance law, criminal law, property law, and laws relating to permitted and forbidden foods, to purity and impurity, and to the detailed regulations for such formal temple ceremonies such as ordination.

READ LEVITICUS CHAPTERS 11, 12 AND 23, 24. These passages are a small part of the Torah Law. It is only by reading some of the Law that you can come to understand the range of matters covered and the amount of detail contained.

In Leviticus you will notice a particular concern with purity and impurity (or, clean and unclean). Purity and impurity are not moral categories but ritual categories. God is said to expect his priests, or perhaps all of his "holy" people, to maintain purity and, should they become impure, to regain purity by ritual bathing. There is nothing wrong, evil, or wicked about impurity; it is normal at certain times. Similarly, one who is pure is not necessarily good, innocent, or morally perfect. Purity is only the state of not being impure, and vice versa. As it is written in the Torah, much of the Law and especially the requirements for maintaining purity, applied principally to the priesthood and not to ordinary people.

Impurity can be transmitted; purity cannot. In other words, a person who is impure can touch another person or touch a bowl of food, and render the person or the bowl impure. Whoever eats the food in the bowl will become impure. The Law is not so much against impurity as against the transmission of impurity, and it is mainly opposed to the transmission of impurity to holy things such as the food offered at the Jerusalem temple. To make a holy thing impure, to return it to a state of profane non-holiness, is a particularly grave infraction of Jewish ritual law. Fortunately, since most people are not priests and rarely have any contact with the holy things of the Jerusalem Temple, purity and impurity are not matters of grave importance to them.

Gentile is the word commonly used to describe all people who are not Jewish; virtually everything in the Gentile world is impure. This is not because there is something immoral about Gentiles but because Gentiles, ignorant of purity laws, pay no attention to them. A Jewish person intent upon maintaining purity would not associate with Gentiles during meals. Can Christians who were Jewish and Christians who were Gentiles come together for meals? Could they celebrate the Communion meal together? This matter was important to several New Testament authors, especially Paul, because it gave rise to a crucial question: must Gentiles who become Christians keep Torah Laws? As we shall see, some of the New Testament authors said yes (for example, Matthew), while others said no (Paul), and some offered a compromise (Luke).

Mark 12:28, 32, 35, 38. The scribes (or lawyers or doctors of the Law) were Jewish legal officials about whom little is known. They were probably similar to local magistrates or justices of the peace today. Scribes were not the same as the Pharisees (see below), although both groups were concerned with Law. The scribes, whose influence declined greatly toward the end of the first century, had formal authority during Jesus' life. The Pharisees did not, although they had acquired it by the time the gospels were being written.

The name "scribe" comes from the historical role of scribes in writing the Torah, which, in those days, had to be copied by hand. A scribe-copyist would have learned to be very exact, for an error could lead to legal complications and would be an offense against God. The scribes probably adhered only to the written Torah while Pharisees believed there was also an unwritten oral Torah. The scribes, therefore, were probably allied not with Pharisees but with the authorities who found the written Torah sufficient.

Mark 12:13–17. Two Jewish groups are mentioned in this passage: the Pharisees and men of Herod's party.

Pharisees were members of what would soon become an important religious and political movement that has since evolved into the Rabbinic Judaism of today. They believed all of the Jewish people should obey all the Law. This sounds like a simple enough idea, but it contains two substantial changes from traditional understandings.

First, the Law from the Pharisees' perspective does not distinguish between priests and people in regard to purity. Therefore, the Pharisees believed, all people were subject to many regulations previously applied only to priests. This especially applied to the habits and procedures of dining. Priests' food was holy, consecrated to God because it came from the tithes of common people and from sacrifices at the temple. To make impure something that was consecrated and holy was a grave offense against God and strictly forbidden. Therefore, priests were required to be extremely careful not to render their consecrated food impure. Pharisees were well-educated Jews who sought to extend to its maximum the concept of the holy people of God. In their opinion, holiness should not be the responsibility of priests alone but of every Jew; every meal should be eaten in an atmosphere of holiness as if it were eaten at the temple, as if the food had been consecrated to God. Thus, the stricter priestly codes of purity were applied even to the common people.

Second, the Pharisees believed the Law included not only the Torah, the five books of Moses, but that it also included a body of legal interpretations supposedly given first to Moses and then passed down by word of mouth to the present day. This has been given the name "oral Torah," due to the method of its transmission. The logic of the situation is this: if all Jewish law comes from God through Moses, and if much later on, 1,500 years after Moses, the Law must be revised, then the revised Law must also come from God through Moses. Since that revised Law is not written anywhere in the Torah, it must be an unwritten Law, an oral Law. This was the Law taught by Pharisees, and it came to be written down in a book called the *Mishnah* around 220 CE, which was expanded into the much larger collection of books called the *Talmud*, around 600 CE. These texts, along with the Hebrew Bible, are the foundation of Rabbinic Judaism in the modern age.

From the perspective of the common people, both the extension of priestly laws of purity to all Jews and the addition of an extensive oral Torah to the written Torah made the attempt to remain obedient much more difficult. Few peasants could even approach the standards set for them by the Pharisees. A religious leader who identified with the peasantry and who suggested they might be acceptable to God without detailed concern for the oral Torah would be opposed by Pharisees; Jesus was one such leader.

To the two meanings of Torah mentioned earlier (the five books of Moses and the Law contained in those books), we must therefore add another: the oral Law and the extended interpretations of the Pharisees. In reading the New Testament and thinking about it, the various definitions of Law must be kept clear. One might say, for example, that Jesus did teach obedience to Law while at the same time clashing with Pharisaic instructors who accused him of opposing the Law. In other words, he may have called for obedience to the Law in the books of Moses without expecting peasant followers to obey strict Pharisaic interpretations of it.

During the time of Jesus, the Pharisees were somewhat influential, but they were a distinct minority. Their power grew enormously during the first century, and by the end of that century they were the dominant force in Judaism. This happened because their base of power and influence was the local synagogue rather than the temple in Jerusalem.

Mark 12:39 refers to the synagogue, where scribes or doctors of the Law are said to have had "chief seats," and "places of honor at feasts." The synagogue was the meeting place of the Jewish community. If you are at all familiar with synagogues in your own town, you already know much of what you need to know about the synagogues of the first century. Although forms, languages, and procedures have changed over the past two thousand years, the basic nature of synagogues and their services have not. Synagogues served both then and now as centers for Jewish community life and as places for community prayer. Every town of substantial size in the Roman Empire had at least one synagogue, and services in all of them were similar. During services the Torah was read aloud and then discussed by experts in the Law. In the first century many of those experts would have been Pharisees; today they are called "rabbis."

In addition to reading and interpreting the Torah, synagogue services included prayer and the singing of psalms. Christians familiar with services that include Bible reading, a sermon, prayers, and hymns will find nothing strange in this;

their services are the direct historical descendants of synagogue services.

The first-century function of the synagogue as the center of community life should also be familiar to Christians and Jews of the twentieth century. Jews went to the synagogue for conversation, for occasional meals, for celebrations and festivals. Important passages in life—birth, maturity, marriage, and death—were formalized in synagogues. Christian churches today fulfill the same roles for Christians as synagogues did, and still do, for Jews.

The legal authority of the synagogue leadership in the first century is not paralleled today in the Christian churches. Churches do not have judicial powers over their members in twenty-first century America. But under the Roman Empire the Jewish people were usually allowed to keep Torah Law. To keep Torah Law meant the establishment of a system of courts and lawyers. The leaders of the community, who were also leaders of the synagogue, were not just religious but also judicial figures and recognized as such by both Jewish and Roman authority. By the time the gospels were written, the Pharisees were first among those community leaders.

In Mark 12:13, the men of Herod's party who are associated with the Pharisees were officials loyal to the government of Herod Antipas. During Jesus' life, Herod Antipas had been installed by Rome as the official "puppet" king of the Galilean region. His father, Herod the Great, ruled Judea and Samaria and Galilee from 37 BCE to 4 BCE. Herod Antipas, a son of Herod the Great, received one-third of his father's empire, including the region of Galilee, and ruled it from 4 BCE to 39 CE, throughout Jesus' lifetime. Both Herod Antipas and his father were titled "King of the Jews," at least officially. Their rule was regarded with suspicion by a substantial number of Jews because they were not descendants of David, the originator of the line of Jewish kings, and so they were theoretically ineligible for the kingship. Furthermore, they were not ethnically Jewish but were members of a family converted from the Idumeans, or Edomites. Finally, they were puppets of Rome without much independent decision-making power and were expected to provide Rome with tax money whole-heartedly. Their policy in regard to Rome came down to this: If you cannot defeat the great power, you had best get along with it. While Judea and Samaria were taken over by Rome in 6 CE and ruled by direct Roman authorities, such as the procurator Pontius Pilate, Galilee remained free of direct Roman rule and was governed by forces of Herod Antipas, not by the Roman military.

It is implied in Luke 1:5 that Jesus was born during the reign of Herod the Great. As Herod died in 4 BCE, Jesus was born somewhat before the year CE 1, which our present calendar implies is his year of birth. King Herod the Great did great things for his people, including massive building projects such as the reconstruction of the temple in Jerusalem, but he never won favor from his people due to the insufficiency of his claims to the kingship and his tactics of violent pressure.

Mark 12:18–27 describes a controversy between Jesus and a group known as the Sadducees. The Sadducees were members of the upper classes. They were often from priestly families, and their center of power was the city of Jerusalem. As people of wealth they sought accommodation with their Roman rulers. They tried to maintain harmony between Rome and the Jewish people, to keep Torah Law as written but not as interpreted through the Pharisaic oral Torah, and to avoid offending the Romans who controlled their nation. Their wealth and position depended on political stability.

The disagreement mentioned in the passage is a technical legal one: to whom is a woman married after her resurrection if she has previously been repeatedly widowed? The Sadducees are not interested in a definitive answer. Rather, they are attempting to show the logical absurdity of the idea of resurrection. Sadducees thought that God's revelation in the Torah was sufficient. The idea of resurrection is not present in Torah, nor is it clearly present anywhere else in the Hebrew Scriptures; therefore, Sadducees did not believe in it. Christians often assume that the Hebrew Bible contains a clear doctrine of heaven and hell, but it does not, and it is questionable whether anything more by way of belief in an afterlife is present in the Hebrew Bible than the idea that the dead may inhabit a shadowy underworld called Sheol.

This is a point on which Pharisees and Sadducees differed: Pharisees did think there would be a resurrection. Since they believed in the new idea of an oral Torah, they were more open to new ideas than Sadducees. In this dispute, Jesus is on the side of the Pharisees.

One significant group of Jewish people is never mentioned in the New Testament: the Essenes. We learn of the Essenes from other sources, the most important of which are Hebrew Bible texts they used and books they wrote. So far as we know, the Essenes were destroyed during the war that took place between Jews and Romans from CE 66 to 70. Aware of the danger, the Essenes from a community in Qumran, near the Dead Sea, hid their books (written on scrolls) in caves. Many of these have been recovered during the past several decades and are known as the Dead Sea scrolls.

The Essenes believed in such absolutely strict application of Torah Laws of purity that many of them left the more thickly populated areas of Palestine and established self-contained communities in desert regions. One such community was at Qumran. Other Essenes sought to maintain strict lives of purity in the cities of Palestine. The Essenes believed that the Jerusalem temple was under the control of illegitimate priests and had been made impure, so they refused to participate in temple ceremonies. Their own ceremonies were focused on their meals. They elevated their dinners into ritual occasions where they dined on food and drink of guaranteed purity.

The Essenes regarded the world in black-and-white terms; the human race was composed of children of light and children of darkness, with no middle ground. They believed God would bring an end to this world in the immediate future, and only children of light like themselves would be saved. During the end times the *messiah* would come (or perhaps two messiahs—one to bring back a perfected priesthood, and one to be king), and the Romans would be driven away forever. A messiah, literally "one who is anointed," is a Jewish king (or sometimes a Jewish priest) whose right to rule comes from God. In times when the legitimacy of Jewish kings was denied, many Jewish people expected God to send a new messiah.

There is no evidence that Jesus was an Essene, but John the Baptist may have been raised in an Essene community. Many Essenes did not marry but adopted and raised other people's children, especially children from priestly families. John's father was a priest (Luke 1:5), and Luke reports about his infant son John that "as the child grew up he became strong in spirit; he lived out in the wilds until the day when he appeared publicly before Israel" (Luke 1:80), which may mean he lived in a desert Essene community. John's practice of baptism may derive from ritual bathing, which Essenes practiced more strictly than did most other Jews and which they may, like John, have regarded as a token of repentance for sin. In his preaching, John quoted a passage from Isaiah about "a voice crying aloud in the wilderness, prepare a way for the Lord; clear a straight path for him" (Luke 3:4), a passage given prominence in important Dead Sea scrolls. John's refusal to eat village food but, rather, to eat "locusts and wild honey" (Mark 1:6), may have stemmed from Essene training, for they believed that villagers' food was ritually impure, while food found in nature was ritually pure. People raised in desert regions regard some species of locusts as good to eat, and the Torah approves of this. If Jesus was influenced by the Essenes, it was probably through John the Baptist.

Many scholars of the New Testament believe Essene practices and beliefs influenced the formation of Christian practice and belief. The Essene belief in the immediate coming of the end of this world and the coming of the messiah of God is thought sometimes to have influenced Christian teaching of the coming of the end and the arrival of God's kingdom. These and other connections between Essene and early Christian ideas have not yet been proven conclusively, however, and may be overstated because we have so much information about the Essenes from the Dead Sea scrolls and so little information about other Jewish movements of the first century.

Mark 12:32–44 deals with events that took place in the temple. Many temple priests were poor farmers who performed sacrifices as seldom as once each year in the temple. John the Baptist's father, Zechariah, was one such priest (Luke 1:5–8). Other priests, however, were very important individuals, members of both the religious and political elite who lived year round in Jerusalem officiating at temple sacrifices. The priests of the temple were allied with the Sadducees, and the two groups overlapped considerably, for many Sadducees were priests. Priests wished not to offend Rome for fear the Romans might interfere with the operation of the temple. The High Priest may have been, in the absence of a legitimate king, the single most important Jewish official.

Priests carried out temple sacrifices daily. Bulls, sheep, and goats were brought to the temple to be ceremonially killed by members of the priesthood. Having killed the animal, the priests would splash its blood on the altar and divide its body according to specifications written in the Torah for particular sacrifices. Some of the animal might be burned on the altar, other parts might go to the priests for their meals, and the remainder would be returned to the offerer for his own meals.

During festival seasons, especially Passover, Jews from all over Palestine and from distant points of the Roman world came to Jerusalem to offer sacrifices. Passover was then and still is today a religious ceremony of remembrance of the beginning of the Jews' exodus from Egypt. At the time of Passover, Jerusalem, usually dominated by conservative forces such as the Sadducees, scribes, and priests, filled with common people from the countryside. This led the occupying Roman forces to fear that revolution would break out. Pontius Pilate, the Roman prefect in charge of the province of Judea from 26 CE to 36 CE, usually did not stay in Jerusalem, but he did come with his troops during the Passover festival to keep civil order.

The story of the tenant farmers' rebellion in Mark 12:1–9 implies the possibility of revolution. There was an organized revolutionary group in Palestine during or shortly after Jesus' lifetime, a movement composed of people known as Zealots, many drawn from the ranks of tenant farmers and peasants. This liberation organization sought through violent activity to drive the Roman armies from the country. During the first century their activities increased until the region exploded into civil war during the years CE 66 to 73.

Zealots do not play a prominent role in the gospels. The prisoner called Barabbas, who was reportedly under arrest at the same time as Jesus (Mark 15:7), had been convicted of violent revolutionary activity and may have been a Zealot. Luke reports that one of Jesus' disciples was known as Simon the Zealot (Luke 6:15). Jesus was not a Zealot; no Zealot would have associated with tax collectors and advocated the payment of Roman taxes as Jesus did. Further, no record exists of Jesus calling for violent expulsion of Roman authority.

Zealots are more important to the New Testament indirectly than directly. Their revolution, their war against Rome, failed completely. Its failure culminated in the physical destruction of the temple in Jerusalem in the year CE 70. That year marks a turning point in the history of the Jewish religion that is perhaps the single most important event in Jewish history since the establishment of the kingdom of David.

During Jesus' life, Judaism was focused on the temple. The duty to perform sacrifices at the temple was as much a part of the Law as any other commandments were. The Sadducees and priests owed their positions of authority to their positions in the temple. The High Priest's great authority stemmed directly from his temple responsibilities. The Pharisees and the synagogues, while of some importance, had nothing like the authority of the temple and its officials.

After CE 70, after the temple had been destroyed, everything changed. Three alternatives were available: (1) Judaism could cease to exist. This did not happen. (2) The temple sacrifices could be offered in other places. The centrality of the temple was so ingrained in Judaism by then that this alternative was not even tried. (3) Judaism might evolve in a different direction, so that the end of sacrifice might be the beginning of something quite different. This is what took place.

After CE 70 most of the Jewish groups we have been considering no longer had power.

The priests no longer had an active role to play in the religion. Although honored in theory, in practice their influence rapidly declined.

The Sadducees failed in their attempt to avoid civil war; Roman trust in them vanished. Their temple-based authority was destroyed. The Sadducees ceased to exist as an influential group.

The scribes, whose formal power was related to that of the priestly authorities in Jerusalem, saw their power rapidly decline, and, like the Sadducees, the scribes soon ceased to exist as an influential group.

The Zealots had been thoroughly and soundly defeated by Roman military power. Although there was another civil war (and another total defeat) in CE 135, for the rest of the first century the remaining Zealots were little more than groups of bandits.

At about this time, the Essenes, too, ceased to exist as a significant movement. It seems likely the Essenes interpreted the civil war to be the beginning of the messianic age, when God would empower a legitimate king to drive out his enemies and establish his kingdom, and that they went out from their desert settlements to take part in it. Most were probably killed by Roman soldiers.

Of the groups mentioned in *Mark 12:1–44,* only the Pharisees came through well. They soon began to set down the legal and religious principles that would govern Judaism for the next two thousand years. Those principles were built upon the assumption that all Jewish people should act in obedience to the Torah, both written and oral. After the destruction of the temple, this principle became policy. Synagogues gained immensely in importance, for they replaced the temple in Jerusalem as the focal point of Jewish life.

The destruction of the temple in CE 70 had significant consequences for the New Testament. For example, as we will see, Paul taught about the sacrificial death of Jesus Christ on the cross while Matthew taught that a central theme of Christianity is the necessity of following Torah Law as interpreted by Jesus Christ. Paul, writing around 55 CE, before the destruction of the temple, reflects the existence of the temple and its sacrifices; Matthew, writing around 85 CE, reflects the Pharisaic renewal of Judaism and its focus on obedience to Torah. The gospels' portrayal of Pharisees as leading authorities of Judaism, and as Jesus' principal rivals, owes less to the conditions present during Jesus' ministry in or around 30 CE than to the perception of the evangelists writing the gospels fifty years later. It is an interesting fact of history that Christianity and Rabbinic Judaism came into being at almost exactly the same time.

Mark 12:38–39 may reflect the growing influence of the Pharisees in the report of Jesus' attack on those who are arrogant in the synagogues. Criticisms of Pharisees appear in the gospels, but nowhere do criticisms of the institution of synagogues appear. The social function of synagogues in the first century was unique. No other institution in all of the empire was so comprehensive in the assistance it offered its people. Jews from Palestine could journey to Greece on business or pleasure and find a Jewish community organized around a synagogue to welcome them on their arrival. Jews could expect some assistance from members of a foreign synagogue if they were without food or shelter or clothing. Jews in legal trouble away from home could turn to the synagogue for assistance. Because synagogues were common, Jews were more at home in the empire as a whole than was any other group, with the exception of the citizens of Rome itself.

Other Religious Groups

The religions of the Roman Empire were many centuries old, and, as they had developed in different cultures with different languages and customs, they were quite diverse. To make it somewhat easier to think about them, let us divide them into three general categories: hearth religion, mystery religion, and imperial religion.

Hearth Religion

Hearth religion was found throughout the empire. It was focused on the heart of the home, the hearth, which was the home's center for warmth, light, and food. Particular deities, varying from place to place or even family to family, were thought to be willing to guide, guard, and assist individuals if properly worshiped. In most of the homes of the empire, an area was set aside for worship. Regularly, often at the time of the new moon, the family would provide food and flowers and other tokens of respect for their gods. Hearth religion had its base in homes but could extend to larger social groups, so that each village and city had deities thought to be its special protectors. Christian devotion to patron saints is akin to, and may have developed historically from, customs of hearth religion.

Mystery Religion

Mystery religion was more formally organized than hearth religion. It is called mystery religion because at the core of its practice were mysteries, sacred rites initiating adherents into the cult. Some mystery religions had several stages of initiation, but the rites were kept secret in all of them. Today, while we know something of the mystery religions, our knowledge is incomplete because their secrets were so well kept. Each mystery religion was separate from the others in terms of its organization, its history, and its specific practices, but they had general features in common. In order to see their common features, we will discuss four specific mystery religions below.

1) The mysteries in Eleusis, a town in Greece, occurred periodically, but individuals were allowed to participate only once during their lives. A procession formed near Athens and, having taken the drug kykeon, proceeded to the small town of Eleusis. There the mysteries of Demeter, the goddess of the earth, were enacted. Although scholars are not certain, most believe the rites included the enactment of the story of Kore-Persephone, daughter of Demeter. Kore was

carried off by the god of the underworld, Hades-Pluton. Demeter searched frantically for her and, failing to find her, began to fast. The fasting of the earth goddess led to the failure of crops until, eventually, Zeus intervened and brought about the release of Kore. This mythological tale symbolizes the cycle of the year. There is a period of growth and plenty when Kore and Demeter are together, and a period of death and potential famine (winter) when Kore and Demeter are separated. Those who were initiated at Eleusis believed their initiation guaranteed them eternal life.

2) The mysteries of Isis began to spread throughout the empire at roughly the same time as did Christianity, but the worship of Isis had long been part of the ancient religion of Egypt. Its mythological and ritual emphasis was on the death and rebirth of Osiris, husband of Isis. Osiris, it was said, had been murdered and dismembered by his antagonist, Seth. Isis searched frantically for Osiris and reassembled him, and he returned to life. Rather than the yearly cycle, the mysteries of Isis symbolized the daily cycle. Osiris, symbol of the sun, rises to the heavens and dies into the underworld. Initiates of the Isis mysteries believed that after their deaths they would live forever with Osiris.

3) The mysteries of Mithra originated in Persia. Their principal mythology concerns the god Mithra's battle with a great bull. After Mithra killed the bull, its body returned to life as the earth's plants and animals. Mithra ascended to heaven and joined the god of the sun. Mithra's initiates believed that after death they, like Mithra, would ascend to the realm of the sun. Mithra's birthday was celebrated on December 25th, near the time of the winter solstice when days become shortest and begin again to lengthen. The empire-wide celebration of Mithra's birthday is thought by some scholars to have led Christians to celebrate the birth of Jesus on the same date.

4) The mysteries of Cybele, which developed in Phrygia in Asia Minor, spread rapidly throughout the empire. The cult worshiped the Great Mother of life, Cybele. Her mysteries are based on the story of her lover Attis who was unfaithful to her. Filled with guilt, Attis castrated himself and died. Cybele eventually brought him back to life. As was the case in Eleusis, the mysteries of Cybele ritually depicted the cycle of the seasons, with Attis taking the role of Kore-Persephone.

The four mystery religions mentioned here had certain motifs in common. Each believed in a deity who died and then rose to life again (Kore-Persephone, Osiris, the Mithraic bull, and Attis). Each believed that through participation in the mysteries and faith in their teachings, individuals could achieve eternal life with the deities. Very little in the New Testament derives directly from any specific mystery cult, but it is clear that the Christian teaching of the death and resurrection of Jesus Christ the Son of God, faith in which leads to eternal life with God, would not have seemed utterly novel to people of the ancient world.

Imperial Religion
Imperial religion in the Roman world was the formal civic worship of the emperor of Rome. This is not the same as Roman religion, which involved worship of traditional Roman gods such as Mars, Jupiter, and Venus, as well as traditional practices we have called hearth religion. Julius Caesar was declared formally deified, but this did not mean he claimed to be God in the Jewish or Christian sense. It meant, rather, that he deserved respect because his accomplishments indicated he had a divine spirit in him. His successor, Octavian, took the name Augustus, which is a religious title meaning one worthy of veneration.

In Mark 12:16 we hear a reference to one of Augustus' coins, or perhaps a coin of Tiberius, who ruled at the time of

Jesus' crucifixion. Such coins bore a variety of inscriptions. On some of his coins, Augustus referred to himself as "son of god," by which he meant little more than that he was the formally adopted son of the deified Julius Caesar. Many Roman coins had on their "tails" side images of various gods or religious ceremonies or altars. Because of these images, and because of the image of the emperor on the "heads" side, religious Jews sought to reduce the circulation of ordinary Roman coins in their territory. Accordingly, Roman law permitted in Palestine the use of special coins that bore no offensive imagery.

The worship of the emperor in the early empire was more like a civil ceremony than a religious event, more like pledging allegiance to the flag than worshiping God. The emperor of the early first century who seems most sincerely to have believed himself to have been a god, Gaius (known also as Caligula), was regarded even by the Romans as insane.

Jews were legally excused by Roman authority from the requirement that they take part in the ceremonies of emperor worship. Gentiles who became members of Christian churches claimed this privilege as well, but to them it was often denied, as only Jews who were acknowledged members of the Jewish community could claim exemption from Roman law. Christians continued to refuse to participate. This led to increasing Roman persecution of Christians, especially in the second and third centuries.

In addition to the varieties of religion discussed above, many other religious and philosophical sects competed for adherents during the early empire. They are a fascinating area for research. One important point must be made: these religions were inferior in their social aspects to synagogue Judaism. Some, such as the cult of Mithra (exclusively for men), were predominantly for one sex or the other, so family life could play little or no role in them. In the synagogue, however, the family was included. Others, such as the mystery rituals at Eleusis, were once-in-a-lifetime events, which might be revisited but never repeated and so had little regular social significance. Synagogues, by contrast, assembled at least once every week.

The Roman religion had appeal primarily to Romans and to political officials who wanted to win favor with Roman authorities. No effort at the conversion of other peoples was contemplated. Judaism, on the other hand, did make an effort to convert other peoples; anyone willing to accept the responsibilities of Judaism, including especially the responsibility for strict obedience to the laws of God found in the Torah, beginning with male circumcision, was welcome to join. Those who did not wish to adopt strict obedience were welcome to affiliate with Judaism and received the title "God-fearer."

People did wish to join. The rapid growth of Christianity is evidence for this, for Christianity (especially as taught by Paul and his followers) offered to Gentiles the possibility of becoming Jewish. Thousands accepted, especially God-fearers, and became Jewish through Christianity. "Jewish," in this sense, means members of the people of God, worshipers of the God revealed in the Torah. It does not, as understood and taught by Paul, include the responsibility for strict obedience to the laws of God found in the Torah (see chapter 3, "Paul").

The Success of Christianity

The fact that Christianity grew rapidly and eventually became dominant in the empire is familiar to most people. But why did people join? What made so many Gentiles eager to adopt this Christian form of Judaism, a form considered inauthentic by the Jews of the synagogues? There are several reasons, listed below.

1. In the Roman Empire the old religions had begun to look rather inadequate. With their many gods, their often morally questionable mythologies, and their statues of human- and animal-headed deities, most of the ancient religions became difficult to defend outside their own locale. In other words, if you were born, lived, and died in a certain region, whatever religion was customary there was probably satisfactory to you, but away from that region, when custom did not provide sufficient evidence for the truth of the religion, traditional religions could prove hard to justify. Philosophers asserted that all of the deities worshiped in the Roman Empire were versions of each other—that, for example, Hermes of Greece and Mercury of Rome and Thoth of Egypt were one and the same. But the evidence of contradictory mythologies, rival priesthoods, and dissimilar rituals made this assertion difficult to maintain seriously.

2. The Torah, the books of Moses, were widely regarded as ancient and were often respected. Although some laws were viewed with suspicion (Sabbath rest was thought sometimes to be laziness), the moral authority of the Torah in general was frequently acknowledged.

3. Judaism offered one God of all the world, not of a region or aspect of the world. There were no images of that God, no embarrassing animal-headed images (as were common in Egypt), no human-headed images (reminiscent of the statues of political leaders). Philosophers of Greece and Rome had defended the concept of the one God; the Jews agreed and claimed they alone worshiped that God.

4. Most religions of the empire were ecumenical; that is, members of various religions were willing to admit the general truth of other religions and to identify others' gods with their own. Judaism, however, was quite adamant that its God was the only God. This was an attractive feature to many people. The feeling that one's religious beliefs are wholly true and the religious beliefs of others who hold different

views are entirely false is psychologically satisfying to people unable to face uncertainty. Christians adopted from Judaism the belief that their God was the only God and that all other worship was directed to demons, idols, and illusions.

5. The Jewish idea of prophecy, that certain special people might receive the Spirit of God and be transformed so as to be able to speak God's words, was extended in Christianity to include all Christian believers. The story of Pentecost (Acts 2) is the story of the Spirit coming to all of Jesus' followers. Paul (Romans 8) indicates that reception of the Spirit is of critical importance and, in 1 Corinthians 11–14, describes some of the manifestations of the Spirit in a Christian community. John's gospel promises that the Spirit, there called the *Paraclete*, will be given to all Christians. The experience of the reception of the Spirit was one of attainment of special supernatural power that was taken to confirm hopes of eternal life. This pleasurable and empowering experience, promised to all who would be Christian, surely motivated many people to enter the Christian movement.

6. The synagogues were an extremely attractive institution. They were adapted to an empire where travel for purposes of trade, tourism, and military service was becoming increasingly common. They were adapted to an urban environment and, in the empire, people frequently came from homes in distant rural regions to live and work in strange cities. The synagogues offered social acceptance and social security to any Jewish person in all regions. No other religion or cult had nearly as comprehensive a social organization.

While Judaism was by no means universally respected and some Gentiles were opposed to Judaism, many others were not. A substantial number of Gentiles who were sympathetic to Judaism subsequently adopted Judaism in the form of Christianity. To do so was to worship a single universal God, be addressed by the revelations in the Torah, be guided by the moral principles of the Torah, and be members of a worldwide network of supportive social centers.

It was through Paul's influence that the most successful branch of the Christian church of the first century offered Gentiles the opportunity to join this attractive religion without the adoption of such Jewish customs (and also Torah laws) as the circumcision of males, avoidance of certain foods (especially pork and shellfish), and concern for the detailed and difficult rules of purity and impurity. The Christian movement offered its members the opportunity to identify themselves with the chosen people of God, to regard the Hebrew Scriptures and especially the Torah as addressed to themselves, to worship the one God, and to receive the Spirit of God in the pentecostal experience. While these ideas and experiences were attractive to many, possibly the most attractive element of all was the opportunity to join the Christian network of churches that arose parallel to the Jewish network of synagogues. In both networks, members were expected or even required to love one another, feed their hungry, visit fellow members in jail, clothe fellow members who were naked, and shelter fellow members who were homeless. In the time of the early empire, when many people were forced by Roman law, urbanization, economic change, and social dislocation to reorient their thinking away from their ancestral ways, it is hard to imagine a more attractive option than this network of churches modeled on the synagogues.

Nazareth and Galilee

Jesus was from the town of Nazareth in Galilee. During his lifetime, Galilee was the Roman-dominated but technically independent kingdom of Herod Antipas. The Gospels of Matthew and Luke report that Jesus was born in Bethlehem in Judea, but their stories differ as to whether his parents traveled there from their home in Nazareth (Luke 2:1–7, which is perhaps the most well-known Biblical narrative of all) or whether his parents were residents in Bethlehem and only later moved to Nazareth (Matt 2:1–5). Many scholars suspect that Bethlehem was written into the story of Jesus because the gospel writers used a prophetic passage from Micah 2:6 as biographical evidence and testimony to Jesus' messiahship. In fact, it is likely that Jesus of Nazareth was born in Nazareth.

Nazareth in Galilee is today a large, mostly Arab administrative center of a prosperous agricultural region. It is located in a moderately arid, quite hilly region looking down on the wide flat fertile plain called Jezreel. During Jesus' lifetime it was an agricultural village that had become in effect a suburb of the major Greco-Roman city Sepphoris. Jesus was born toward the end of the lifetime of Herod the Great, who died in the year 4 BCE The conventional date of Jesus' birth (year 1) is off by five or six years. When Herod the Great died, rebellious anti-Roman rioting occurred in Sepphoris that was violently suppressed by Roman soldiers and most of the city was destroyed. The son of Herod the Great, Herod Antipas, who had become the king of the Galilee began to rebuild the city, and throughout Jesus' life Sepphoris was reconstructed so as to resume its status as a major Greco-Roman urban area where a substantial population of the wealthy educated leadership of Galilee made their homes. Sepphoris was the capital of Galilee until Jesus was around 20 years old, at which time Herod Antipas moved his capital's location to the city of Tiberias on the shores of the Sea of Galilee.

Jesus is said to have been a *"tekton"* (Mark 6:3), a word that is usually translated "carpenter," but *"tekton"* can also mean more generally, "construction-worker." Nazareth is about an hour's walk from Sepphoris, roughly four miles, and any *tekton* looking for steady work would have found employment opportunities in Sepphoris. It is much more likely that Jesus of Nazareth commuted by foot to work in Sepphoris than that he stayed home in Nazareth trying to make a living as a local village woodworker. It may be difficult to imagine Jesus as a professional construction worker living in the suburb of a major regional capital city, instead of as a village carpenter in a town given over to small-time farming and sheep herding, but that was what he was.

The word "*Ioudaios*" in Greek means two things in English. This can cause some difficulty when reading the New Testament because translators must always choose one of two different English words whenever "*Ioudaios*" or its plural, "*Ioudaioi*," appears in the Greek. On the one hand, the word *Ioudaios* means "Judean," an inhabitant of a particular geographic region, the capital of which was Jerusalem and the borders of which usually went no more than 25 miles north of Jerusalem, ending at the border of Samaria. Galilee was further north, separated from Judea by Samaria. Judea was an established geographical region and its inhabitants were *Ioudaioi*. In this sense, Jesus was not *Ioudaios*, he was Galilean. However, *Ioudaios* is also translated by the English word "Jewish," because the religion of the Judeans was Judeanism, which our language shortens to "Judaism." The question then is, to what extent did Jesus of Galilee practice the religion of the Judeans? The simple answer is commonly given that Jesus was Jewish and everyone knows that, end of problem, but the reality was not that simple.

The histories told within the books of the Hebrew Bible begin with the time of David and of Solomon, roughly 1000 BCE to 930 BCE. After Solomon, their territory split into two separate and independent political and geographic entities, a northern state called "Israel" and a southern state called "Judea." Galilee was part of the northern state. The books of Kings and Chronicles in the Hebrew Bible discuss the dynastic and political affairs of these two separate kingdoms. The northern kingdom, Israel, was conquered by the Assyrians in 722 BCE and it ceased to exist as an independent kingdom. Much of the population of Israel, including many people of Galilee, was forcibly removed and replaced by foreigners. Eventually the region was conquered by the Babylonians, and then by the Persians, and then by the Greeks. It never was part of Judea until most of the region, including Galilee, was briefly conquered by the Judeans in 104 BCE only to come under Roman domination in 63 BCE. The Romans gave control over the adjacent regions of Judea, Samaria and Galilee to Herod the Great in 37 BCE, who ruled as a Jewish king, but since Herod was the son of an Idumean ("Edomite") father and an Arabian mother his dedication to the Jewish religion was more a matter of practical political necessity than a result of his personal ethnic heritage.

The historical background of Galilee means that one needs to think of Jesus and his home culture in a rather complex way. He was not Judean but Galilean. His Judaism was Galilean Judaism and not the official Judaism of the region around Jerusalem. His relationship to the temple of the Judeans and the Torah of the Judeans was certainly influenced by his having grown up in Nazareth. He would have had a very different religious background if he had grown up in Bethlehem, which was within walking-distance of Jerusalem, the capital of Judea, rather than in Nazareth, within walking-distance of Sepphoris, the capital of Galilee.

End-of Chapter Exercises

1. Describe some of the major changes brought about by the Roman Empire. Why is it important to understand this historical context when reading the New Testament?

2. Differentiate the Scribes, Pharisees, Sadducees, Essenes, and Zealots. In which social class did members of each group generally belong? What were the primary concerns of each group?
3. There are cultural "food laws" in America. For example, large four-legged creatures may be eaten but thou shalt not eat six-legged creatures. Identify 2 or 3 other such laws and customs. Describe your emotional response to the idea of eating such "impure" foods. How, for example, would you feel if you observed someone eating a bowl of worms?

Bibliography

Crossan, John Dominic and Jonathan L. Reed. *Excavating Jesus: Beneath the Stones, Behind the Texts.* New York NY: HarperCollins, 2002.

Ferguson, Everett. *Backgrounds of Early Christianity.* Grand Rapids MI: Eerdmans 2003.

Foerster, Werner. *From the Exile to Christ: An Historical Introduction to Palestinian Judaism.* Philadelphia: Fortress Press, 1964.

Freyne, Sean. *Jesus, a Jewish Galilean: A New Reading of the Jesus Story.* Edinburgh: T & T Clark, 2005.

Gager, John G. *Kingdom and Community.* Englewood Cliffs: Prentice Hall, 1975.

Grant, Michael. *The World of Rome.* New York: New American Library, 1961.

Horsley, Richard. *Jesus in Context: Power, People, and Performance.* Minneapolis MN: Fortress, 2008.

Kee, Howard C. *Christian Origins in Sociological Perspective.* Philadelphia: Westminster Press, 1977.

Malherbe, Abraham J. *Social Aspects of Early Christianity.* Philadelphia: Fortress Press, 1983.

Meeks, Wayne A. *The First Urban Christians.* New Haven: Yale University Press, 1983.

Sanders, E. P. *Jesus and Judaism*. Philadelphia: Fortress Press, 1985.

Scott, Julius. *The Jewish Backgrounds of the New Testament*. Grand Rapids MI: Baker Academic, 2000.

Stark, Rodney. *Cities of God*. San Francisco CA: HarperSanFrancisco, 2006.

Paul's Letters

Dashed lines: indirect influence
Double lines: oral transmission
Single thick lines: use of written source
Thin lines: followers, admirers & imitators

CHAPTER 3

Paul's Letters

OBJECTIVES
- Situate Paul in relation to Jesus and the early leaders of the Christian movement
- Explore controversies that arose from Paul's mission to gentile believers
- Discover patterns of ideas in Paul's letters that form the basis for important ideas in the later Christian church

Author, Date, and Place of Origin

Other than Jesus himself, the most important person in the Christian tradition was a man named Paul, whose ideas form the foundation of all subsequent Christian doctrine and belief. Oddly enough, we have no books or even pamphlets written by Paul, and we have no reason to think that he ever wrote any. What we do have in the New Testament are some personal letters that Paul wrote to churches—letters that are the subject of more study, scrutiny, debate and reflection than any other letters ever written.

Paul lived from roughly 10 CE to roughly 65 CE. Information about his life story can be found in some of his letters (especially Galatians and Second Corinthians) and in Luke's book the Acts of the Apostles. Paul was born to Jewish parents in Tarsus, a city of substantial size and influence located in Asia Minor (present-day Turkey). Luke informs us that Paul held Roman citizenship, presumably inherited from his father, which gave him social prestige and legal privileges. The name "Paul" is his Latin name, but he had a Hebrew name as well, "Saul," (who was the first King of Israel, preceding David). Paul was well educated, both in the Greek tradition (as shown by his excellent writing and his knowledge of Greek philosophical themes) and in the Jewish tradition (as shown by his skill in argumentation based on Jewish Scripture). He may even have studied with one of the greatest Jewish teachers of the first century, Rabbi Gamaliel (Acts 22:3). He was a professional maker of tents, a trade allowing him to make a living in any reasonably sized town. So he had social status from his citizenship, ethnic background, and occupation.

We do not, of course, know for sure what he looked like, but he took no pride in his appearance or physical presence (2 Cor 10:10). The Acts of Paul, a set of legendary second-century stories about Paul with almost no historical validity, does contain a description of Paul that is not the sort of thing writers of legends invent for their heroes. It may conceivably be accurate: "A man small of stature, with a bald head and crooked legs, in a good state of body with eyebrows meeting and nose somewhat hooked, full of friendliness."

As he thinks back over his youthful life, Paul regards himself as a righteous, Law-fulfilling Jew. Upon learning of Christians in the first years after the crucifixion, he persecuted them. Having heard of a community of Christians in Damascus, Syria, Paul set off to continue his persecution there (Gal 1:13–17). He was probably in his early twenties at the time.

The greatest event in Paul's life took place during that journey somewhere on the road from Jerusalem to Damascus; Paul believed that God revealed Jesus Christ to him. Paul seems to have immediately been convinced that Jesus Christ was Son of God, that he had died for the sins of all people, that salvation came only through faith in Christ, and that he, Paul, having thus seen the risen Christ, had been appointed apostle to the Gentile world.

At this point he began to travel into Gentile regions seeking to establish communities of people who would live in accordance with his vision of God's expectations. He was amazingly successful, establishing groups loyal to him (loyal to his gospel, he would say) in such areas as Macedonia, Corinth, Ephesus, Thessalonika, and Galatia. Acts reports that Paul arrived in Rome and was arrested. Later traditions declare he was executed in Rome; this is thought to have taken place around the year CE 65.

It would serve no useful purpose to go into detail here about his life and travels. Many books contain such details, as best as scholars can figure them out. What is important for our purpose is to understand his overall perspective.

Of the twenty-seven books in the New Testament, fourteen are customarily attributed to Paul of Tarsus. All but one of these fourteen are letters; the exception is Hebrews, which is more like an essay or a sermon. Some of the letters attributed to Paul were written by Paul himself; others were written by followers of his who wished to carry forward his tradition and ideas by writing in his name.

Scholars can usually distinguish Paul's authorship from that of those who wrote in his name by analyzing the style and content of the writing. There is general agreement that Paul's letters to Christians in Rome, in Corinth, in Galatia, in Philippi, and in Thessalonika are authentically his. The short personal letter entitled Philemon is also undoubtedly Paul's. These form a solid body of information on Paul's style of writing and pattern of ideas. Other letters can then be compared with those and judgments made as to whether they deviate so far they could not come from him or whether they are sufficiently close to his style they should be attributed to him.

Scholars have counted each word and variety of grammatical construction in Paul's letters to Rome, Corinth, Galatia, Philippi, and Thessalonika. From this they have determined the frequency of Paul's use of terms and phrases. A letter attributed to Paul that uses words and grammatical constructions with the same frequency as they are used in other letters known to be his is probably written by Paul. If that letter also contains ideas known to be his, then it is certainly written by Paul. But a letter attributed to Paul containing many words that never otherwise occur in Paul's letters, does not have the same frequency of word use, has atypical grammatical constructions, and includes ideas inconsistent with those known to be Paul's was probably written in Paul's name by somebody else.

Virtually no analytical scholars believe 1 Timothy, 2 Timothy, Titus, or Hebrews were written by Paul. Hebrews reflects his style and concepts not at all and it is not a letter but an essay or sermon. The other three letters, collectively called "the Pastorals," come from a later period of the church. This is evident from the developed patterns of leadership and organization in the churches to which they are written. Paul's churches were in the process of formation, while the Pastorals are written to churches that have been established for a considerable period of time. The author of the Pastorals does know something about Paul's ideas, but he does not interpret them in the same way Paul himself does. Further, his style of writing is not Paul's.

Paul probably did not write the letter to the Ephesians, although that letter was written by a follower of his who was greatly influenced by him. The style of Ephesians is significantly different from that of the letters certainly written by Paul, and the ideas of Ephesians, although Pauline, are not sufficiently similar to Paul's to have come from him. Some scholars now believe that Ephesians was written as a cover letter or introduction to the rest of Paul's letter.

Two letters are in dispute. Did Paul write Colossians and 2 Thessalonians, or did he not? Since Paul was brilliant and inventive, one cannot be too rigid in categorizing ideas as his or not-his. He may have changed his mind or come up with startling ideas that do not appear in the letters he wrote. But neither of those letters seems fully consistent with Paul's thought and they contain stylistic elements absent from his other letters. Further, 2 Thessalonians seems, in part, to be a rewritten version of 1 Thessalonians. Accordingly, many analytical scholars tend to leave Colossians and 2 Thessalonians aside in writing about Paul and regard them as having been written by associates of his who developed his thought in their own ways; but the question of their authenticity is far from being settled and a good many eminently respectable scholars regard one or both as having been written by Paul himself.

Instead of being a cause for disappointment, the discovery that some of the letters customarily attributed to Paul were written by others should be a source of pleasure. It means the range of ideas and opinions in the New Testament is greater than it would have been if Paul had written all fourteen letters. For example, the Pastorals give insight into the state of Christianity in the early part of the second century, and Hebrews reveals Christianity as interpreted through Hellenistic Judaism. Colossians develops beyond Paul toward an even more exalted conception of Jesus in whom "everything in heaven and on earth was created, not only things visible but also the invisible orders of thrones, sovereignties, authorities, and powers: the whole universe has been created through him and for him" (Col 1:16).

The dates given below for Paul's letters are approximate (as are the dates of all New Testament documents), but here the range of uncertainty is a matter of a few years rather than of a decade or more:

- 1 Thessalonians: ca. CE 51
- 1 Corinthians: ca. CE 54
- 2 Corinthians: ca. CE 55
- Galatians: ca. CE 56

- Philippians: ca. CE 56
- Philemon: ca. CE 56
- Romans: ca. CE 59
- Colossians (?): ca. CE 61

When you read Paul's letters carefully, you may notice that his line of thought occasionally stops abruptly and shifts to another subject or that he suddenly seems to pick up a line of thinking he left many chapters earlier. Some letters seem to end twice. A convincing theory regarding these sudden shifts is that certain short letters of Paul's were combined at a later date to create longer letters.

Each of Paul's letters contains different emphases, and each is written to address a somewhat different set of problems, but on central points concerning Jesus Christ, salvation, faith, and morals they present the same general system of ideas. Paul's letters are letters not theological treatises or carefully composed sermons. They were not designed to present a general system of ideas but to respond to conditions in communities and to respond to particular problems. They assume that readers are already familiar with Paul's thinking.

In every instance except in the letter to Romans Paul is writing to people who have had long and sustained contact with him personally and so he writes to remind readers of what he thinks they should already know. Even the letter to the Romans, which is written to a community Paul has not yet visited, assumes that members of the community know of Paul's gospel, although he believes many of them are likely to have misunderstood it. For nearly two thousand years, Christians have sought to make clear systematic sense out of Paul's letters, but never with complete success. Great minds have worked on the problem and have always found themselves slightly, but significantly, in disagreement. When you, then, read Paul's letters and find yourself sometimes puzzled, don't despair but, rather, regard yourself as joining a community of distinguished sometimes puzzled readers.

Paul's ways of thinking and expressing himself were somewhat different from those of ordinary people. His ideas work within a particular view of reality that is his own and that he felt he had received from God. Within his particular frame of reference much of his thinking makes logical sense. Outside his frame of reference he cannot make sense. To understand him, therefore, we must try to enter his frame of reference uncritically and sympathetically.

Paul speaks of two separate ways of being human and preaches a gospel declaring that people should shift from the one way to the other way. This shift is not just a change of habits or attitude; it is a shift to a whole different category of being. Here are some of the characteristics of the two alternatives:

- Guilty // Justified
- Cursed // Blessed
- Alienated from God // Approved by God
- Less than potential // Ideal
- Seeks God's approval by trying to follow Torah Law // Finds approval from God by having Faith
- Believes in the necessity of following the Law of Moses // Follows the Law of Christ
- Tempted by the power of the flesh // Assisted by the power of the Spirit
- Oriented toward the material // Oriented toward the spiritual
- Destined to die // Destined to rise
- Some are physical descendants of Abraham // All are spiritual descendants of Abraham

This list might be lengthened considerably. There is no logical limit to such a list because it stems from the premise that for each significant aspect of human life and each aspect of religious theory, there is an aspect reflecting faith in Christ and an aspect not reflecting such faith.

Paul does not clearly define "faith" in any of his letters. Christians have sought to do this for him over a period of two thousand years, but rather than creating one solution they have created many denominations. Faith definitely involves trust in God, belief in Christ, acceptance of Christ's death as a death for all humanity, and acceptance of the idea that through faith people may be justified, or made righteous, in the eyes of God.

Paul is less interested in an abstract definition of faith than in the effects of faith. Those effects include communal love, moral living and confidence in one's salvation. Paul uses the effects of faith to reason back to a practical definition of faith. In other words, those who show the effects of faith are shown to be correct in thinking they have understood faith correctly. In the absence of the effects, faith is questionable. Faith enables Christians to receive the Spirit of God. The Spirit of God enables people to resist the temptation to sin and so to follow the way of Christ at least moderately well. Paul does not think Christians are all entirely moral, but he also doesn't think they should act immorally. Christians, guided by the Spirit, should be able to behave more morally than non-Christians, even if they cannot achieve perfection. The Spirit enables Christians to perform observable acts, including healing, miraculous powers, prophecy, and speech "in tongues" (1 Cor 12:7–11). Because they have the Spirit, Christians, in theory at least, should be able to act as Jesus acted, both in the sense of obedience to God and in the sense of exercising supernatural power.

Temptations from the flesh always exist. Temptations from the material world, old habits, false gospels—all can still threaten faith. So Paul honestly admits that the good he wants to do, he often cannot do. While the Spirit is willing, the flesh is weak. Paul does not believe in a hell or in eternal punishment. Death is annihilation, which is punishment enough.

The most visible effects of faith come from the Spirit, as it enables the working of miracles and other signs and guides Christians in proper behavior. When they all have the same Spirit, which is the Spirit of the person Jesus Christ, they are all in that sense one person. In Paul's mind it logically follows from the fact of all Christians being one person in Christ that they are united with Christ and are Sons and heirs of God; they are a new creation, and constitute the body of Christ (Paul uses all these ways of expressing it). Paul speaks most dramatically of identification with Christ when he writes, "I have been crucified with Christ: the life I now live is not my life, but the life which Christ lives in me" (Gal 2:20). But he does not regard himself uniquely to be a person in whom Christ lives; he assumes this applies to all who have received the Spirit of Christ.

In the community, which is the body of Christ, there are to be no social divisions; there are indeed no separate people, and so "in Christ there is no such thing as Jew and Greek, slave and freeman, male and female; for you are all one person in Christ Jesus" (Gal 3:28). Elsewhere he writes, "For Christ is like a single body with its many limbs and organs, which, many as they are together make up one body. For indeed we were all brought into one body by baptism, in the one Spirit, whether we are Jews or Greeks, whether slaves or free men, and the one Holy Spirit was poured out for all of us to drink" (1 Cor 12:12–13). How should people who are all the same person behave? They should love one another.

A body who is "one person in Christ Jesus" cannot allow social distinctions based on former religion or sex or wealth (Gal 3:28) or powers given by the Spirit (1 Cor 12:4) or roles within the church (1 Cor 12:29) ever to be a source of division. To Paul, Christian unity is absolutely essential. The Torah Law of Moses, therefore, if useful, should lead to unity, but in the real world of Jews and Gentiles, the Law of Moses led to disunity and diversion. The Law is detailed regarding permitted and forbidden foods; since the Pharisees interpreted the Law to make it even more restrictive with complex rules of purity and impurity, the social effects of following the Torah Law included the refusal by observant Jews to dine with non-Jews. Gentiles did not keep, or even know anything about, the Law's purity and impurity restrictions and had no reason not to dine on such forbidden foods as ham and shrimp. For a Christian group whose main ritual occasions were frequent celebrations of the Lord's Supper—at that time a real, not a symbolic, meal—this meant that adherence to Torah Law would either lead to a split within the body of Christ or to the necessity that all Christians follow the Torah Law. Neither alternative was acceptable to Paul, the first because disunity contradicted his thesis that all Christians are one in Christ and the second because it contradicted his thesis that only faith, not obedience to Law, brings salvation.

Paul believed the effort to achieve God's approval through following Law was the opposite of faith. Faith allows one to receive a gift that we call "grace." Following Law to achieve God's favor shows you have not accepted this gift through faith. To make a commonplace analogy: if you need a thousand dollars and a friend or relative informs you they have deposited a thousand dollars in your bank account, yet you continue as before to work overtime to earn the thousand dollars, such behavior indicates you really do not think the money is in the bank waiting for you. That is one way to look at the question of Law; seeking salvation through Law indicates you have not taken seriously the idea you have already attained salvation through faith. Paul, further, does not believe salvation can be attained by obedience to Law because he regards the attempt to be saved through Law as boasting, as demanding God give a reward for proper behavior. In Paul's opinion, people cannot earn salvation. It is a gift accepted through faith.

Not seeking salvation through Law, however, is not the same as disregarding all Law. Paul cautions Christians against using faith as an excuse for sinning. He is emphatic that Christians must not think they have God's permission to live immorally. He also contends that following Torah Law may be necessary to keep from offending those who are not Christians or do not understand that the Law cannot bring salvation. His position is not "never follow the Torah Law" but "never seek salvation through the Torah Law."

The crucial factor for Paul is motivation. If your motivation for following the Torah Law is to win God's approval, your failure is inevitable and you have opted not to have faith. If, on the other hand, your motivation is to keep from offending people, to live morally, to win others to the gospel, then you have done nothing wrong at all.

In recent years a "New Persepective on Paul" has been a central focus of many New Testament scholars. They argue that the classic perspective on Paul, the claim that Paul was opposed to the Jewish religion's idea that salvation can come through obedience to the Law of Moses, implies that Judaism is a religion based only in a legalistic doctrine of salvation or, more specifically, a legalistic doctrine of justification. These scholars are convinced that this is not an accurate portrayal of Judaism and that in fact Judaism is a religion based on faith in the one God and on grace, defined as the inclusion of Jewish people into God's chosen people by God's will alone rather than by their being rewarded for their behaviors. When Paul argues against the works of Law, they believe, he means the particular ceremonies of Jewish religion that are never practiced by Gentiles: keeping Sabbath, requiring circumcision, concern with kosher practices as regards foods. Because these ethnically specific practices serve to separate Jews from Gentiles, Paul is said to have found them unacceptable practices in the Christian community that contained Jews and Gentiles together. But as for the moral and legal commandments that did not divide people ethnically, Paul is said not to have argued against them. This new perspective is not universally accepted, however, and there are many scholars who maintain the classical perspective that Paul believed that seeking salvation through obedience to God's Law was indeed a principal factor in the Jewish religion and that Paul thought it was now replaced with the belief that salvation comes only through faith in Jesus Christ.

Some textbooks on the New Testament give as much space to Paul's letters as to all the gospels put together. The authors of such textbooks are looking at the New Testament as a collection of documents, equating a document such as, say, Paul's letter titled First Corinthians to Mark's gospel and, as a result, giving these two documents equal attention. In contrast, I think it is better to regard the New Testament as a collection not of documents but of Christian *authors*, a collection of diverse points of view. Accordingly, Paul and Mark are equally authors and equally have significant points of view, even though the former wrote many documents and the latter wrote but one. With this perspective in mind, I will consider Paul's Letter to the Galatians in greatest detail. I will do so for several reasons: in Galatians, the "apostle to the Gentiles" speaks especially to Gentile Christians, spelling out central themes of his thought rather clearly; also, in Galatians more than in any other letter, Paul discusses his own life; finally, it is a short and manageable letter. Having examined Galatians we will turn our attention to Paul's masterpiece, his Letter to the Romans and then briefly examine his other letters. In an introductory book such as this, our goal is to discuss the basic principles of Paul's thought, not fully to analyze all of his letters. You will certainly learn more about Paul by reading Paul than by reading this book or any other discussion of his letters.

1 Thessalonians

This is the oldest piece of Christian writing we have. It dates from about 51 CE before any of the gospels were written. As Paul often does in his letters, he takes time to defend himself against various accusations: here he declares that he has no base motives, does not seek to deceive, does not flatter, seeks no praise and that he worked for his living rather than accepted money from the community (2:4–9). He speaks very bitterly of "the Jews, who killed the Lord Jesus and the prophets and drove us out," but this must not be taken to be his true assessment of Judaism or the Jewish people. In his letter to the Romans, Paul writes at length very favorably about Jews and Judaism.

Perhaps the principal motivation for this letter was a perceived need to explain to the Thessalonian Christians that the physical death of believers ought not be taken to be a contradiction of Paul's gospel. Rather, he writes, Christians who have died will be brought to life again . . . they "sleep" until that occurs. Paul believes that the end of this world and the second coming of the Lord will occur in a very short time, certainly during his own lifetime. He speaks of "we who are left alive until the Lord comes," at which time there will be heard the word of command, the sound of the archangel's voice, God's trumpet call. Then the Lord will descend, the Christian dead will rise and "we who are left alive" will be caught up in the clouds to meet the Lord in the air. This passage (4:13–18) is the one to which evangelical Christians appeal when they speak of "the rapture." Paul evidently refers to a traditional saying of Jesus in 5:1–2, when he refers to the day of the Lord coming like a thief in the night (Matt 24:43–44 // Luke 12:39–40).

Galatians

READ PAUL'S LETTER TO THE GALATIANS AT LEAST TWICE (IT IS QUITE SHORT BUT QUITE COMPLEX). UNDERLINE EVERY REFERENCE TO LAW AND TO CIRCUMCISION. The term "circumcision" means, to Paul, accepting the necessity of following the Law to win God's approval. He chose this symbol because a male Jewish baby first obeyed Torah when, on the eighth day after his birth, he was circumcised. Paul is not so much concerned with circumcision itself as with circumcision as a symbolic act demonstrating one's determination to follow the Law. In this symbolic sense, persons of either sex might accept circumcision. For Gentile men, of course, the acceptance was more than symbolic and was, in the days before anesthetic or antiseptic, a very serious decision.

Jesus' disciple Peter is the person called "Cephas" in Galatians. His original name was Simon. Jesus gave him the Aramaic name Cephas, but he is now universally known as Peter. Peter is a Greek translation of Cephas; both words mean "the rock." It may sound funny, but the correct English translation of the nickname Cephas (Peter) is "Rocky."

Torah Law in Galatians

Having read Galatians carefully, you will have noticed the letter is highly argumentative. The Gentile Christian community in Galatia is evidently in the process of deciding to follow Torah Law. The people, therefore, intend to accept circumcision. Paul is adamant; they should not do this. The passages you have underlined assert repeatedly that Law and faith are contradictory. You may do the one or the other, but not both. To feel a need to keep the Law is to demonstrate a lack of faith. Paul's strongest statement to that effect is: "Mark my words: I, Paul, say to you that if you receive circumcision Christ will do you no good at all" (5:2), indicating, incidentally, that the Galatians had not yet taken this step. Justification, or righteousness in the eyes of God, comes through faith in Christ Jesus, not through following Law.

This opposition between faith and Law is spelled out clearly in Galatians. Paul writes (2:21), "If righteousness comes by Law, then Christ died for nothing." Paul believes that since Jesus' death, people have the potential to shift from one category to another, from fallen people to perfected people. Should there be no need to shift, if righteousness is already available, what would have been the point of Jesus' death? Nothing significant would have changed; the Law would lead to righteousness just as much before as after. It is as essential to Paul's theory that Law does not bring righteousness and justification but faith that does so. Why did the Son of God have to die on a cross? That's Paul's question. If you answer that Christ's death brings one more optional way to salvation, Paul will not accept it. For Christ's death to have been necessary, it must provide the only way to salvation.

Paul argues against Law as a way to salvation in various ways. Paul writes, "Tell me now, you who are so anxious to be under Law, will you not listen to what the Law says?" (4:21). Here he uses the term in two ways—Law as the seeking of justification by obedience to rules, and Law as the stories in the Torah. In this instance, he uses the story of Abraham found in Genesis 12–25. The allegory in Galatians 4:21–31, for example, is based on the story that Abraham had two sons, one by his slave girl Hagar and the other by his elderly wife Sarah, whose pregnancy was said to have come about in fulfillment of God's promise. Paul claims that the offspring of Sarah represents those who have faith and are free from Law, while the offspring of Hagar represents those who seek righteousness through the Law given to Moses on Mount Sinai. Paul clearly accepts the authority of Torah as divinely revealed allegorical stories even though he argues against Torah as a required set of ordinances. Because he understands those stories as allegories he feels free to interpret them in light of his own gospel, a gospel he believed to have been revealed to him by God. Christians should understand that although Jewish rabbis also read Torah allegorically, and instances of this are found even in the Dead Sea Scrolls, Paul's Christian allegorical readings would have been incomprehensible to knowledgeable Jewish people. To non-Jews, to the Gentiles to whom Paul came as apostle, his allegorical readings evidently did make good sense.

All Jewish people traced their ancestry back to Abraham and Sarah. Genesis contains the story of God's establishment of a covenant with Abraham and, through him, with Abraham's offspring (or "issue"). The covenant included the following promise (Genesis 12:2–3): "I will make you into a great nation, I will bless you and make your name so great that it shall be used in blessings: Those that bless you I will bless, those that curse you, I will execrate. All the families on earth will pray to be blessed as you are blessed." This promise was made to Abraham and his offspring. The Jewish people identified themselves as Abraham's offspring and regarded themselves as a people whose duty to the covenant included the obligation to keep the Law of Moses.

Paul believes the promise made to Abraham and his offspring is valid. In what would have come as a staggering surprise to any Jewish audience, Paul goes on to declare that

Abraham's offspring is Christ and, in accordance with his theory that Christians are one person through the Spirit of Christ, the offspring of Abraham is, therefore, any person who has faith in Christ and so does not seek righteousness through Law. According to him, Abraham's true offspring were the Christians of Paul's Gentile churches, for they had faith in Christ. Jews would have thought this theory turned Scripture absolutely upside down. Paul's rationale is that Abraham received the promises and covenant because "Abraham put his faith in the Lord and the Lord counted that faith to him as righteousness" (Genesis 15:6). The offspring of faithful Abraham are only those people who have faith. Paul assumes what the Genesis passage means by faith is exactly what he means by faith: faith in Jesus Christ.

Today's readers rarely realize how radical Paul's ideas are. He claims that the promises made to Abraham and the covenant on which the Jewish people had based their national and religious identity for centuries were made all along only to such non-Jews (Gentiles) and Jews as were willing to renounce the obligation of obedience to the Law by accepting that they had become righteous through their faith in Christ. In Paul's opinion the "new covenant" is the final version of the old, making explicit what the old covenant implied.

Paul encourages Gentile Galatians in the Christian community to think of themselves in a Jewish fashion, as heirs to the promise to Abraham and as members of the covenant—a new covenant in Jesus' blood (1 Cor 11:25). They could consider themselves the ones to whom the Torah really refers and to whom it belongs, those who correctly worship the One God who was revealed to Abraham and Moses and who spoke through the prophets.

What of the Jews? In his Letter to the Romans, Paul writes to a Jewish Christian audience and is careful to be highly complimentary to Jews and the Jewish religion. Yet his conclusion remains, as in Galatians, that true Jews, true Israel, are those who have faith in Christ. Such people were, primarily, Gentiles. Jews are welcome to join Paul's communities of faith, and he profoundly respects the fact that the Torah was revealed to them—indeed, he regards that revelation as a mark of God's special favor—but, in the final analysis, to be Jewish without faith in Christ Jesus and to seek to become righteous by obedience to Torah would not enable people to be justified in the eyes of God.

Paul offers Gentiles a way of being "Jewish" that does not entail the rigors of Judaism, that does not involve the painful and dangerous circumcision, and that did not require any change in eating habits. Then, as today, eating was the central event of social life. Imagine being unable to dine with business colleagues, friends at their homes, or relatives who married members of other religious groups, and you will see the social consequences of the Mosaic food laws when taken seriously. Such laws create strong group cohesion, but at the cost of separation from those outside that group. While Judaism was an attractive option to many Gentiles (see chapter 2, "Judaism and the Roman Empire"), to become "Jewish" through faith rather than through obedience to Law was an even more attractive option. Gentiles who followed Paul's gospel might believe themselves to have the benefits of Judaism without the social difficulties usually encountered by converts to Judaism who sought to follow Torah Law.

Gentiles evidently did wish to enter the covenant and receive the promises of Abraham through faith in Christ. Their desire to do so led to the rapid spread of the Christian religion. Jewish people, on the other hand, considered themselves already to be in the covenant, to be heirs to the promises of God, and to be the people of God. The men already were circumcised and surely most Jews then, like most Jews today, believed they had lived throughout their lives in reasonable accordance with the Law. Most Jews were confident that had they broken the law and then sincerely asked God's forgiveness, they would be forgiven. Paul offered to Gentiles the opportunity to enter Judaism without the Law, but there is no reason to think any substantial number of Jewish people would be interested in accepting that offer for themselves.

Jewish people believed God would forgive failure to keep his Law if people were sorry, repentant, and determined to do better. For them it was not that complicated a matter; God's forgiveness was repeatedly announced in the Hebrew scriptures. It would be nonsense for the prophets to have demanded repentance if repentance did no good. Judaism affirms that God forgives sin and God will approve as righteous those who seek to obey his Law and who repent when they fail.

Here we find difficulty in Paul's line of reasoning, because, if Paul's theory is to work, repentance must be impossible. He argues, "Those who rely on obedience to the Law are under a curse; for Scripture says, 'A curse is on all who do not persevere in doing everything that is written in the Book of the Law.' It is evident that no one is ever justified before God in terms of Law" (Gal 3:10, quoting Deuteronomy 27:26). This argument, and, in fact, Paul's whole perspective, depends on there being no forgiveness for those who break God's Law. If God forgives those who repent, then the "curse" would apply only to those who will not repent, and Paul is absolutely convinced his theory, his revelation, applies to all humanity. Those who repent must not have some kind of advantage over those who do not repent, in order for Paul's perspective to make sense.

If God forgives, then those who break the Law can repent and be forgiven. If people can repent and be forgiven, then people can obtain righteousness through Law, provided they sincerely try to keep it and repent when they fail. This is the belief of Jews today and it was the belief of Jews in Paul's day. If that is true, however, then from Paul's perspective, "Christ died for nothing." Does salvation come *only* through faith in Christ or *also* through faith in Christ? For Paul, the answer is "only through faith in Christ."

The Situation in Galatia

As the letter to the Galatians begins, Paul states the problem he intends to solve: "I am astonished to find you turning so quickly away from him who called you by grace, and following a different gospel" (1:6). Evidently, other Christians have brought a gospel to the church in Galatia. Their gospel includes the requirement that Christians, whether born Gentile or Jewish, must keep Torah Law. If men are not circumcised, they must be circumcised. The food laws must be kept. The Christians who preached this message are apparently near to success in convincing a church founded and instructed by Paul that Paul's teachings are unreliable. Evidently some or all of the Galatian Christians are trying to keep the Law of Moses (4:21) and so are moving away from the Pauline point of view that salvation comes through faith and grace. Paul seems furious:

"You stupid Galatians! You must have been bewitched—you, before whose eyes Jesus Christ was openly displayed upon his cross! Answer me one question: did you receive the Spirit by keeping the Law or by believing . . . [my] gospel message? Can it be that you are so stupid? You started with the spiritual; do you now look to the material to make you perfect? I ask then: when God gives you the Spirit and works miracles among you, why is this? Is it because you keep the Law, or is it because you have faith in . . . [my] gospel message?" (3:1–5).

The Law, material, is opposed to Faith, spiritual. Paul believes some of those in Galatia who have become Christians have now been convinced to return to behaviors and beliefs characteristic of their life before their conversion. This would make Paul's whole work with them a failure. No wonder he is upset. The Galatian Christians accepted his gospel; they had evidence provided by the Spirit and miracles worked through the Spirit affirming his gospel. Now they are adopting a perspective contradicting his gospel.

What might lead the Galatians, who probably never heard of Jesus Christ before the arrival of Paul, suddenly to turn away from Paul's teachings to those of other Christians? Those other Christians must have had substantial authority to enable them to convince people that Paul was wrong and that the Law of Moses must be obeyed. If Galatian Christians follow strangers rather than Paul, who brought them the gospel, we must assume that the strangers had strong arguments to support their claim that their gospel was superior to Paul's. An effort to understand Paul's letters requires an effort to understand the perspectives of the audience of those letters (a perspective with which Paul himself is usually not sympathetic). In reading Galatians, one should try to comprehend how it might have been that Paul's Christians would have been tempted to turn away from Paul. Some powerful motivations must have been at work.

Clues to the identity of Paul's opponents come from Paul's self-defense. Paul defends himself in two ways. First, he argues both from scripture and from the principles of his theory of salvation from faith, that seeking salvation by following the Law opposes the good results of faith. Second, he defends himself personally. He does this in the first section of Galatians, 1:1–2:16.

Apparently the claim had been made that Paul was appointed to the status of apostle by one or more human beings, for at the beginning of his letter he takes pains to defend himself from such a charge. Presumably, there were Christian authorities who claimed the right to appoint apostles. Either these authorities denied ever having appointed Paul, or they thought their appointment of him gave them the right to control him. Paul responds with the assertion that he is not an apostle by human appointment or commission but by commission from Jesus Christ and from God (1:1).

When Paul outlines his past (1:12–2:14), he does not simply tell a story; he tries to prove that his knowledge of Jesus Christ did not come from human instruction at all but from direct revelation. After his initial persecution of Christians, Paul believes God revealed His Son to him [literally, "in" him] in order that he might proclaim God's Son to the Gentiles. Immediately thereafter, Paul went to Arabia and then returned to Damascus in Syria. It was after three years that Paul went to Jerusalem to meet Peter (Cephas). He stayed there only two weeks and saw only Peter and James. This section is worded to demonstrate that although Paul did meet Peter and James, he did not go to them for instruction, and that his acquaintance with them was very limited.

"Fourteen years later," he again went to Jerusalem. There he met privately with James, Peter, and John, who agreed that Paul should bring the gospel to the Gentiles while they should bring the gospel to the Jews. Paul also agreed to collect money to send to them.

He strongly insists that he went to Jerusalem only twice in seventeen years and that while he was there little happened other than that James, Peter, and John agreed he should bring the gospel to the Gentiles. Without their permission, he had already been doing this for several years. Paul insists his account is true. He claims, "What I write is plain truth; before God I am not lying" (1:20). Those are powerful words.

Paul's argument in outlining his career contains two key points: first, that he was not appointed by any human being; second, that he did not learn his gospel from any human being. His appointment and his gospel were both given to him directly when God revealed the Son to him. Not Peter nor James nor John nor their associates commissioned him or taught him; on that point he is adamant. It is interesting to note that this means that Paul's knowledge of "the historical Jesus" (whom James and Peter and John knew personally) was limited, even close to non-existent. His argument here in Galatians is that he had little such knowledge and wanted little, and that he seized no opportunities to get more. Knowledge of Christ the Son of God that God had revealed to him was, in his mind, more than sufficient by itself.

Paul would be telling us all this only if it were essential to his defense against his opponents in Galatia. Those opponents must have claimed Paul was appointed an apostle by humans and learned his gospel from humans; otherwise it would be pointless for Paul to seek to prove such claims false. Since their gospel differed from his regarding the Law, Paul's opponents presumably claimed that whatever he had learned from humans he had learned badly, and that whoever had appointed him an apostle wished to cancel the appointment or wished to assert authority over him so that he would no longer teach freedom from Law.

We do not know exactly who came to Galatia and raised these problems for Paul and his community. Many scholars use such terms as Judaizers or Jewish-Christians, with the implication they constitute a branch of the early church independent both of Paul and of the authorities in Jerusalem. This is possible but not likely. At this very early date in the history of the Christian movement, it is hard to imagine there were Christian groups who both kept the Law and urged Gentile Christians to keep the Law, and who were also distinct from or in opposition to the leaders of the church in Jerusalem.

A more convincing explanation is that those who came to Galatia were sent by James or by the church in Jerusalem, which was led by James up to the time of his death in 62 CE. We know James believed that Christians must follow Torah Law. As Paul presents it, if Christians representing James arrived Galatia to reform Paul's Christian community, then the Christians representing James were breaking the agreement Paul had made previously with James, Peter, and John that he, i.e. Paul, would go to Gentiles while they would go to Jews.

Were the Christians in Galatia "Christians" (in the sense of a separate religious category) or were they "Jews"? From Paul's perspective, the answer is that faithful Christians are the descendants of Abraham, the people of God, and therefore they are "Jews." Another way of putting this is that Paul declared the covenant between God and his people now open to Gentiles who have faith in Jesus Christ; thus, Christians are those who, through faith, have joined in the covenant between God and His chosen people.

Suppose then the Galatians, feeling and believing themselves to have become Jewish through their faith, encountered Christians of Jewish ancestry—Christians who had seen Jesus or, at least, had met his brother James, his disciples, and friends of Jesus such as Peter and John—who said, "Nonsense! You must have faith in Jesus Christ *and* you must obey the Law of God, repenting any sins you may commit, receiving forgiveness in Jesus' name." The Galatian Christians might have countered, "But Paul said the Law and faith were opposed," and might have heard in response, "What does Paul know? He never met Jesus. Everything he learned he learned from those who did know Jesus, especially our friends who are leaders of the church in Jerusalem. They allowed him to be an apostle. He has no grounds to contradict them."

The Galatians seem to have met such people and nearly to have been convinced that salvation requires obedience to God's Law. Paul hears about this and angrily, defensively, responds with his letter.

As before, in the city of Antioch (2:11–14), Paul in Galatia is in conflict with Jesus' brother James and Jesus' most important disciple, Peter (Cephas). Paul cannot claim anything like their knowledge of the life, teaching, and personality of Jesus. Rather, he claims knowledge of Jesus the risen Christ and Lord, knowledge given him directly by the risen Christ. It was not James or Peter but God who appointed Paul an apostle. God's Son taught him, not James or Peter. The Galatians should listen to him, and through him God, rather than listen to representatives of James or Peter.

Toward the end of his letter to the Galatians Paul addresses another problem, one occurring frequently in his letters. If Christians are free from the necessity to follow the Law, are they therefore free to do anything they want no matter how wild and irresponsible? Of course not. In the concluding chapters of his letter Paul is careful to emphasize that Christians must act in a moral and loving fashion despite their freedom from Law.

Romans

Paul's letter entitled Romans written in c. 59 CE is his masterpiece, his most sustained and systematic effort to communicate his thoughts on Christ, salvation, sin, and Law. READ THE LETTER TO THE ROMANS. UNDERLINE REFERENCES TO FAITH, JUSTIFICATION AND RIGHTEOUSNESS.

Paul's Letter to the Romans contains lengthier and more complex versions of the same arguments as are in the letter to the Galatians and so, because it is so densely and complexly argued, it is less accessible to ordinary readers than Galatians is. In Galatians, Paul addressed an audience of Gentiles. In Romans, his audience included both Jewish and Gentile Christians, and the Jewish Christians may have been in the majority. Thus, Romans contains several arguments that the Jewish tradition and the Jewish people are favored by God, but Paul does not downgrade Gentiles.

The Gentiles and the Law

Toward the beginning of Romans (1:18–2:17), Paul argues against the idea that because God is the God of the Jews, and because the Jews were given God's Law, the Gentiles are irrelevant to God's plan. This idea arises from reasoning that if the problem of salvation concerns people's obedience to God's Law, and if God, who is just, would act unjustly should he punish people for disobedience to a Law they never knew, then God would neither reward nor punish Gentiles. Paul argues that the Gentiles indeed have the Law, or at least knowledge of God and God's commands equivalent to the Law: They obtain this knowledge from reasoning about the natural world or perhaps, as we might put it, from their consciences. Paul writes, "For all that may be known of God by men lies plain before their eyes; indeed God himself has disclosed it to them. His invisible attributes, that is to say his everlasting power and deity, have been visible, ever since the world began, to the eye of reason, in the things he has made. There is therefore no possible defense for their conduct; knowing God, they have refused to honor him as God, or to render him thanks" (1:19–21). Through careful thought about the world, Gentiles can come to know the nature and requirements of God. In Paul's opinion, therefore, Gentiles are just as subject to God's judgment as Jews and just as capable of achieving righteousness as Jews are.

This line of reasoning would naturally raise the question of whether Jews have any special relationship to God at all, or whether they are simply one more ethnic group out of many. Paul wishes to argue that Jews do have a special place in God's plan while maintaining the position that "God has no favorites" (2:11–12). Jews have the advantage over Gentiles, in theory at least, because they have received God's Law directly and therefore, unlike the Gentiles, do not have to puzzle it out for themselves by reflection on the world. Paul thus concedes the Jews have a special relationship to God. Yet he denies that "special" means "superior": "Are we Jews any better off? No, not at all! For we have already drawn up the accusation that Jews and Greeks alike are all under the power of sin" (2:9). God is the God of Jews and Gentiles equally.

Paul seems to argue two points simultaneously, and while they may seem contradictory, they are not. He argues that the Jews were given the Law on Mount Sinai and, had they been able to keep the Law, would have had the advantage over Gentiles. As they did not keep it (in Paul's opinion), their advantage has been canceled, leaving them in the same situation as the Gentiles. Still, they were first to receive special consideration by God (Torah Law), and so the Jews come first and Gentiles last. In Romans 11, Paul symbolizes Judaism as a domestic variety of olive tree that has been consecrated to God. Some branches are pruned off the domestic tree (Judaism), and some branches of a wild variety of olive tree (Gentiles) are grafted onto it. These wild branches now share the nutrients provided by the roots and the sap of the consecrated tree, and all parts constitute the same tree. Because of their lack of faith, the old branches were pruned off; because of their faith, the new branches are grafted on.

In Romans 11, especially, Paul argues that the salvation of the Gentiles is intended, in part, to provide motivation for Jews to be saved. Paul finds Jews somewhat less receptive to the gospel than the Gentiles are but believes that condition to be temporary: "This partial blindness has come upon Israel only until the Gentiles have been admitted in full strength; when that has happened, the whole of Israel will be saved" (11:26). It is unlikely that Jewish audiences then or now have found this prospect comforting, or even acceptable.

Righteousness Through Faith

For Paul "righteousness" is a key principle; if God finds a person righteous, or justified, that person is approved by God and so, Paul believes, will never spiritually die. But Paul believes humanity is sinful, unwilling to admit God is sovereign over all life, and incapable of living in accordance with God's will. Thus, God cannot approve of humanity in the absence of complete transformation. As Paul understands it, that transformation can only come through faith.

One term Paul frequently uses to express the approval of God is *justification*, which usually means "to make righteous." In Paul's opinion, people try to make themselves righteous, but in this they cannot succeed. Only God can justify people. Should a person, through faith in Christ Jesus, admit they are sinful and concede that God has the right to punish sin, then that person is open for justification. When the person has faith in Jesus Christ, understands that Jesus died for the sins of all humanity, and receives the Spirit of Christ, that person is justified, or righteous, before God. This process of justification through faith can be called "salvation," or "redemption," or even "expiation," a word most often used in reference to cleansing through sacrifice. Jesus Christ was a sacrifice for expiation, Paul believes, and through faith in his death for sin, the expiation of the sins of faithful individuals becomes effective.

Although individuals may receive justification through their faith, this does not guarantee they will subsequently live moral lives or, regardless of their behavior, rise to life with Christ after death. Strengthened with the Spirit, Christians should be better able to avoid sin than other people, but sin (conceived as a power counteracting the will of God) continues to urge people to go against God. In Romans 7, Paul uses the first person ("I"), but this is not just self-description. The "I" of this chapter refers to all those with faith in Christ.

Paul writes, "I do not even acknowledge my own actions as mine, for what I do is not what I want to do, but what I detest. But if what I do is against my will, it means that I agree with the law and hold it to be admirable. But as things are, it is no longer I who perform the action, but sin that lodges in me" (7:15–18). This is, of course, a pessimistic view of the human situation. It is countered by a statement found a little later in Romans in which Paul, speaking of Christians like himself, writes, "You are on the spiritual level if only God's Spirit dwells within you; and if a man does not possess the Spirit of Christ he is no Christian. But if Christ is dwelling within you, then although the body is a dead thing because you sinned, yet the Spirit is life itself because you have been justified" (8:9–11). This reminds one of the passage in Galatians wherein Paul claims "to prove that you are sons, God has sent into your hearts the Spirit of his Son, crying 'Abba! Father!' You are therefore no longer a slave but a son, and if a son, then also by God's own act an heir" (Gal 4:6–7). In fact, Paul recalled that thought when writing Romans, for he continues on in chapter 8 to write, "All who are moved by the Spirit of God are Sons of God. The Spirit you have received is not a Spirit of slavery leading you back into a life of fear, but a Spirit that makes us Sons, enabling us to cry 'Abba! Father!' In that cry the Spirit of God joins with our spirit in testifying that we are God's children; and if children, then heirs" (Rom 8:14–15). (Note: In many English translations, a small "s" for "sons" rather than a capital "S" for "Sons" is a translator's decision designed to distinguish Jesus the Son of God from other people who are sons of God; Greek manuscripts do not make this distinction.) All Christians, Paul believes, have received a Spirit making them children [Sons] of God. As such they are saved, justified, righteous—heirs to the promise God made to Abraham.

Paul seems to shift from pessimism to enthusiastic optimism in a few short lines in this section of Romans. The Spirit of God in a person will war against its opposite, the spirit of sin, but final victory does not occur during a person's lifetime. Thus, a person who has received the Spirit of God should seek to do what is right with the aid of the

Spirit, but that person should not be overconfident; the temptations of the spirit of sin, which he sometimes calls the "flesh," will continue. Paul optimistically believes Christians will be saved through their faith and that through the assistance of the Spirit they will be able to behave in a reasonably loving fashion.

In Romans 12–15, Paul outlines the course of conduct appropriate for Christians in whom God's Spirit dwells. This is not a re-creation of the Law through the back door, although some have accused Paul of doing so. Rather, Paul gives general advice based on the principle that as all Christians are united in faith, they must behave in ways appropriate to that state of union. If Christians are all one person in Christ Jesus, they must love one another as themselves, not just in a poetic way but in a way directing their behavior.

1 Corinthians

READ FIRST CORINTHIANS AND UNDERLINE PASSAGES THAT IDENTIFY SPECIFIC PROBLEMS ADDRESSED BY PAUL: for example, 1:11–12 specifies a problem relating to divisions among the Christian community, 8:1 defines a problem having to do with whether Christians can eat food consecrated to heathen deities.

Paul wrote First Corinthians to comment on specific problems he believed to exist in the Corinthian Christian community. Readers can infer the theology and Christology of Paul from the letter, but this letter was not written to be a treatise on those subjects.

First Corinthians is part of a longer correspondence, more of which is preserved in the composite letter called Second Corinthians. Like other letters of Paul's, this one has a formal style. It begins with greetings and continues with a thanksgiving statement (1:1–9). Then comes the body of the letter, a section which in his letters frequently concludes with *parenesis*, an exhortation to behave properly (16:13–18). Galatians 5:1–6:10 is a more extended example of parenesis.

The first portion of the first Corinthians letter, 1:10–6:20, is critical of Christians who believe that they have a special wisdom that elevates them above other Christians. Paul writes, with irony, that his gospel is a message of foolishness and weakness, not of wisdom and self-aggrandizement. He combines this idea with the crucial theme of the crucifixion of Jesus and argues that the message of the cross, which seems like foolishness, is in fact the manifestation of the wisdom of God.

First Corinthians is particularly significant for the insight it gives into early Christian ritual life. Here we find the first recorded discussion of the ritual of the communion meal (10:14–17, 11:17–34, etc.). We hear about the practice of public prayer and prophecy in the church meetings (14:1–19, etc.), a practice evidently carried out by men and women alike (11:13). But in another passage, one that causes considerable dismay to many readers, Paul declares that women should not speak aloud in church (14:34–35). Scholarship is divided on the issue of whether Paul wrote this passage or whether it was written later (at about the same time as the Pastorals) and inserted into First Corinthians. Those who think it is a later insertion argue the following: the passage contradicts other passages in Paul's letters that indicate that women did speak in churches; it contradicts the principle that "in Christ there is neither male nor female;" the flow of the letter is smoother if the passage is removed (i.e. if 14:26–33 carries directly into 14:36–40, the passage makes clear sense); and Paul is not prone to arguing that Christian services must be "as the Law directs."

Those who accepted Paul's gospel and received the grace of God received also the Spirit of Christ. The Spirit of Christ was not conceived to be an abstract state of being but a powerful and practical new experience, giving an individual special power. That special power included increased ability to resist temptations and to do special things. Paul lists various possibilities in 1 Corinthians 12:7–11: "In each of us the Spirit is manifested in one particular way, for some useful purpose. One man, through the Spirit . . . can put the deepest knowledge into words. Another, by the same Spirit, is granted faith; another, by the one Spirit, gifts of healing, and another miraculous powers; another has the gift of prophecy, and another ability to distinguish true spirits from false; yet another has the gift of ecstatic utterance of different kinds, and another the ability to interpret it. But all these gifts are the work of one and the same Spirit, distributing them separately to each individual at will." The gifts of the Spirit were seen by Paul to validate his work and his gospel (Gal 3:1–5) and to provide evidence for its truth.

His churches, composed of people filled with Spirit who encountered the Spirit through enthusiastic experiences, tended sometimes toward chaos. In 1 Corinthians 11 to the end, Paul tries to bring order to community meetings where the display of spiritual gifts had been leading to disorder. One of his main points is that speaking in tongues (technically: *glossolalia*) has no useful effect upon a communal audience unless that speech can be translated into comprehensible language (for them, Greek). While this is sometimes taken to be an effort by Paul to downplay the importance of speech in tongues, he shows great respect for that capacity when used properly. In fact he claims that he speaks in tongues more than anyone in the community (14:18). Paul does argue, however, that spiritual gifts of any sort are subordinate to the capacity for love. His classic passage on love is found in chapter 13: "I may speak in tongues of men or of angels, but if I am without love, I am a sounding gong or a clanging cymbal. I may have the gift of prophecy, and know every hidden truth; I may have faith strong enough to move mountains; but if I have no love, I am nothing . . ." (1 Cor 13:1–3). These words were written to emphasize his principle that nothing should come ahead of Christian unity through love—not even the exercise of the gifts of God's Spirit.

2 Corinthians

It is likely that Second Corinthians is a composite of letters rather than one sustained piece of communication. <u>READ THE LETTER CALLED SECOND CORINTHIANS, BUT TRY DOING SO IN THE FOLLOWING ORDER:</u>

1. The "Tearful Letter" (10:1–13:14)
2. Paul defends himself (2:14–6:13, 7:2–4)
3. Goodwill returns (1:1–2:13, 7:5–16)
4. Letter recommending Titus (8:1–24)
5. Letter about the collection (9:1–15)
6. A fragment some think was not written by Paul but by someone critical of his teachings (6:14–7:1) . . . Can you see why?

Evidently, other Christian itinerant apostles have come to Corinth and delivered what Paul believes is a message of another Jesus, another spirit, another gospel (11:4). They have had some success among the Corinthian Christians, and Paul is outraged. He responds with bitter irony claiming that while he does not wish to boast, as he believes those other apostles boast, he nevertheless could boast if he chose to do so. And for several paragraphs he does just this. In the process, he provides very interesting biographical material, particularly in 11:21–12:10. Speaking of himself in the third person, he tells of an experience fourteen years past (i.e.

about 41 CE) when he entered the third level of the heavens and heard secret supernatural words.

As he did in the beginning of First Corinthians, Paul contrasts power and weakness, choosing, ironically, to brag about his weakness as he bragged, in First Corinthians, about his supposed foolishness (see also 2 Cor 11:16–21). Paul would have his audience believe that his weakness is, in reality, the power of God. "Hence," he says, "I am well content, for Christ's sake, with weakness, contempt, persecution, hardship, and frustration; for when I am weak, then I am strong" (12:10).

Paul's opponents come across in his letters extremely badly. We know about them only what he tells us, and he is not interested whatsoever in giving their points of view a fair assessment. But it is a good mental exercise to try and surmise what their point of view might have been and what they might have said critically of Paul. His opponents were (presumably) sincere Christians who were active in a very early stage of the Christian church, and they may well have had significant and valuable points of view of their own.

Philippians

See if this letter doesn't make more sense if you consider it originally to have been three letters:

1. A letter thanking the Philippians (1:1–3:1)
2. A fragment of a polemical letter (3:2–4:9, 21–23)
3. Another letter thanking the Philippians (4:10–20)

Philippians contains a passage of principal importance for the development of Christian thought about Jesus Christ: 2:6–11. This is sometimes called "the Christ Hymn" because of its poetic structure. Most scholars today believe that it was quoted by Paul, not composed by him, because it contains words and emphases rare or unknown elsewhere in Paul's writing. On the other hand, it is likely that Paul made some changes in the Christ Hymn, probably adding the phrase "death on a cross" and possibly adding the phrase "in heaven, on earth, and in the depths." This hymn was probably in use in Christian liturgies in Philippi and perhaps elsewhere.

Paul's angry argument in chapter 3 is similar to his angry arguments in his letter to the Galatians. Here, especially in 3:9, one can see the kind of uncompromising statements that, in part, gave rise to the Protestant reformers' insistence that salvation comes by faith alone. Verses 3:12–14 echo a theme found elsewhere in Paul's letters: the perfection of salvation has not happened yet. Paul believes that Christians are transformed now, by the Spirit, into people whose ultimate salvation is guaranteed but has not yet occurred. This is sometimes called Paul's *eschatological reservation*, meaning that perfection must not be claimed now (as perhaps some Corinthian Christians claimed, evidenced in Paul's sarcastic response in 1 Cor 4:8) but anticipated at the time of the return of the Lord (see 1 Thess 4:15–18 in light of Phil 3:20–21).

Philemon

This letter is written to accompany the slave Onesimus, who is being returned to his master Philemon. Onesimus is probably the same person referred to in Colossians 4:7–9 as a native of Colossae; if so, Philemon also lives in Colossae. Paul urges Philemon to look favorably on Onesimus despite the fact that Philemon had the legal right to punish him severely.

Paul here seems to accept the institution of slavery. Elsewhere in his letters, he urges slaves and servants to be obedient to their masters and urges Christians in general to accept the orders of the civil government. Paul's revolutionary ideas were confined to the sphere of religion. He does not seem to have had any intention to urge people to seek the restructuring of secular society.

Colossians

The question of Paul's authorship of this letter is disputed but there are as many scholars who affirm it is Paul's as deny that it is. It actually makes sense, however to say that the letter is *both* by Paul *and* that it isn't. Here's why: the letter opens with a double greeting, from Paul and Timothy. As with most or all of Paul's letters, this one was dictated rather than handwritten. In fact, in the last sentence Paul makes a point of saying that he writes that final sentence himself, and we should understand that a scribe wrote the rest from dictation. Dictation to scribes was common practice in the ancient world both for illiterate and literate people. In the case of the letter to the Colossians, it may well be that the dictation came mainly from Timothy rather than from Paul, even though Paul was present in the room at the time listening in. If Paul was present while Timothy dictated the letter, then the Letter to the Colossians is not quite a letter of Paul's, Timothy having dictated it, but nevertheless it had Paul's approval and Paul even literally signed off on it in the final sentence.

The letter to the Colossians contains the most elevated concept of the nature of Christ to be found in any Pauline letter. Paul declares him to be "the image of the invisible God; his is primacy over all created things. In him everything in heaven and on earth was created, not only things visible but also the invisible orders of thrones, sovereignties, authorities, and powers: the whole universe has been created through him and for him. And he exists before everything, and all things are held together in him," (1:15–17), and "in Christ the complete being of the Godhead dwells embodied, and in him you have been brought to completion" (2:9–10). These exalted views, which probably are related to the identification of Jesus Christ with God's Wisdom (cf. Proverbs

8:22–31 and 1 Cor 1:24) may not correspond completely with other statements of Paul's about Christ. The Christ Hymn that Paul cites approvingly in Philippians derives from a rather different image of Christ than the Colossians hymn; in the Christ Hymn, Christ was described as the one who voluntarily emptied himself of divinity. That said, Paul's ideas may have evolved over time and been expressed differently in different circumstances. Indeed, it would not be unlikely that, as his ideas evolved, he came to hold a more elevated vision of Christ's nature.

Recurring Themes

The remainder of our consideration of Paul will follow a format used in the other chapters of this book. The following recurring themes in each New Testament book will be discussed: sources, Jesus' life, Jesus' death, eschatology, Torah Law, community, and controversies. In subsequent chapters, there will be discussion of the interaction of ideas between the document under consideration and those already considered. Of course the section on interactions will continually expand as more documents have been studied. This format will allow the summary of material already presented and also allow the introduction of significant new information.

Sources

Paul declares that the main and essential source for his ideas and teachings is the revelation he received from God. All other sources of information—human teachings, as he would put it—are secondary. "Without consulting any human being" (Gal 1:16), Paul began his ministry. He did not feel the need to learn from anyone but God and Christ. This is not to say he did not learn from any other Christians. He must have done so, but he placed little value on that knowledge and does not use the "teachings of Jesus" as sources for the principal ideas of his gospel. We need to bear in mind that Paul tells us that before his experience of Christ, he was actively persecuting the Christian movement. A persecutor always believes that he understands what it is that he is persecuting, and so Paul surely believed that he understood the basics of the Christian movement before he joined it. It is significant that Paul affirms that he joined the movement that he previously had opposed and so, in Paul's mind, he is not coming up with anything new.

On certain occasions Paul seems to refer to traditions he received from human beings. For example, when he gives an account of the Lord's Supper, he writes, "The tradition which I handed on to you came to me from the Lord himself" (1 Cor 11:23). Scholars usually treat the term "tradition" as governing that sentence, which implies that Paul's knowledge of the Lord's Supper comes from other people to whom it was a crucial event recalled from Jesus' life. Another point of view, however, is that "the Lord himself" spoke of the matter to Paul in a revelation. Paul's denial, in Galatians, of the influence of human information on his thought would support this idea. The sentence as it stands is ambiguous. It may mean the Lord himself revealed to Paul an account subsequently passed on as a tradition, one eventually written down by Mark and then adapted by Matthew and Luke. John, Q, and Thomas do not record this tradition.

We may be certain Paul knew something of Jesus' life and of his sayings. Therefore, oral tradition must have had some influence in shaping his point of view. Indeed, Paul does not insist that he refused ever to know anything about the "historical" Jesus. But from Paul's own perspective, historical traditions were not nearly as important in the formation of his thought and beliefs as was private revelation from the Lord.

Jesus

Paul's interest in the events of Jesus' life is limited. He never discusses in any detail Jesus' birth, miracles or teachings. Once in a while, Paul quotes words spoken by Jesus, but usually to support his own teachings and even then not in a way that indicates that he relies on Jesus' words for his own ideas. If we knew of Jesus' life and teachings only through Paul's letters, we could say little beyond that Jesus was born "under the Law" and that he was condemned by Pilate and crucified.

We do not know what, if anything, Paul told strangers about Jesus' life to lead them to faith. From his letters it does not seem likely he told them tales of Jesus' miracles, for he never refers to them. Paul would not have denied Jesus did any or all of the miracles attributed to him in the miracles sources. Rather, Paul would have argued they were details of little importance compared to the cosmic importance of Christ's death for the sins of all people and Christ's resurrection, which gave all people the opportunity to choose to rise from the dead with him. Similarly, Paul does not consider his gospel a version or continuation of the oral "gospel" spoken by Jesus and transmitted by tradition. He might not have denied that Jesus said what traditions said he said, but he does not anywhere indicate that he is dependent on, or even particularly interested in, explaining and carrying on the traditions of Jesus' sayings.

Jesus' death is of crucial significance to Paul. When Christ died, he died for the sins of all people; thus the option of accepting Christ's death rather than having to die one's own death became available to anyone. This, for Paul, was the most important event in human history since the fall of Adam. It provided the opportunity to achieve eternal life, to be justified through faith, and thus to be united with Christ and be children of God (Gal 3:26). The idea of "the sacrifice of Christ on the cross" comes from Paul; "sacrifice" is another way of indicating that Jesus' death brings forgiveness of sins and escape from death to anyone with faith.

Eschatology

Eschatology is a term referring to ideas about the end of things, particularly the idea of the end of this world. The prevalent eschatology of the New Testament is the idea that this world will soon come to an end and will be replaced with another improved world called the "Kingdom of God." Paul's clearest statements about the coming end of this world can be found in his first letter to the Thessalonians. There, he makes clear the end of this world will come quickly and that one mark of Christian life is that Christians should "wait expectantly for the appearance from heaven of [God's] Son Jesus . . ." (1:10). Paul believed they would wait a short time; he speaks of "we who are left alive until the Lord comes" (4:15), confident the Lord will return during his own lifetime, though he also says that no one knows exactly when this event will take place.

The faithful who are embodied in flesh now will receive immortality and new non-flesh bodies. Paul reveals this secret in 1 Corinthians 15:51–53: "Listen! I will unfold a mystery: we shall not all die, but we shall all be changed in a flash, in the twinkling of an eye, at the last trumpet-call. For the trumpet will sound, and the dead will rise immortal, and we shall be changed. This perishable being must be clothed with the imperishable, and what is mortal must be clothed with immortality." Note that Paul expects that he and most of his audience will be alive when this happens.

Paul's expectation of the end of this world and the return of the Lord Jesus Christ in a short time affects his ideas about how people should live. For example, he believes it might be best to avoid such long-term commitments as marriage since the remaining time is so short.

When the Lord returns those who are in the Lord will be more perfectly with him, free from constraints brought about by material life. Paul's perspective on the world's end is optimistic for himself and his followers, but others will suffer and die: "While they are talking of peace and security, all at once calamity is upon them, sudden as the pangs that come upon a woman with child; and there will be no escape" (1 Thess 5:3).

There is no Judgment Day for Paul; nor does he anywhere mention hell or eternal punishment. The common concept of Judgment Day contradicts Paul's essential ideas. To be judged whether you have or have not lived in obedience to God's intentions falls into the category of Law rather than faith. Those who have faith will be with Christ; those who do not will die and exist no more. The judicial idea of judgment, with people on trial before God or Christ, has no place in Paul's system of ideas.

Torah Law

Much of this chapter has dealt with the Law as Paul conceived of it. His ideas come down to this: (1) Although the Law may provide useful instruction in morality, anyone who seeks to be justified in the eyes of God by following it is doomed to failure. All will break it and so all will be cursed. (2) Faith in Christ brings about justification in the eyes of God. Anyone already justified by faith ought not to seek justification through following Law. (3) Anyone may follow the Torah Law if it is convenient; no one should live immorally or feel under any deliberate obligation to break the Law. The second point caused Paul considerable trouble. His followers occasionally believed freedom from Law meant freedom to do anything at all, and his opponents accused him of teaching immorality. He repeatedly denies any such intention. His letters insist that Christians are not free to behave immorally and that such behavior will lose them the rewards their faith would otherwise bring them.

Paul thinks the Law could have unacceptable social consequences. Since Christian unity is essential, the Law should be put aside for the sake of that unity, as demonstrated in the case of the food Laws addressed by Paul in his letter to the Galatians. It is on this point that Paul disagreed with Peter and Barnabas in Antioch (Gal 2:11–14).

Paul's message to Gentiles includes the important point that Gentiles can become members of God's community ("Jews") through faith without following the Law of the Jews. It should not be surprising he ran into opposition from Jewish Christians who insisted upon the contrary, that to be members of God's community one must necessarily follow God's Law. This may have been the most significant conflict within the Christian movement during the first century. By the second century, Paul's perspective prevailed.

Community

Paul was probably the founder of the Christian communities to which he wrote, with the exception of the community in Rome. His letters show he felt responsible for those communities, and, even when absent, felt he had the right to exert influence and control. To what extent the members of the communities thought of Paul as their leader, in his absence, is unclear, but certainly their respect for him gave him strong influence.

Controversy

Paul wrote his letters because of controversies and, therefore, controversies fill them. Because we have only Paul's side of the argument, and Paul has no interest in detailing, much less explaining, the positions taken by his opponents, it is usually unclear exactly what the controversies were about or with whom Paul found himself in disagreement. Sometimes, as in 1 Corinthians and Romans, Paul apparently was engaged in more than one argument at once. In Galatians, Paul argues against Jewish Christians who seek to convince his Gentile Christians they should follow the Law. Paul's defense indicates that his opponents represented, or claimed to represent, the Jerusalem church, whose principal figures were James, Peter, and John. As we have but the one letter to go by, we do not know who won, but in the long run Paul's perspective on the Law came to be that of the whole Christian church.

End-of-Chapter Exercises

1. Why can't a person find salvation through the Law, according to Paul? If you believed that following the Law of God is a path to salvation, how might you respond to Paul?
2. What did you discover when you read 2 Corinthians in the suggested order on page 89? How important is the order of a text to its meaning?
3. In Galatians 4 Paul makes an allegorical argument based on the story of Abraham. Read Genesis 15:1–22:19 and judge to what extent Paul's interpretation of the story is valid.

Bibliography

Betz, Hans Dieter. *Galatians*. Philadelphia: Fortress Press, 1979.

Bryan, Christopher. *A Preface to Romans: Notes on the Epistle in its Literary and Cultural Setting*. New York NY: Oxford University Press, 2000.

Crossan, John Dominic, and Jonathan Reed. *In Search of Paul*. San Francisco: HarperCollins, 2004.

Davies, W. D. *Paul and Rabbinic Judaism: Some Elements in Pauline Theology.* 4th ed. Philadelphia: Fortress Press, 1980.

Hock, R. F. *The Social Content of Paul's Ministry.* Philadelphia: Fortress Press, 1980.

Horrell, David. *An Introduction to the Study of Paul.* Edinburgh: T&T Clark, 2006

Jewett, Robert. *A Chronology of Paul's Life.* Philadelphia: Fortress Press, 1979.

Lockwood, Gregory. *1 Corinthians: Concordia Commentary.* St. Louis MO: Concordia Publishing House, 2000.

Muddiman, John and John Barton. *The Pauline Epistles: Oxford Bible Commentary.* New York NY: Oxford University Press, 2010.

Perrin, Norman, and Dennis Duling. *The New Testament: An Introduction.* New York: Harcourt Brace Jovanovich, 1982.

Sanders, E. P. *Paul, the Law, and the Jewish People.* Philadelphia: Fortress Press, 1983.

Sandmel, Samuel. *The Genius of Paul: A Study in History.* Philadelphia: Fortress Press, 1979.

Schnelle, Udo. *Apostle Paul: His Life and Theology.* Grand Rapids MI: Baker Academic, 2005.

Theissen, Gerd. *The Social Setting of Pauline Christianity.* Philadelphia: Fortress Press, 1982.

Gospel Sources

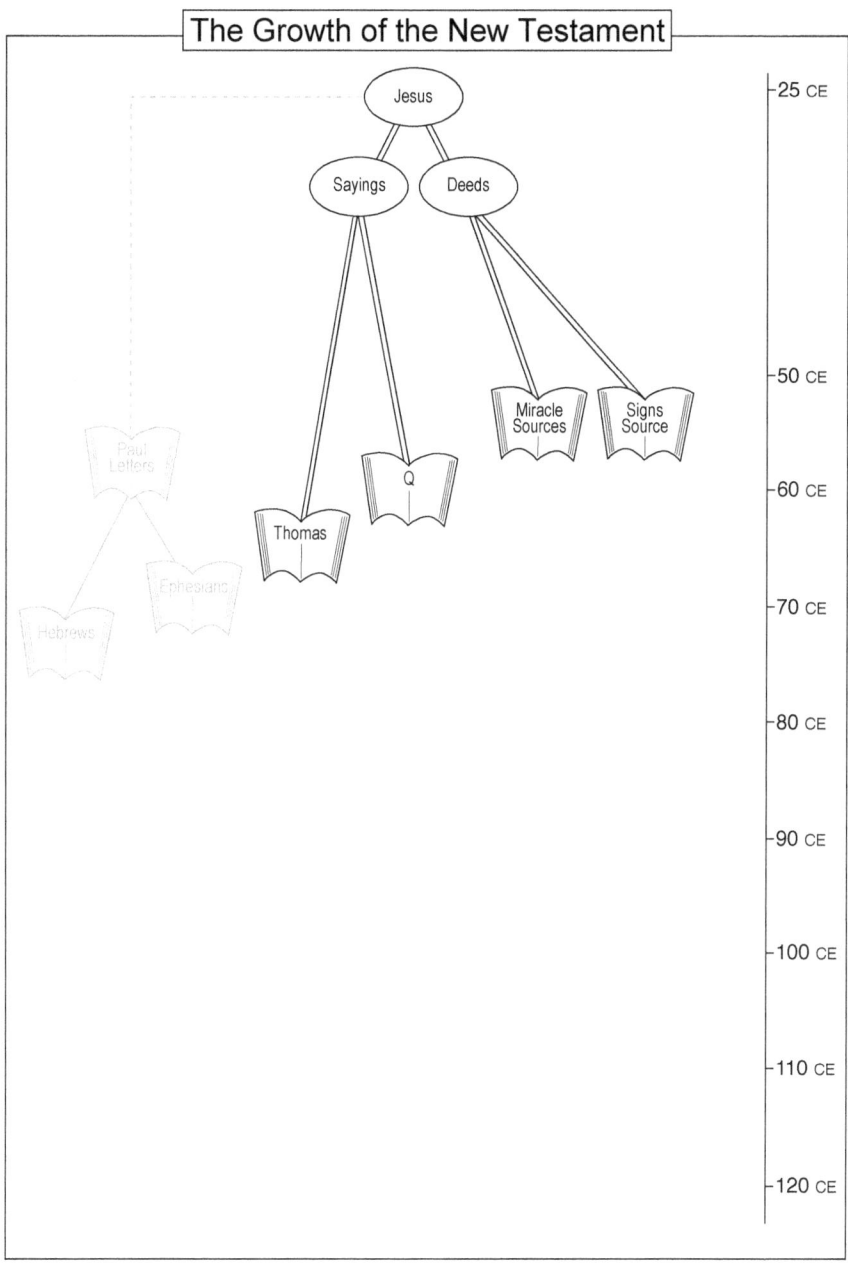

Dashed lines: indirect influence
Double lines: oral transmission
Single thick lines: use of written source
Thin lines: followers, admirers & imitators

CHAPTER 4

Gospel Sources

OBJECTIVES

- Differentiate the gospels of the NT in terms of dates written, sources, and key themes
- Learn how to do *form criticism* via an in-depth analysis of Q source
- Discover the issues raised by the presence of miracle stories in the gospels

Analytical scholars of the New Testament reject two extreme views of the New Testament gospels: They believe neither that the gospels are fictions invented entirely from writers' imaginations, nor that the gospels are precise transcriptions by eyewitnesses. In agreement with the preface to Luke's gospel, analytical scholars believe that the evangelists used a variety of oral and written sources to compose their books. Some of those written sources can be recovered and studied separately from the gospels in which they are included, so that even if today we do not have physical manuscripts of those sources, we can still read them. To study them is to study approaches to an understanding of Jesus that existed before some or all of the gospels were written. Two important sources are (1) collections of miracle stories and (2) collections of sayings of Jesus, and we will study both in this chapter.

The Miracles Sources

Mark, Matthew, and Luke begin their accounts of Jesus' ministry in the same way. After his baptism, Jesus amazes many of those whom he encounters by healing diseased people and driving out what they thought were disease-causing demons. At the very beginning of his gospel Mark writes, "They brought to him all who were ill or possessed by devils; and the whole town was there, gathered at the door. He healed many who suffered from various diseases, and drove out many devils." Soon, "all through Galilee he went, preaching in the synagogues and casting out the devils" (1:39). Similarly, Matthew reports that shortly after his baptism "he went round the whole of Galilee, teaching in the synagogues, preaching the gospel of the Kingdom, and curing whatever illness or infirmity there was among the people. His fame reached the whole of Syria; and sufferers from every kind of illness, racked with pain, possessed by devils, epileptic, or paralyzed, were all brought to him, and he cured them. Great crowds also followed him, from Galilee and the Ten Towns, from Jerusalem and Judaea, and from Transjordan" (4:23–25). Luke also introduces Jesus' activities this way (4:40), and John writes toward the beginning of his gospel, "While he was in Jerusalem for Passover many gave their allegiance to him when they saw the signs he performed" (2:23).

The evangelists intended to show that the initial perception people had of Jesus was that he was a miracle worker, which is to say, a healer. Jesus is portrayed as a physician of his time, and in that time medical practice and what we now call religion, or magic, or miracles, were wholly intertwined. Throughout the gospels, we are given reports of miracles that could just as well be understood as examples of ancient medical practice. Exorcism, for example, is a medical technique in nearly all pre-modern cultures. Mark begins with a report of Jesus healing Simon's mother-in-law who was ill in bed with fever (1:30), then gives reports of the cure of a leper (1:42) and of a paralyzed man (2:4), then of a man with a withered arm (3:1), and so forth. While it is probably correct to think of Jesus during his early life as a *tekton*, a carpenter or construction worker, Jesus is described in the New Testament as a physician during his later life.

Where did these stories come from? Presumably they arose from events in Jesus' lifetime. Then, early on, they were passed from one person to another orally, by word-of-mouth. Naturally, during the oral transmission of stories, details were dropped and elements were added. At first the stories were told in the Aramaic language used by Jesus and his disciples; later they were told in Greek as the Christian movement took hold in regions outside of Palestine.

Many scholars believe that in addition to oral traditions, Mark and John used written texts as sources for the miracle stories in their gospels. These sources took the form of booklets or sections of scrolls that were themselves written compilations of orally transmitted stories. The first written accounts circulated among Christian leaders who used them as sources for preaching intended to convince people that Jesus was an exceptional, important, and divinely guided person. It is impossible to say for certain, but the miracle sources were probably first written a decade or two after the crucifixion, in roughly 40–60 CE. The names of their authors are unknown.

Some early Christians (like some twenty-first century Christians) based their beliefs and their arguments that Jesus was Christ on the evidence of his miracle-working ability. Peter is quoted in Acts as stating, "I speak of Jesus of Nazareth, a man singled out by God and made known to you through miracles, portents, and signs, which God worked among you through him, as you well know" (2:22). Luke's Acts of the Apostles frequently stresses the importance of miracles in establishing the legitimacy of the apostles, and, according to Acts, working miracles was a principal activity of Jesus during his life.

Nature Miracles and Healing Miracles

Stories of Jesus' miracles can be divided into two major categories: nature miracles and healing miracles. Walking on water, stilling storms, and turning water into wine are examples of nature miracles because the laws of nature are, apparently, overcome. Those who are convinced the laws of nature apply to all times and all circumstances do not believe nature miracles can happen. When Jesus is reported to have healed leprosy, cured blindness, enabled crippled people to walk, or cast out demons, he has performed healing miracles. Healing can result from many things, and even though modern medicine may not be able to explain how a cure happens, the fact that an explanation is lacking does not prove natural law has been broken. Faith healing occurs today both in religious settings and in doctors' offices; faith in a healer can, by itself, through what is known as the "placebo" effect, lead to recovery.

In ancient times almost all medical practice was religious in one way or another, and almost all cures were thought to include an element of divine intervention. A skeptical person today, however, will assume that the main factor in religious healing is the placebo effect, which takes advantage of the human mind's tendency to assist physical healing—or at least the reduction of symptomatic pain—when it is confident that healing is taking place. In other words, the more one has faith that one is being healed by whatever means, modern or ancient, the more likely it is that one's mind will facilitate the healing process. The placebo effect describes a secular faith-healing analogous to religious faith-healing, and it is not at all unreasonable to think that this type of healing is reasonably effective. It has been the main form of medical practice for the human race for thousands of years. The idea that Jesus healed people by virtue of the faith they had in his power as a healer is one upon which both religious and non-religious people can agree.

The idea that Jesus was a person who inspired physically sick or mentally ill people to have faith in his powers as a healer and the idea that he could forgive sins are closely related. Theological explanations for physical or mental illness in the ancient world were common. It was often thought that distress was the result of angering God or the gods. If a person became seriously ill or paralyzed or blind then it was often believed the person (or perhaps the person's parents) had offended God and therefore God was punishing the offense, or sin, with illness (John 9:2). If a sick person believed Jesus had the ability to forgive sin, this would lead to the elimination of the manifestation of sin, the sickness (Mark 2:1–12), and so forgiveness could be a healing procedure.

People often interpreted disease, especially mental illness but also physical illness and bodily disabilities, as the work of demons. A distant analogy for this is the common modern supposition that disease is caused by germs. We may not know which germ brings a disease (a virus? a bacterium? a protozoan?), and we may not be able to see the germ, but we are certain some germ is responsible. A physician is a specialist in determining the name of the germ (say, streptococcus, or the flu virus) and then prescribing the proper treatment for that particular organism. In a similar way, ancient healers were expected to identify particular demons by name, know their natures, and design treatments (exorcisms) to get rid of the demons. As offenses against God were thought to cause illnesses, the powers of God were thought to cast out demons and so eliminate the symptoms attributed to demons. But such curing was often temporary and symptoms might re-occur as Jesus said: "When an unclean spirit comes out of a man it wanders over the deserts seeking a resting-place; and if it finds none, it says, 'I will go back to the home I left.' So it returns and finds the house swept clean, and tidy. Off it goes and collects seven other spirits more wicked than itself, and they all come in and settle down; and in the end the man's plight is worse than before" (Luke 11:24–26). Some, perhaps many, of Jesus' closest followers were people whose faith in Jesus led them to be cured; Mary Magdalene, it is said, had seven demons before Jesus exorcised them (Luke 8:1–3).

Faith healers or miracle workers were persons thought to have particular access to the powers of God, but if people did not have faith in a healer, his or her success rate would be low. For example, in Nazareth, where people knew Jesus well, "he could work no miracle there, except that he put his hands on a few sick people and healed them; and he was taken aback by their want of faith" (Mark 6:5–6). A proverb attributed to Jesus is associated with this passage: "A prophet is not acceptable in his own village; a physician does not heal those who know him" (Gospel of Thomas 31). In the first century (as in any century), healers who depended on the faith of those who came to them might expect to find little faith among their own childhood acquaintances.

Christians in the first century interpreted Jesus' ability to do healing miracles as evidence that he had special access to the powers of God. As God had unlimited power, Jesus' access to it meant that his capabilities were immense. This idea led eventually to the development of stories crediting him with performing even nature miracles, miracles outside the realm of historical credibility, such as withering a tree on command (Mark 11:12–20), raising the dead (Luke 8:49–56), and turning water into wine (John 2:11). The fact that Mark's gospel begins with Jesus' reception of the Holy Spirit indicates that in Mark's opinion Jesus' access to the power of God came through the Spirit within him.

To some people, faith in Jesus meant faith in his powers. These people concluded that he was divinely empowered—perhaps a new prophet or an ancient prophet come back to life (Mark 6:15–16, 8:28; John 6:14). This was the central point of view of the miracle sources.

The Signs Source in John's Gospel

It is probably the case that the author of the Gospel of John used a written list of miracles attributed to Jesus. The list evidently began with the water-into-wine miracle at the wedding in Cana in Galilee (John 2:1–11) and continued with the healing of an official's son (John 4:46–54), also reported to have taken place in Cana in Galilee. The two stories are separated in John's gospel by accounts of Jesus' journey to Jerusalem for a Passover and his cleansing of the temple there, a journey through Judea, and a story of his coming to Samaria. Yet the fact that both miracle stories take place in the same village is a solid clue the stories were originally in sequence. In addition, these two little miracle stories, like the others in John's miracle source, share common language that does not reflect the unique ideas and modes of expression of the great majority of other passages in John's gospel. This is evidence that the miracle stories were originally written down by someone other than the final author of the Gospel of John. Significantly, the first story ends, "This deed at Cana in Galilee is the first of the signs by which Jesus revealed his glory and led his disciples to believe in him," and the second story concludes similarly: "This was now the second sign which Jesus performed after coming down from Judaea into Galilee." The fact the stories are numbered first and second is another clue that they originally belonged in sequence.

In John's gospel, the term "sign" (*semeia* in Greek) is used instead of "miracle," and therefore scholars frequently call the miracles source in John the "Signs Source." In addition to the first two stories placed in the village of Cana in Galilee, located about nine miles north of Nazareth, the collection contained at least five more miracle stories. In writing his gospel, John edited, revised, and commented on his miracle source's accounts. John 6 is an extensive commentary on the miracle of loaves and fishes; chapter 9 is an extensively rewritten account of a miracle wherein Jesus gives sight to a blind man; and the original story of the raising of Lazarus in chapter 11 is rewritten with substantial additions of ideas and expressions characteristic of the author of the Gospel of John. Despite John's revisions, however, enough of the original source can be observed and recovered to make its re-creation possible.

<u>THE SIGNS SOURCE HAS TO BE RE-CREATED BY YOU. HERE IS HOW: UNDERLINE THE FOLLOWING PASSAGES, OR TAKE A HIGH-LIGHTING MARKER AND COLOR THEM IN. READ THEM CARE-FULLY.</u> (A verse indicated as 31a means only the first part of verse 31, 28b means only the second part of verse 28).

- John 2:1, 3, 5–11
- John 4:46–47, 49–54
- John 5:2–15
- John 6:1–5, 7–14
- John 6:16–21
- John 9:1–3, 6–17
- John 11:1, 3, 17–20, 28b, 32–35, 38–39, 41, 43–45
- John 20:30–31a
- John 21:1–14

You will need to underline scattered lines in the story of the raising of Lazarus and elsewhere because the remaining lines were added by the author of John to supplement and interpret the stories he received in the Semeia source. Unfortunately, it is by no means certain exactly which lines are from the source and which are from John. Those listed above are a good guess, but not a conclusive list. John 20:30–31a is probably the original conclusion of the *Semeia* source.

<u>NOW THAT YOU HAVE THE RAW MATERIAL FOR EXAMINA-TION AND ANALYSIS OF A VERY EARLY CHRISTIAN DOCUMENT, READ IT.</u> In reading these accounts, you are not reading John but a pre-gospel document John used. This can be exciting;

you are reading material about Jesus written before any evangelist wrote. The signs source in John reveals its central point of view in several passages:

> This deed at Cana in Galilee is the first of the signs by which Jesus revealed his glory and led his disciples to believe in him (John 2:11).
>
> The father noted that this was the exact time when Jesus had said to him, "Your son will live," and he and all his household became believers (John 4:53).
>
> When the people saw the sign Jesus had performed, the word went round, "Surely this must be the prophet that was to come into the world" (John 6:14).
>
> Now many of the Jews who had come to visit Mary and had seen what Jesus did, put their faith in him (John 11:45).
>
> There were indeed many other signs that Jesus performed in the presence of his disciples, which are not recorded in this book. Those here written have been recorded in order that you may hold the faith that Jesus is the Christ (John 20:30–31).

In this set of stories, miracles are evidence, part of the following cause-and-effect sequence: "Jesus did such and such, which led people to believe in him; if you concede he did such-and-such, you, too, should believe in him."

The source tells us that some people concluded he was "the prophet who was to come into the world" and also that people ought to conceive of him as the Christ. The meanings and implications of the terms "prophet" and "Christ" existing in the twenty-first century derive from the whole collection of New Testament texts, and from two thousand years of denominational speculation about those texts. It is wrong to presume that the meanings you associate with these terms are the same ones held by first-century Christians. Indeed, even in the New Testament different authors use different terms in different ways. What the word "Christ" meant to Paul, for example, is a different thing from what it meant to the compilers of miracles. The terms "prophet" and "Christ" were applied to Jesus, and the compilers of miracle stories used evidence of miracles to justify the use of the terms—to convince people to have faith in Jesus. What exactly they meant by "Christ" we cannot know.

Miracle Stories in Mark's Gospel

Mark used both oral and written sources in writing his gospel. It is likely that among those sources were written lists of miracles, sources probably quite similar in structure and point of view to the miracles source used by John. Mark probably used two similar written sources, because there clearly is duplication among the miracles reported, but it would be stretching our limited knowledge too far to attempt to state precisely which stories were taken from which source.

<u>HIGHLIGHT OR UNDERLINE THE FOLLOWING PASSAGES AND READ THEM MORE THAN ONCE.</u>
- Mark 3:1–5
- Mark 4:35–41
- Mark 5:2–20
- Mark 5:22–23, 35–42
- Mark 5:25–34
- Mark 6:35–44
- Mark 6:46–51
- Mark 7:25–30
- Mark 7:32–35
- Mark 8:1–10
- Mark 8:22–25

Remember, you are not reading a gospel; this is not Mark, but a source used by Mark. In fact, as we shall see, Mark was not altogether sympathetic to the point of view of the miracles sources he used, and he has Jesus tell people to keep silence about miracles that Jesus does. In one instance, Mark has placed one story in the middle of another to indicate the passage of time.

The groups of stories you have underlined in Mark and John are probably not the only collections of miracle stories that circulated in written form prior to the composition of the gospels, but they are the only ones we can reconstruct. Other stories were handed down by oral tradition, but evidently not many others, since the Gospels of Matthew and Luke contain very few stories that are not also in the Gospel of Mark. The many letters in the New Testament contain no detailed miracle stories at all.

The miracle stories in Mark occasionally show a difference in point of view from the stories in John. For example, the stories in Mark frequently assume that faith is necessary to produce a miracle, while the stories in John often presume faith was brought about because miracles occurred. This may just show two ways of looking at the same thing, for in Mark's gospel the miracles done by Jesus often led to others having faith in him.

The miracle sources do not agree on the methods Jesus used to do remarkable things. Sometimes miracles just happened, as when Jesus is said to have taken a few loaves and fishes, blessed them, and broke and distributed them to thousands of people (Mark 6:41, 8:6; John 6:11). In another instance, Jesus was apparently not aware that a healing by his power was taken place until it was over, for in the story of the woman suffering from hemorrhages, she touched his clothes and he, "aware that power had gone out of him, turned round in the crowd and asked, 'Who touched my clothes?'" (Mark 5:30). In other cases, Jesus went though procedures of some complexity to achieve the desired result. In healing a man who was deaf and had an impediment in his speech,

Jesus "took the man aside, away from the crowd, put his fingers into his ears, spat, and touched his tongue. Then, looking up to heaven, he sighed, and said to him, 'Ephphatha,' which means 'Be opened'" (Mark 7:33–34). This miracle was not a spontaneous result of the person's faith but the result of a somewhat elaborate set of actions on Jesus' part. The same is true for a story told in John 9:6–7 about a man blind from birth. Jesus "spat on the ground and made a paste with the spittle; he spread it on the man's eyes, and said to him, 'Go and wash in the pool of Siloam.' The man went away and washed, and when he returned he could see." If the miraculous cures attributed to Jesus happened spontaneously through people's faith in Jesus, it is hard to imagine that a few decades later anyone in the Christian movement would want to claim Jesus used such techniques as making a compound of mud and spit and then rubbing it on the eyes of a sightless man. It is likely that earlier traditions telling about Jesus' miracles contained reports of more detailed procedures and that later accounts tended to locate the cause of miracles in simple commands.

Recurring Themes

Sources

Miracle stories came into being in three different ways. These are not competing explanations; all three are probably true for different stories.

1. Jesus of Nazareth was known in his lifetime as a healer who had the ability to cast out demons, who had access to the Spirit of God to assist him, and who was therefore able to counteract the effects of sin. People in the first century would have found it reasonable that, if illness was due to sin and if Jesus cured illness, Jesus thereby cured the effects of sin and so could forgive sin. There is no particular reason for

a skeptical student to refuse to believe that some people of Jesus' own time had faith in his abilities to cure them. Stories of Jesus' healings and exorcisms circulated during his lifetime and thereafter. Our first source, therefore, is a collection of stories told and retold by word of mouth. The stories transmitted in this way would have been somewhat altered over time, as is inevitable in oral story transmission, and a major alteration at the beginning of oral retelling was the switch in language from Aramaic to the Greek tales that came to be written into the gospels. The impression given by the healing and exorcism stories, that Jesus went about Galilee and Judea curing those who had faith in his abilities and that people believed he cast out demons from those who felt themselves to be possessed, is historically reliable.

2. Miracle stories existed less as historical documents than as arguments to prove the special excellence of Jesus in order to convince people to adopt the Christian faith. Christians presumed that since Jesus did many awe-inspiring miracles, it would be appropriate to heighten the miraculous elements in stories or even to create awe-inspiring stories to convince others that Jesus deserved special respect. The nature miracles probably originated from this tendency.

3. The miracle source in John depicts people as concluding on the basis of Jesus' actions that he was a great prophet. Mark also shows that people thought of Jesus as a prophet because of his miracles. Some people apparently concluded Jesus was not a new prophet but a prophet returned to life: "The fame of Jesus had spread; and people were saying, 'John the Baptist has been raised to life, and that is why these miraculous powers are at work in him.' Other said, 'It is Elijah.' Others again, 'He is a prophet like one of the old prophets'" (Mark 6:14–15).

If people interpreted Jesus' miracles as those of a prophet, and they wished to know what kinds of miracles prophets did, they would turn to Hebrew Scriptures to find out. Chapter 4 of the book entitled 2 Kings is a collection of miracle stories much like the collections in the Gospels of John and Mark. This collection contains accounts of miracles supposedly done by the prophet Elisha. At least one and perhaps more of the miracles attributed to Jesus were designed to show that Jesus not only could do what the ancient prophet Elisha did but could do so on a considerably larger scale. The account in 2 Kings 4:42–44 of the miraculous feeding of one hundred men underlies the story of Jesus feeding thousands with a few loaves and fishes.

In summary, miracle stories originated from three sources: oral traditions of Jesus' activities as a healer and exorcist, legends created to heighten people's reverence for him, and accounts based on Hebrew Bible prophetic models.

Jesus

For the miracle sources, the life of Jesus was obviously of principal importance. What he did counted most; what he said or taught counted little. The conclusion reached by the source in John and the sources in Mark is that the many miracles Jesus did during his life give convincing evidence he was a great prophet and/or the Christ. We should, however, be cautious about drawing complex conclusions about what those terms meant to people in ancient times.

Jesus' death does not seem to have much interested those who put together the miracle collections. Some scholars have argued that the story of Jesus' resurrection was contained in John's miracles source, but this is not the opinion of the majority. Even if it had been contained there, it would have been considered no more than a great miracle, and the miracles sources give no hint of a belief that salvation came through the death of Jesus.

Eschatology

The miracles sources, as far as we can determine, have no interest in eschatology.

Torah Law

Two stories (or two versions of one original story) in our sources have to do with a point of Torah Law. In John 5:2–15 (and also Mark 3:1–5) Jesus heals a crippled man on the Sabbath. According to Torah Law, no work was allowed on the Sabbath. Did healings count as work? Yes, they did, but exceptions were made in emergency situations, and saving a life on the Sabbath would not have been condemned but praised. Indeed, saving a life on the Sabbath was required according to Jewish Law even if work was involved. If there was any legal problem with Jesus' Sabbath healings it was that the healings were not always life-or-death emergencies; a handicapped person could be expected to wait a few hours in order to be healed when the Sabbath was over.

In the case described in John's gospel, the problem is perhaps not that the man was healed but that Jesus told him to carry his bed. From a conservative perspective on Law, carrying a bed on the Sabbath constitutes work. Well before the time of Jesus, Judaism possessed a strong tradition that works of mercy and kindness could take precedence over strict detailed adherence to the Law. As a Sabbath healer, Jesus might have been considered a liberal interpreter of Law, but his death was not a direct result of his healing people on the Sabbath. No Pharisees or scribes or other legal authorities would have threatened his life for that reason.

Community

The miracle stories provide few clues about the community or communities that compiled and used them. We do know that many early Christians believed that Jesus expected them to become workers of miracles (that is, healings and exorcisms) and so the stories of healings by Jesus were used as examples of the sorts of healing that his followers might be expected to perform. Since the purpose of the miracle stories is to convince their audience that Jesus is the Christ or a great prophet, miracle stories must have derived from groups dedicated to the proposition that belief in Jesus should be spread to others. This means that the communities involved were not secret sects or self-enclosed cult groups but communities openly seeking new members.

The Sayings Source Q

Everyone who has read the New Testament has noticed substantial repetition in the first three books. Having read Matthew, one finds Mark to contain much of the same material. Having read Matthew and Mark, one finds story after story in Luke to be the same as one has read before. In the Gospel of John, however, the stories change, the style of Jesus' sayings changes, and, for the first time since Matthew, one seems to be reading a very different account.

Matthew, Mark, and Luke, when their stories are set side by side, look very similar. They are called the *synoptic gospels*. The term "synoptic" comes from the Greek and means "seen together." Clearly, the three have a special relationship, but what is it? Are all three versions of a lost original gospel? Did Matthew revise Mark and then Luke revise Matthew? Is Mark a shorter version of both Matthew and Luke? Many theories have been offered during the past century, but the one now accepted by the vast majority of New Testament experts is called the *Two Document Hypothesis*, or *Two Document Theory*.

The Two Document Hypothesis is quite simple. It is as follows: Mark wrote the first gospel. Matthew and Luke each read Mark and decided that it should be revised. Among other things, Matthew and Luke wished to improve Mark's gospel by adding substantially more of the sayings of Jesus passed down by tradition. Both Matthew and Luke independently added sayings to Mark's gospel and, therefore, each gospel contains sayings the other does not have. However the great majority of sayings added by Matthew and Luke to Mark are the same ones, frequently using the same wording. They cannot have taken all of those same sayings in the same wording from oral tradition; they must have used a common written source. Both Matthew and Luke used the same written collection of sayings as a source for the material they used to supplement Mark's gospel. We can tell that they are not just dependent on oral sayings traditions because quite often the same Greek phrases and terminology are used by Matthew and by Luke in material they do not borrow from Mark.

You can imagine, then, Matthew at his desk in one town and Luke at a desk in another town. Both have before them two written documents, a copy of the Gospel of Mark and a copy of the same list of sayings in Greek attributed to Jesus. Both of them used those two documents to compose their own gospels. This is the meaning of the term "Two Document Hypothesis," that two documents were used by Matthew and by Luke in the writing of their gospels.

Another principal hypothesis is known as the *Griesbach Hypothesis*, after the German scholar who constructed it. A minority of New Testament scholars believe it to be true, but they are firm in their confidence that ultimately it will win over many other experts. The Griesbach Hypothesis is based, in part, on the observation that there are a few passages in Matthew, Luke, and Mark where the versions in Matthew and Luke are identical, but the Mark version is different. How can this be, they wonder, if both of the others used Mark as a source? The Griesbach Hypothesis holds that Matthew was the first gospel, and Luke was a rewritten form of Matthew. Mark then made a synopsis of both Matthew and Luke in producing his much shorter gospel.

What is called the *Farrer Hypothesis* also has its supporters, who argue that it makes most sense to believe that Mark wrote the first gospel, then Matthew revised Mark by incorporating into it a considerable number of new sayings of Jesus. Luke later on took Mark's gospel and Matthew's gospel and wove them together to make the book we call the Gospel of Luke.

In this book, as is the practice in almost all introductory books to the New Testament, we will follow the Two Document Hypothesis. The scholars who adhere to the Griesbach and Farrer hypotheses are few in number and, while they make interesting arguments in support of their points of view, not very many New Testament experts have been convinced by them.

The German scholars who first theorized that Matthew and Luke used the same sayings collection as their written source for sayings of Jesus called that collection the "source." The word for source in German is *Quelle*. This became abbreviated to "Q," and the term "Q" is now universally used for that sayings collection. Q does not now exist in separate written form; it was probably considered superfluous after it was incorporated into both Matthew's and Luke's gospels, and Christian scribes stopped copying it.

Every passage in Matthew and Luke can be put into one of three categories: (1) unique material shared with no other New Testament document, such as the different stories of Jesus' birth found in the two gospels; (2) material Matthew and/or Luke borrowed from the Gospel of Mark; and (3) material Matthew and Luke borrowed from their common source for sayings, Q. Remember, Mark did not use the source Q. The common material in Matthew and Luke, the passages they both have and Mark does not have, is Q.

The existence of Q has received strong support with the discovery in 1945 of an ancient Christian collection of more than 114 sayings attributed to Jesus called the *Gospel of Thomas*. It is just what Q was thought to be—a list of sayings one after the other without much commentary and with no stories or biography attached. It is about the same length as Q is thought to have been, and it shares about a third of its sayings with Q. While Q remains hypothetical in the sense that no physical manuscript of it has come down to us from the ancient world, the hypothesis that Christians in early times wrote down lists of the sayings of Jesus is confirmed by the existence of the Gospel of Thomas. A brief discussion of the history and nature of the Gospel of Thomas along with a discussion of its relationship to the New Testament can be found as an appendix to this textbook.

The Origin of Q

Because Matthew and Luke so frequently use identical Greek phrases when borrowing from Q, we know the Q material was written in Greek. The ideas and way of life reflected in Q are primitive, meaning they do not reflect the more sophisticated concepts of Christ and of Christian community structure that developed as the early church developed. Certainly Q was in existence before the writing of Matthew and Luke, but much more than this we really cannot say; the best guess for the date of Q is somewhere between 50 and 70 CE. As to the author of Q, no name is attached to it. Probably if it had not disappeared, some name would have been attached to it in the second century and it might have been called the Gospel of Andrew or the Gospel of Simon. This happened with the similar sayings collection called the Gospel of Thomas, which was not written by the apostle Thomas.

Some early Christians put the Q collection together by choosing, from the sayings known to them, those they thought to be of particular interest and importance. The sayings they selected reflect not only aspects of Jesus' teachings but also aspects of their own teaching and their way of life. People usually do not try to preserve traditions with which they are in disagreement or which cast doubt upon their own way of life. In speaking of the Q material, then, we should think not of one person but of a group of people, the "Q people," or the "Q community." Scholars sometimes refer to the "Q community," but as the term community evokes the idea of a settled group, a village or a neighborhood, "Q people" is preferable. The Q people left a record of their activities in the sayings they created or preserved. As with all material in the New Testament, we should be careful not to attribute all sayings in Q to Jesus himself. Some, possibly most, sayings in Q derive from sayings of Jesus, but others do not. Further, the selection made by the Q people of sayings attributed to Jesus may give a distorted notion of his main themes. They are the ones who made the selection; Jesus did not.

In several places, the sayings in Q describe a way of life, and we will examine that way of life in the next few pages. Scholars differ, however, on whether the way of life described in Q was lived by the Q people or only valued by them. This leads to the question, were the people who compiled the Q sayings itinerant Christian prophets, or were they individuals living in a more settled community who respected and assisted itinerant Christian prophets? In either case, a particular way of life, strange by our standards, was valued and implicitly lived. We shall assume in this book that the Q sayings were compiled by people who lived in accordance with them even though that is not altogether certain.

Reading Q
The Q "document" can be recovered, read, and discussed. YOU SHOULD NOW UNDERLINE OR HIGHLIGHT THE PASSAGES LUKE HAS TAKEN FROM Q. There are two related, but rarely absolutely identical, versions of each passage, one from Luke's gospel and one from Matthew's, and the dual versions can be compared by using a book of gospel parallels or underlining or highlighting both sets. The sayings are not completely identical in the two gospels, for both Matthew and Luke felt free to revise them in accordance with what they thought Jesus would have said. It appears that, while Luke did occasionally take the opportunity to change elements of sayings when it fit his purposes, Matthew did this more often and also extensively changed the order of the sayings to construct five major speeches, while Luke more often left the Q order alone. For the sake of clarity, we use the passages as they are found in Luke to study Q below. While scholars disagree about the exact details of which parts of Luke's sayings come from Q, the following list is the generally agreed upon set— UNDERLINE OR HIGHLIGHT THE Q SAYINGS IN YOUR BIBLE IN THE VERSION FOUND IN LUKE'S GOSPEL OR, IF YOU WANT TO BE THOROUGH, IN MATTHEW'S GOSPEL, AS WELL:

- Luke 3:7–9 / Matt 3:7–10
- Luke 3:16–17 / Matt 3:11–12
- Luke 4:1–13 / Matt 4:1–4, 9–12, 5–7, 13
- Luke 6:12, 17, 20 / Matt 5:1–2
- Luke 6:30–23 / Matt 5:3, 6, 4, 11–12
- Luke 6:24–26 / probable
- Luke 6:27–36 / Matt 5:44, 39–42; 7:12; 5:46–47, 45, 48
- Luke 6:37–38 / Matt 7:1–2

- Luke 6:38–40 / Matt 15:14; 10:24–25
- Luke 6:41–42 / Matt 7:3–5
- Luke 6:43–4 / Matt 7:16–20; 12:33–35
- Luke 6:46–49 / Matt 7:21, 24–27
- Luke 7:1–10 / Matt 7:28; 8:5–10, 13
- Luke 7:18–20, 22–23 / Matt 11:2–6
- Luke 7:24–28 / Matt 11:7–11
- Luke 16:16 / Matt 11:12–13
- Luke 7:31–35 / Matt 11:16–19
- Luke 9:56–62 / Matt 8:19–22
- Luke 10:2–12 / Matt 9:37–38; 10:7–16
- Luke 10:13–15 / Matt 11:21–24
- Luke 10:16 / Matt 10:40
- Luke 10:21–22 / Matt 11:25–27
- Luke 10:23–24 / Matt 13:16–17
- Luke 11:2–4 / Matt 6:9–13
- Luke 11:9–13 / Matt 7:7–11
- Luke 11:14–23 / Matt 12:22–30
- Luke 11:24–26 / Matt 12:43–45
- Luke 11:27–28 / probable
- Luke 11:16, 29–32 / Matt 12:38–42
- Luke 11:3 / Matt 5:15
- Luke 11:34–36 / Matt 6:22–23
- Luke 11:42 / Matt 23:23
- Luke 11:39–40 / Matt 23:25–26
- Luke 11:43 / Matt 23:6–7
- Luke 11:44 / Matt 23:27–28
- Luke 11:46 / Matt 23:4
- Luke 11:47–48 / Matt 23:29–32
- Luke 11:49–51 / Matt 23:34–36
- Luke 11:52 / Matt 23:13
- Luke 12:2–3 / Matt 10:26–27
- Luke 12:4–7 / Matt 10:28–31
- Luke 12:8–9 / Matt 10:32–33
- Luke 12:10 / Matt 12:32

- Luke 12:11–12 / Matt 10:19
- Luke 12:13–14 / probable
- Luke 12:16–21 / probable
- Luke 12:22–31 / Matt 6:25–33
- Luke 12:33–34 / Matt 6:19–21
- Luke 12:39–40 / Matt 24:43–44
- Luke 12:42–46 / Matt 24:45–51
- Luke 12:49, 51–53 / Matt 10:34–36
- Luke 12:54–56 / Matt 16:2–3
- Luke 12:57–59 / Matt 5:25–26
- Luke 13:18–21 / Matt 13:31–33
- Luke 24–27 / Matt 7:13–14, 22–23
- Luke 13:28–30 / Matt 8:11–12; 20:16
- Luke 13:34–35 / Matt 23:37–39
- Luke 14:11, 18:14 / Matt 23:12
- Luke 14:16–24 / Matt 22:1–10
- Luke 14:26–27, 17:33 / Matt 10:37–39
- Luke 14:34–35 / Matt 5:13
- Luke 15:4–10 / Matt 18:12–13
- Luke 16:13 / Matt 6:24
- Luke 16:16 / Matt 11:12–13
- Luke 16:17 / Matt 5:18
- Luke 16:18 / Matt 5:32
- Luke 17:1–2 / Matt 18:6–7
- Luke 17:3–4 / Matt 18:15, 21–22
- Luke 17:6 / Matt 17:20
- Luke 17:22–24, 26–30, 34–35, 37 / Matt 24:26–28, 37, 39–41
- Luke 19:12–26 / Matt 25:14–30
- Luke 22:28–30 / Matt 19:28

<u>NOW, HAVING RECONSTRUCTED Q BY ISOLATING IT IN LUKE (AND, IF YOU WISH, MATTHEW), GO BACK AND READ IT CAREFULLY.</u> Nobody can underline or highlight and read carefully at the same time. Remember, you are not reading Luke's gospel when reading the Q material in Luke. Luke must have

agreed generally with the Q material or he would not have used it, but Luke's ideas are not identical to those in Q and must be considered separately. In reading the Q material, you are reading a separate and different document than the Gospel of Luke (or Matthew).

See if you can locate evidence for the lifestyle of the people in the Q sayings. What do the Q sayings convey about the Kingdom of God? What does Jesus say in the Q sayings that you find surprising?

Q Way of Life, Q Ideas

While scholarship on the New Testament has made great advances during the past hundred years, the main technique of scholars remains the same. We read the material over and over again and try to make sense of it in its own context and to take it seriously as it stands. In other words, we must presume Q and the other New Testament materials mean what they say. Sayings and ideas that do not sound right to us cannot be wished away, rewritten, or ignored. This is particularly important in analyzing Q, for, fortunately or unfortunately, the Q version of Jesus' sayings often reveals perspectives on human life and Christian expectations alien to us today.

Q can best be understood by first looking at the way of life of the Q people, including their reactions to their society. Then we can examine their ideas about Jesus and their vision of the future in the context of their behavior rather than in the abstract.

The Q people were itinerant, which means that they moved from town to town and depended on the charity of those who accepted them as prophets. They were poor, hungry, and afraid. Their way of life is depicted in Q in a long passage in which Jesus is said to be giving instructions to his disciples. It appears twice in Luke, once borrowed from Mark (Luke 9:2–6) and once from Q (Luke 10:2–12). In these passages, early Christian prophets are depicted as impoverished people, whether by choice or by necessity. They possessed neither walking stick nor pack, neither bread nor money, neither purses nor shoes; they did not even have a change of clothes. They had no place to sleep, and their principal image of themselves was as tenant farmers (laborers harvesting an absentee landlord's crop). The Q people regarded themselves as the last in a long line of Jewish prophets, who (in their opinion) had been sent from God to the Jewish people but had been rejected, persecuted, and killed by the people to whom they had been sent. In Luke 11:49–51, the following is said in reference to both the prophets of the Hebrew Scriptures and Q prophets: "'I will send them prophets and messengers; and some of these they will persecute and kill'; so that this generation will have to answer for the blood of all the prophets shed since the foundation of the world."

Using your imagination, picture the people who followed this way of life. They were dirty. They were hungry. They were rude, for they would "exchange no greetings on the road." They were entirely dependent on the kindness of strangers, even though the strangers they encountered were themselves poor Galilean villagers.

The Q people would come to a small village and hope to be welcomed. Their duty was to announce that "The kingdom of God has come close to you," but there was no guarantee anyone would agree. They might bestow their blessing (their "peace") on a house, but that might make no difference; they still might be rejected. Then their blessing, their peace, would be removed from the house and returned to them.

They sought the repentance of the people. Repentance did not mean feeling sorry for misdeeds but rather a radical change of life in light of the prospect that "the kingdom of God has come close." Their evidence for the truth of their message was their ability to heal the sick and to cast out demons, but this alone was not necessarily good enough. Luke 10:13–15 indicates that in the Galilean villages of Chorazin,

Bethsaida, and Capernaum such healings had been done, but few cared or repented, and therefore presumably few gave the Q people food or a place to lay their heads and rest. Notice, incidentally, Q does not say that the non-Jewish areas of Tyre and Sidon did accept them, only that *if* they had gone there, Tyre and Sidon would have been more impressed than some Galilean villages were.

Q Sayings, Spirit Sayings

Among the most famous of all Q passages are the *Beatitudes*. They are found in Luke 6:20–23 and announce that poor, hungry, unhappy people will inherit the Kingdom of God. The Q people were not primarily concerned with just any poor person but with those specific poor people who were prophets of Jesus and of God. This does not mean that whatever you do for any poor or humble person you do for Jesus; a more accurate interpretation of this teaching would be that when you listen to Q prophets or assist them you assist Jesus, and when you reject them you reject Jesus. By rejecting Jesus you reject God, as we hear in Luke 10:16: "Whoever listens to you listens to me; whoever rejects you rejects me. And whoever rejects me rejects the One who sent me." Similarly, in Matthew 10:40: "To receive you is to receive me, and to receive me is to receive the One who sent me." It is also one of the very few Q sayings found in John: "He who receives any messenger of mine receives me; receiving me, he receives the one who sent me" (13:20). Although Q has several distinctive points of view, in this matter it is in accord with most of the rest of the New Testament. Even an author who repudiates this point of view by weakening it (Mark 9:37) shows he is aware of it.

The Q people did not believe they were to carry on the mission of Jesus only by repeating sayings they had memorized. Rather, they were able to do as he did because they now had the Spirit Jesus had. The Spirit is the crucial link. They believed that there is a Spirit of God able to possess people. Jesus, at his baptism, received this Spirit, and so one may regard the sayings of Jesus as the sayings of God through this Spirit. New Testament gospels agree that a divine Spirit came to Jesus' followers after his crucifixion. This entitled his followers to speak words from the Spirit or to have their statements attributed to the Spirit. Therefore, to listen to them was to listen to God's Spirit. To disbelieve them was to disbelieve God's Spirit, and to reject them was to reject God's Spirit. From this perspective, just as Jesus spoke and one thereby heard God's Spirit, so, too, would one would hear God's Spirit when a Q person spoke, and this would be the same thing as hearing Jesus. For this reason, the Q people reasoned that they, like Jesus, were prophets of God. If one wrote down what a Q person said, one wrote down what the Spirit of God said. According to this view, such written sayings could be attributed to the Spirit of God (see Luke 10:21) or to Jesus without making a false claim.

Many people are astonished to discover that some sayings attributed to Jesus in the New Testament were not said by Jesus but came into existence well after his crucifixion. When one considers, however, that his early followers believed they too had the Spirit Jesus had, then what is surprising is not that some of their sayings were attributed to him but that so many of his original personal sayings survived word-of-mouth transmission and translation from Aramaic to Greek, and are available to us at all.

Q Mission

The Q people believed themselves to be of great, even cosmic, importance, conveying God's message to people, proving their message true by healing the sick. But often they were rejected by those to whom they came. Rejection did not just hurt their pride; it threatened them with starvation, for they were poor people with serious concern for basic survival. RE-READ THE Q PASSAGES LUKE 12:22–31. Certainly Q people hoped God would take care of them, but what they needed most was food to keep them alive and clothes to cover their bodies. Of course they set their minds on food and drink; of course they worried. Who would not in their circumstances?

The Q people's vision of the Kingdom of God was of a place where there was plenty to eat and plenty to drink: "You shall eat and drink at my table in my kingdom" (Luke 22:30). As to the people who so often rejected them, "There will be wailing and grinding of teeth there, when you see Abraham, Isaac, and Jacob, and all the prophets, in the kingdom of God, and yourselves thrown out. From east and west people will come, from north and south, for the feast in the kingdom of God" (Luke 13:28–30).

Most Q people were probably from the ranks of tenant farmers, shepherds, fishermen, and other impoverished groups. They left their homes, went on the road to various villages, and announced the imminent arrival of the Kingdom of God. But what of the people they left at home when they went on the road? To understand Q it is necessary to imagine the condition of families when a spouse or parent suddenly took off, never to return. This would have been an emotional tearing apart of the nuclear family structure, leaving scars on all concerned. Yet this tearing apart, this repudiation of basic family obligations, was demanded and expected.

From the Q people's perspective, families were social units working against the possibility of going forth and preaching the coming of the Kingdom of God. Families, therefore, were to be put aside along with other normal elements of human social life, business, planting of crops, building houses, and so forth (Luke 17:26–30). Some sayings in Q are called "hard sayings" because they reject the values many Christians have believed to be of major importance. But the radical perspective of Q as a whole is consistent. Consider these:

> If anyone comes to me and does not hate his father and mother, wife and children, brothers and sisters, even his own life, he cannot be a disciple of mine (Luke 14:26).

> Do you suppose I came to establish peace on earth? No indeed, I have come to bring division. For from now on, five members of a family will be divided, three against two and two against three; father against son and son against father, mother against daughter and daughter against mother, mother against son's wife and son's wife against her mother-in-law (Luke 12:52).

> Jesus said to a man, "Follow me," but the man replied, "Let me go and bury my father first." Jesus said, "Leave the dead to bury their dead; you must go and announce the kingdom of God" (Luke 9:59).

Although some exaggeration is present in these sayings, the Q people presumably did what these sayings expect them to do. They did leave their families; they did cause division within their families; they did repudiate even the ordinary duties to their families, including sometimes the burial of their fathers. What of the rest of social life? It was condemned. As every Jewish person of the time knew, only Noah's family were righteous enough to be saved from the flood; only Lot was righteous enough to be saved when God sent fire and sulfur to destroy the town of Sodom. Everyone else died. They deserved to die because, according to Q (Luke 17:26–30), they ate, drank, married, bought, sold, planted, and built. Following a normal social life does not enable one to go and announce the coming of the Kingdom of God, and so such normal life is implicitly condemned. The Q people did not value what we now value and, indeed, did not value what most people then valued. They valued only one thing: the Kingdom of God.

Since the Kingdom of God is their main interest, we might expect them to describe it in some detail, but Q sayings do not do this. It is only mentioned in a few places and described little. From what we know we can say this: The Kingdom of God is a condition coming to earth in a very short time. The desires of the Q people (especially for food and drink) will be satisfied. Those who have believed the pronouncements of its coming and repented will be welcomed into it; those who have not will be destroyed.

This radical perspective cannot be compared to later Christian notions of an ethereal heaven up there for those who die and are acceptable in God's eyes. The Q notion of the Kingdom of God is of something coming here soon. People do not die and eventually go there; it will come here, quickly, in a matter of months or, at most, a few years. When it comes, the condition of human life will be entirely changed and only a few people will be permitted to survive and enter it. When it comes, it will be like the flood of Noah or the fire and brimstone that destroyed the towns Sodom and Gomorrah. The kingdom is a promise for those who repent, but a threat for the rest of the world (Luke 17:22–34).

The Q sayings do not give many directions for behavior in advance of the coming kingdom. Repentance is necessary. To repudiate normal social and family life and go forth to warn others is necessary. Some of the Q sayings taken to be moral principles are probably more in the line of practical advice. For people who have no staff, no money, no means of defense, it only makes sense that "when a man hits you on the cheek, offer him the other cheek too; when a man takes your coat, let him have your shirt as well. Give to everyone who asks you; when a man takes what is yours, do not demand it back" (Luke 6:29–31). This advice is similar to that given novice bank tellers: if people come to rob the bank, give them the money in front of you, and give them what is in the drawer as well; don't try to resist. People visiting large cities are advised to give muggers what they want, never to be heroes, and so forth. But the Q material does contain one great moral principle, one way of looking at human relationships special to the Q people and in accord with their perspective on the world. It may well be a perspective going back to Jesus. It is fairly simple, and it comes down to this: "Do to your fellow human beings what you wish God to do to you on the day of judgment." Luke 6 contains this advice:

> You must love your enemies and do good; and lend without expecting any return; and you will have a rich reward: you will be sons of the Most High, because he himself is kind to the ungrateful and wicked. Be compassionate as your Father is compassionate. Pass no judgment, and you will not be judged; do not condemn, and you will not be condemned; acquit, and you will be acquitted; give and gifts will be given to you (Luke 6:35–38).

The principle here is, if you expect God to forgive you, you must forgive others. If you expect God to be compassionate to you, you must be compassionate to others. This is not a set of abstract principles but practical advice. Given that the Kingdom of God will come soon, that Jesus will return as judge and few will survive to enjoy the kingdom, how can you behave so as to be able to enter it? You must act to other people the way you wish God to act to you on that great and terrible day.

It is ironic the Q people found it necessary to act in a rather uncharitable fashion toward their own families in order to proclaim the necessity of charitable behavior to the Palestinian world in general.

Form Criticism

New Testament scholars use a variety of techniques to analyze biblical texts. Rather than discuss them all at the same time, this book will introduce several of them at relevant points. The first is called *form criticism*.

Form criticism, or form analysis, is a technique for analyzing specific New Testament *pericopes*. A pericope (pronounced "purr-*ick*-uh-pee") is a single unit of tradition, a saying or story that can be taken from its gospel context and analyzed independently. Since most of the sayings and stories in the gospels were transmitted by word of mouth (oral tradition) before being written down, the analysis of individual pericopes can, scholars hope, lead to some understanding of the teachings of Christians prior to the writing of gospels. A primary skill of the form analyst is the ability to distinguish the original form of a saying or story from its form in the gospels.

Generally, form criticism is applied to sayings and stories found in Mark, Matthew, Luke, and the newly discovered Gospel of Thomas. The sayings of Jesus in the Gospel of John are rarely derived from oral tradition, and so form analysis is not as often applied to them.

Form analysts organize sayings and stories into categories. The following are some of the most important of those categories:

Proverbs are short pithy sayings. Their meaning is immediately obvious. Some may have been spoken first by Jesus, but many proverbs attributed to him were probably in circulation prior to his lifetime. "Do not be anxious about tomorrow; tomorrow will look after itself" (Matt 6:34) is a proverb and so is Luke 6:39: "If a blind man leads another blind man they both will fall into the ditch."

Parables, a characteristic form of Jesus' teaching, are short stories making a point. Jesus' parables, however, seem to have been deliberately designed to be somewhat ambiguous, and their point is rarely obvious. Many form analysts believe those parables found in the New Testament that make a clear and unambiguous point are probably not from Jesus. Here is an example of one of Jesus' parables:

> A sower went out to sow. And it happened that as he sowed, some seed fell along the footpath; and the birds came and ate it up. Some seed fell on rocky ground, where it had little soil, and it sprouted quickly because it had no depth of earth; but when the sun rose the young corn was scorched, and as it had no root it withered away. Some seed fell among thistles; and the thistles shot up and choked the corn, and it yielded no crop. And some of the seed fell into good soil, where it came up and grew, and bore fruit; and the yield was thirtyfold, sixtyfold, even a hundredfold (Mark 4:3–9).

Explanations of parables in the New Testament are composed by the gospel writers or other members of the early church. Jesus seems to have left his audiences to seek their own understanding of his parables and not to have explained them himself. Following the parable quoted immediately above, for example, Mark gives a lengthy explanation beginning, "The sower sows the word. Those along the footpath are people in whom the word is sown, but no sooner have they heard it than Satan comes and carries off the word which has been sown in them," and so on (Mark 4:14–20).

Apocalyptic sayings are predictions and descriptions of events to take place at the time of the end of this world. The word "apocalyptic" refers to revelations of the supernatural world, especially regarding the end of time and usually including final catastrophes and the raising of the dead. Mark 13 contains many such sayings, such as, "When you hear the noise of battle near at hand and the news of battles far away, do not be alarmed. Such things are bound to happen; but the end is still to come" (Mark 13:7).

Community rules derive from a time later than Jesus when the structured church was coming into being, such as, "If someone sues you, come to terms with him promptly while you are both on your way to court; otherwise he may hand you over to the judge, and the judge to the constable, and you will be put in jail" (Matt 5:25).

Similarly, the miracle stories discussed in this chapter are divided into categories. Some of the most prominent are healings, exorcisms, and nature miracles.

After having categorized New Testament pericopes, form analysts proceed to theorize about the purpose of the category during the time when oral tradition was the main form of Christian preaching. Each category, they believe, played a particular role in preaching Christian doctrine or in teaching moral principles or in organizing Christian communities. The purpose of each category is called its *Sitz im Leben*, German for "situation in life." Scholars sometimes refer to the Sitz im Leben of a particular pericope as its reason for existence: "Pericope X continued to exist because it served purpose Y." Form analysts believe that sayings without specific usefulness to the later community would have been forgotten.

Form criticism seldom leads to definitive conclusions. Rarely do two scholars come up with exactly the same categories or agree completely as to which sayings fit which categories. The attempt to determine a periscope's Sitz im Leben cannot help but be speculative. Still, historical scholarship can rarely be definitive, and so, although form analysis is less well respected today than it was a few decades ago, you should be aware of it and know what a form critic does.

Recurring Themes
Sources

Jesus spoke in Aramaic and his disciples remembered some of what he said. They, in turn, told others in Aramaic what he said. From one person to another his sayings were repeated and, with each transmission, changes might have taken place. Eventually, the sayings were translated from Aramaic to Greek, and today we know them only in their Greek form. One of the main sources for the Q sayings is material in the Aramaic language, originating with Jesus, passed down by word of mouth (with some inevitable changes), translated into Greek and eventually written down.

There is another source for Q sayings. Many of Jesus' followers (including the Q people) felt that the Spirit Jesus had received was one that they also had received. The Spirit that gave Jesus his knowledge of divine things also gave them such knowledge. As it was the same Spirit, to listen to them was to listen to Jesus (Luke 10:16). Accordingly, on some occasions, things said by later Christian prophets were taken down and attributed to Jesus. There is nothing dishonest about this procedure, but it does greatly complicate the task of trying to determine what Jesus himself said as distinct from what his later followers said in his name.

The sources for Q, then, are two: the sayings of Jesus transmitted by word of mouth until finally written down in Greek, and the Spirit-inspired sayings of some of Jesus' later followers that were attributed to him.

Jesus

Jesus' life was of great importance to the Q people, forming, they thought, a model for how they should live their lives and providing them with the key for their hopes for the future. Although Jesus was thought to be in the line of persecuted prophets going back all the way to Abel (Luke 11:51), he was certainly much more than a prophet. Even John the Baptist, described as inferior to the least person in the Kingdom of God, was more than a prophet (Luke 7:27–28). However, specific events that later Christians found immensely important play no role at all in Q. It has no virgin-birth story, no discussion of crucifixion, and no mention of resurrection.

A key term in Q is "Son of Man" but, despite the best efforts of scholars over the past decades, the background of this term is still obscure. The term sometimes is used in a cosmic sense in the New Testament as a heavenly being or an angel in the form of a man. But the only place in the Hebrew Scriptures which uses the term in a cosmic sense is in Daniel 7:13–14, in which a being who looks like a human being—literally "like a son of man"—appears in what early Christians took to be a scene reflecting the second coming of Christ. This passage strongly influenced early Christian thinking, including that of the Q people, and in later times a phrase from Daniel 7:14 was even added to the Lord's Prayer ("for thine is the kingdom and the power and the glory forever").

But "son of man" has another meaning: In Aramaic "son of man" was ordinarily used to mean a human being in general, or "a person like me," a way it is sometimes used in Q sayings. For example, "Foxes have their holes, the birds their roosts; but the son of man has nowhere to lay his head" (Luke 9:58) means that, unlike the animals, "people like me" have nowhere to lay their heads. It is sometimes hard to determine whether this common usage was intended in sayings, or whether one should read them with the image of the cosmic Son of Man in mind.

Son of Man is the term used most often for Jesus in Q. During his life on earth Jesus proved his special role in bringing about the Kingdom of God by his actions and by his words, and some thought the kingdom was beginning to be present in his ministry. But the Q people focused most of their attention on the near future, not on the present. In the near future would come the "Day of the Son of Man." Suddenly the Son of Man would come to earth in judgment (Luke 12:40; 17:26–30), and at that time only those who responded positively to Jesus and his messengers would be approved by the Son of Man. From the Q perspective, both Jesus and the Q people were entitled to say, "Anyone who acknowledges me before men, the Son of Man will acknowledge before the angels of God; but he who disowns me before men will be disowned before the angels of God."

While Q uses the term "Son of Man" to refer to Jesus, it is not always clear that Jesus and the Son of Man are one and the same. Some Q sayings can be read to imply Jesus and the Son of Man are the same, others that Jesus is speaking of the Son of Man as someone else, such as God's agent at the end of this world, as is indicated in Luke 17:23–24, 26–30. But is this Jesus? Neither here nor elsewhere is it absolutely clear. Nevertheless, while it does not seem likely that Jesus openly and directly declared himself to be a cosmic Son of Man to come, the Q people probably believed he did so and included sayings to that effect in their collection.

Jesus' death was of no apparent interest to the Q people, for his death and his resurrection are not mentioned. Considering that Jesus' death and resurrection were of substantial importance to other branches of the early church it is surprising the Q material does not mention them. The word for cross is used only once: "No one who does not carry his cross and come with me can be a disciple of mine" (Luke 14:27), but this saying probably derived from a common saying meaning "shoulder a terrible burden" and does not refer to Jesus' own crucifixion. The Gospel of Thomas, which, like Q, does not show any interest in Jesus' death and resurrection, contains the same saying (as saying 55), and there, too, it is the only time the word "cross" is used.

Eschatology

For Q people the end of this world was a matter of utmost urgency. It was expected immediately, certainly within their lifetimes. This world, they thought, will end after a time of destruction. On the Day of the Son of Man, the whole world will be judged, and those who have not already repented will be destroyed. The remaining few will enter the Kingdom of God. Following logically from Q's stress on repentance is the fact that those who thought themselves most righteous will be least likely to repent; those who felt themselves poor, sinners, or outcasts will be most likely to change their ways. Q favors the poor and condemns such leaders as those Pharisees who were thought to be so convinced of their own righteousness that they saw no need for repentance.

It is possible to understand the Q sayings as implying that on the Day of the Son of Man, Jesus, who came first in disguise, will return in glory and be known by all to be God's agent. On the other hand, it is possible to understand the Q sayings to mean that Jesus predicted that the Day of the Son of Man would occur, but that he did not think that he himself was that Son of Man. In any event, when that great day comes it will be too late to repent. Those who had been hungry, poor, weeping, and persecuted for the sake of the Son of Man (Q people and those who accepted them), will soon begin to feast and drink in the Kingdom of God. All others will die.

Torah Law

The Q people preserved the saying, "It is easier for heaven and earth to come to an end than for one dot or stroke of the Law to lose its force" (Luke 16:27), so we can conclude they thought the Law should be obeyed. Following the Law, however, was not all that was necessary to be saved from destruction on the Day of the Son of Man. One must also forgive others and be compassionate to others if one hoped to find God willing to forgive and be compassionate. In light of this, the passage in Luke 16:16—"Until John, it was the Law and the prophets: since then, there is the good news of the kingdom of God, and everyone forces his way in"—cannot be taken to mean the Law is over and done with any more than that prophets ceased to exist. Rather, the good news of the kingdom was added to the previous messages of the Law and the prophets. People were encouraged to follow the Law in detail while keeping in mind the necessity of living in accordance with more abstract moral principles.

Consider the following example: Torah Law requires that 10 percent of agricultural produce must be supplied to the priests. People often applied this to major crops only, but some more strict legalists found it also to apply to small garden herbs. The Q attitude would have supported the latter sort of detailed concern but also insisted that such concern must be accompanied by concern for the general principles of justice and love of God: "Alas for you Pharisees! You pay tithes of mint and rue and every garden herb, but have no care for justice and the love of God. It is these you should have practiced *without neglecting the others*" (Luke 11:42).

Community

The startlingly radical style of life of the Q people has been surveyed in the preceding pages. To summarize it, let us look at the Lord's prayer, which is a Q passage (Luke 11:2–4). The idea that God's name should be hallowed expresses traditional Jewish piety, urging that God be respected, glorified, and obeyed. "Thy kingdom come" reflects the Q desire that the Day of the Son of Man arrive so they might enter the kingdom. "Give us each day our daily bread" is not a vague generality but a serious request by people who probably went many days with no bread or food at all. "And forgive us our sins, for we too forgive all who have done us wrong" reflects their key moral principle: as people forgive other people, so they anticipate God will forgive them. Finally, the often-misunderstood last clause (which does *not* refer to temptation to sin), "And do not bring us to the test," means the Q people hoped to avoid the times of testing, the period of tribulation when the fires and destruction they anticipated would be let loose upon the world. Even those who felt confident God would forgive them and that they would be acknowledged by the Son of Man before the angels of God, were frightened of the prospect of such terrible times and asked God to let them avoid it.

Controversy

There is no sign in Q of any controversies within the Christian community. Jesus' disciples, insofar as they are mentioned at all, are mentioned favorably. Q perhaps reflects the kind of preaching you would have heard from Peter, James, John, and the other historical friends and associates of Jesus.

On the other hand, passages between Luke 11:39 and 11:53 show the Q people in conflict with Pharisaic Judaism. They accused the Pharisees of concerning themselves only with detailed legal observance and not with principles of love and justice, and the Pharisees were thought to be guilty of the persecution of God's prophets. Neither accusation is true of all Pharisees, but it is not hard to imagine that people who thought themselves to be prophets would have resented religious leaders (including Pharisees) who did not accept them, did not repent on command, and who probably insisted (as Christian and Jewish religious leaders might do today) that Q itinerants be driven away or locked up. Nothing in Q would have given the Pharisees any grounds under Torah Law to insist Q people be killed. However, the announcement that a new kingdom of the Jewish God would come and replace the existing (Roman administered) kingdom was a serious crime under Roman law, so Roman authorities could easily have interpreted the message of the Q people to be an illegal prediction or plot to replace the empire of Rome by an empire under Jewish leadership. Some Q people might have been executed by Roman authorities. Their founder was.

Interactions

Q and Miracles Sources

The miracle stories and the Q sayings collection do not contradict one another, but they are certainly different. The one focuses on action, the other on words. Miracle tales sought to convince people Jesus was the Christ or a great prophet, while the Q sayings were less concerned with people's ability to identify Jesus correctly and more concerned with people's willingness to commit themselves to a new repentant and compassionate form of life. The miracle sources show Jesus to be willing, even determined, to reveal himself as Christ; the Q sayings show him more ambiguously as Son of Man.

The Miracles Sources and Paul

The miracles sources argue that faith in Jesus as Christ should be based on his miraculous power. This is not Paul's position. Faith for him is faith in Christ leading to transformation, not simply faith that Jesus was in fact Christ. Through the Spirit Christians receive, they can perform miracles, and those miracles serve as evidence that faith is effective. As all Christians can do miracles of some sort or another, to argue that Jesus did miracles would be, from Paul's perspective, simply to argue that Jesus had the Spirit. Jesus, to Paul, was much more than just somebody with the Spirit.

The Q Source and Paul

For Q, following the Law was essential; the questions raised in Q only reflect differences of opinion about which parts of the Law take precedence over others. Repentance leading to forgiveness and ultimately to God's approval is a central theme of Q, as it is for Judaism generally, while for Paul only grace through faith leads to God's approval. The fact that Q does not find Jesus' crucifixion to be a crucial factor for salvation means that Q Christianity and Pauline Christianity were significantly different.

Paul and Q agree on one major point, however: Both believe that Jesus will return soon, and at that time faithful Christians will be saved.

End-of-Chapter Exercises

1. How did NT scholars come to the conclusion that gospel writers shared sources like Miracles and Q?
2. Define form criticism. What kinds of information can form criticism provide you?
3. What might be some of the consequences of incorporating older texts into a newer one? If, for example, you wanted to write a new version of a gospel for the modern era, you would probably borrow bits and pieces of Mark, Matthew, Luke, and John to do so. What would you need to do to ensure that your interpretation of events is the one your readers accept?

Bibliography

Boring, Eugene. *Sayings of the Risen Jesus.* Cambridge: Cambridge University Press, 1982.

Davies, Stevan. *The Gospel of Thomas Annotated and Explained.* Woodstock VT: Skylight Paths Press, 2002.

Edwards, Richard A. *A Theology of Q.* Philadelphia: Fortress Press, 1976.

Fortna, R. T. *The Gospel of Signs.* Cambridge: Cambridge University Press, 1970.

Goodacre, Mark. *The Case Against Q: Studies in Markan Priority and the Synoptic Problem*. Harrisburg: Trinity Press International, 2002.

Havener, Ivan. *Q: The Sayings of Jesus*. Wilmington: Glazier, 1986.

Hengel, Martin. *Four Gospels and the One Gospel of Jesus Christ*. Trinity Press, 2000.

Kee, Howard C. *Miracle in the Early Christian World*. New Haven: Yale University Press, 1983.

Keller, Ernst. *Miracles in Dispute*. London: SCM Press, 1984.

Kloppenborg, John. *Excavating Q: The History and Setting of the Sayings Gospel*. Minneapolis MN: Fortress Press, 2002.

Mack, Burton. *The Lost Gospel: The Book of Q and Christian Origins*. San Francisco: Harper, 1993.

Reumann, John. *Jesus in the Church's Gospels: Modern Scholarship and the Earliest Sources*. Philadelphia: Fortress Press, 1983.

Smith, Morton. *Jesus the Magician*. New York: Harper & Row, 1978.

Theissen, Gerd. *The Miracle Stories of the Early Christian Tradition*. Philadelphia: Fortress Press, 1983.

The Gospel of Mark

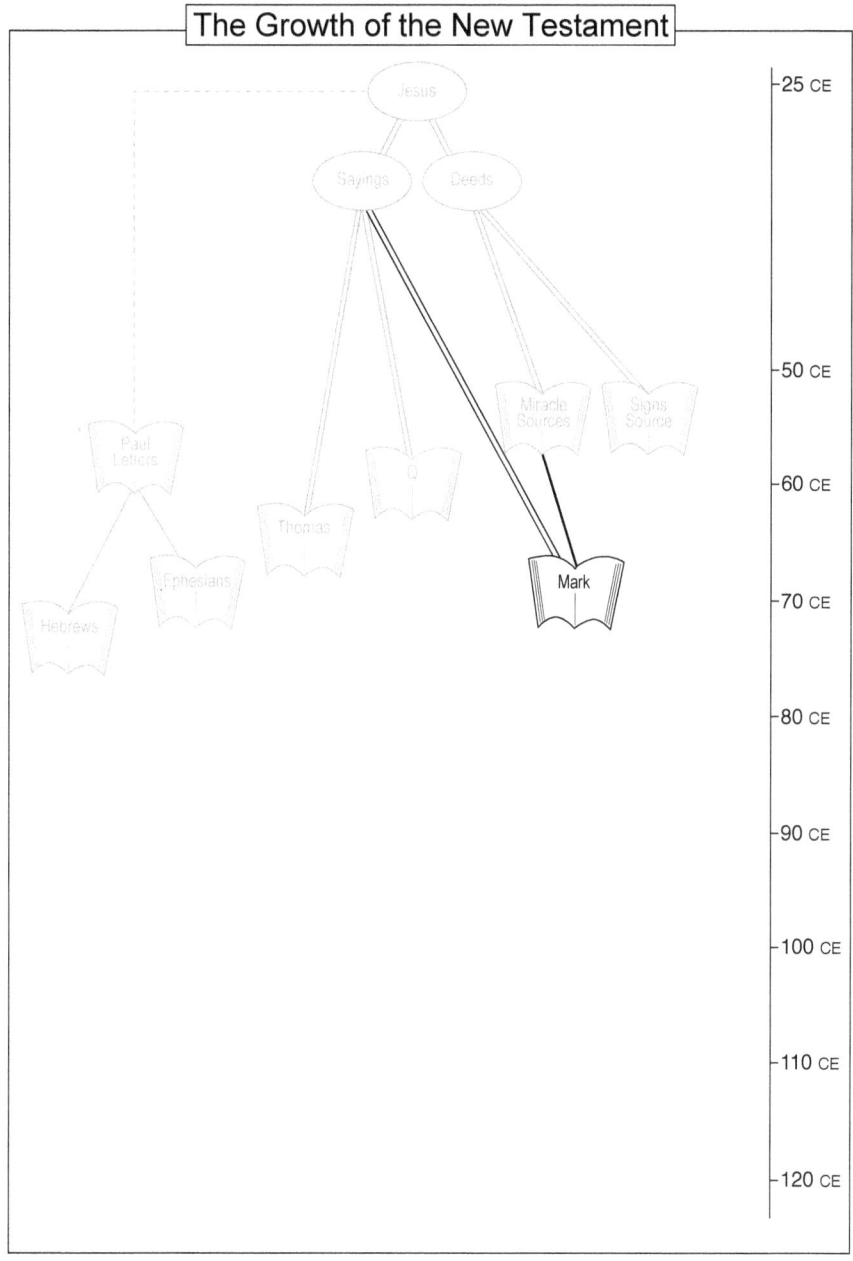

Dashed lines: indirect influence
Double lines: oral transmission
Single thick lines: use of written source
Thin lines: followers, admirers & imitators

CHAPTER 5

The Gospel of Mark

OBJECTIVES

- Begin identifying each gospel's representation of John the Baptist, Pontius Pilate, and Jesus as exemplary of the unique goals of each gospel writer
- Learn how scholars use *text criticism* to determine which aspects of Mark are original and which are later additions and/or revisions (e.g. the ending)
- Evaluate Mark's often negative depictions of Jesus' disciples & family

READ MARK FROM VERSE 1:1 TO VERSE 16:8 AND UNDERLINE ALL REFERENCES TO JESUS' DISCIPLES, TO JESUS' FAMILY, AND TO JESUS' DEMANDS FOR SILENCE OR SECRECY. BE SURE TO USE A DIFFERENT COLORED PEN OR HIGHLIGHTER WHENEVER YOU ARE UNDERLINING DIFFERENT KINDS OF MATERIAL. IF, FOR EXAMPLE, YOU HAVE USED YELLOW TO HIGHLIGHT MARK'S MIRACLE STORIES, USE PINK OR BLUE TO HIGHLIGHT OTHER MATERIAL. In the following pages, we will be examining Mark's ideas about Jesus' followers and family as well as possible reasons for Jesus' commands for silence, so it will be useful to isolate passages concerned with those subjects. As with other New Testament material, one reading is never enough. Gospels are not difficult reading, but readers raised in Christian countries approach them with many preconceptions. Repeated reading lets a gospel's own messages come through; with a single reading one will frequently find only what one expected to find.

Author, Date, and Place of Origin

The Gospel of Mark is usually dated around the year CE 70. Like the dates for all the gospels, this date is approximate and may be off by a half decade or so. The reason for the date CE 70 is that chapter 13 suggests Mark knew about the Jewish insurrection against Rome and the resulting destruction of the temple in Jerusalem in CE 70. We have no other evidence about Mark's date.

An early tradition says that Mark's gospel originated in Rome. Mark does not know Palestinian geography well and assumes his readers know little of Palestinian Judaism (7:1–8). There is, however, no solid evidence that Mark is Roman in origin, and the few Latin terms used in the gospel are terms that would have been used commonly throughout the empire.

The Beginning of the Gospel

The Gospel of Mark starts at an interesting point. Having introduced John the Baptist, immediately Mark gives a short account of the baptism of Jesus. Quickly he tells of the arrest of John, and of Jesus coming into Galilee proclaiming the gospel of God: "The time has come; the kingdom of God is upon you; repent, and believe the Gospel" (1:15). Jesus immediately selects Andrew and Simon to follow him and they quickly do so. The repeated use of "immediately" and "quickly" in the sentences above gives you an example of one trait of Mark's writing. Unlike the other evangelists, he introduces many of his paragraphs with "immediately," as though to give his gospel a sense of rushing and urgency, a tendency supplemented by later passages urging people to "keep awake!" (13:35, 37). Mark's use of Greek is not at all sophisticated, and his writing style is clumsy. Like Matthew and Luke, who both revised Mark, modern translators generally work to improve Mark's style.

Notice that this gospel does not begin with an account of Jesus' cosmic origin (as John's poem about the "Word" does) or of his birth (as Matthew's does) or of his birth and childhood (as Luke's does). For Mark, Jesus' importance began at the time of his baptism, at the moment when the Spirit, as a dove, descended and a voice spoke from heaven saying, "Thou art my Son, my Beloved; on thee my favour rests" (1:11). The fact that Mark begins the gospel with Jesus' baptism entitles us to believe he knew nothing of the story of Jesus' virgin birth. Therefore, from the outset, Mark's perspective contrasts somewhat with that of the other evangelists. It contrasts least with John's, for, although John places Jesus in a cosmic setting with an introductory poem, John's story of Jesus' life begins with Jesus' encounter with John the Baptist just as Mark's does. Even Luke, who has the most extensive account of the birth of Jesus of any gospel writer, begins a summary of Jesus' life story in the book of Acts with Jesus' baptism: "Starting from Galilee after the baptism proclaimed by John . . . God anointed him with the Holy Spirit and with power. He went about doing good and healing all who were oppressed by the devil, for God was with him" (Acts 10:37–39).

As we study each gospel, we will briefly examine the roles of two individuals, one prominent at the beginning, the other at the end of Jesus' life ministry: John the Baptist and Pontius Pilate. Each of the four evangelists was faced with similar problems regarding those individuals, and each of the four chose somewhat different ways to solve those problems. Comparing the gospels in this regard will show something of how evangelists went about solving the problems they faced.

John the Baptist

It is historically likely that John the Baptist believed he had a mission from God to baptize people "in token of repentance, for the forgiveness of sins" (Mark 1:4), that John baptized

Jesus, and that, when he was baptized, Jesus believed he received God's Holy Spirit. At this point Jesus began the mission leading ultimately to his crucifixion. Two difficulties arise for the evangelists: First, was Jesus sinful, then repentant, then willing to submit to baptism? Second, does the fact that John baptized Jesus imply John is superior to Jesus, as the followers of John surely would have claimed? No evangelist believed Jesus sinful, nor did any believe John superior.

Mark introduces John at the very beginning of his gospel. He outlines John's mission in the passage quoted above (Mark 1:4) and categorically states that Jesus "was baptized in the Jordan by John" (Mark 1:9). To demonstrate John's inferiority to Jesus, Mark reports that John said, "After me comes one who is mightier than I. I am not fit to unfasten his shoes. I have baptized you with water; he will baptize you with the Holy Spirit" (1:8). It is likely John said these words, but it is debatable whether he meant them to refer to Jesus or to God, whom John expected would come in the immediate future to usher in his kingdom. Mark presumably believes that John's statement demonstrated John's inferiority to Jesus. Mark does not explicitly contradict the assumption one could draw from 1:4 that Jesus, like others who came for baptism, came in response to John's call for repentance.

Pontius Pilate

The problems the evangelists faced in regard to Pontius Pilate are more urgent and more difficult than the problems they faced in regard to John the Baptist. Pontius Pilate was a prefect appointed by Rome, and was the chief Roman official in Palestine during Jesus' life. As far as we can determine historically, Pilate brought Jesus to trial (perhaps after a preliminary examination of his case by the Jewish court, the Sanhedrin) and found him guilty of treason and ordered his execution. Precisely what Jesus did that Pilate thought treasonous is uncertain, but it is possible Jesus' announcement of the coming of the Kingdom of the Jewish God (and thus, implicitly, the end of Roman control of Palestine) would have been sufficient for a charge of treason.

The evangelists, and Christians generally, did not seek the overthrow of the Roman Empire and did not intend to be traitors. While Jews were legally excused from offering formal sacrifices to images of the emperor because they regarded the ceremony as idol worship, Roman law contained no similar provisions for Christians who similarly refused to offer sacrifices. Thus Christians, by refusing to offer sacrifices to the emperor's image, created the impression that they were traitors, an impression seemingly confirmed by the fact that Christians worshiped a legally convicted traitor as the Son of God. Thus Christians throughout the empire were in danger of execution from their seemingly anti-Roman beliefs.

The fact of Jesus' execution was well known and could not be denied. Christians did not believe him to have been a traitor to the empire. Evangelists, therefore, were faced with the difficult task of demonstrating that a person legally convicted and executed of treason was not a traitor. Toward the end of their gospels, the four evangelists wrote differing accounts of Jesus' trial before Pilate and Pilate's decision to execute Jesus. They shared the desire to demonstrate that Pilate did not believe Jesus to be a traitor and even that Pilate had found him innocent. The responsibility for Jesus' execution is said not to be Pilate's at all but rather to be the responsibility of the only non-Roman people present: the leaders of the Jewish people, or the Jewish people as a whole.

In Mark's account, the "chief priests and the whole council [Sanhedrin] tried to find some evidence against Jesus to warrant a death-sentence, but failed to find any" (14:55). However, after Jesus admits he is the Messiah, the Son of the Blessed One, "their judgment was unanimous: that he was guilty and should be put to death" (14:61–64) on the grounds of blasphemy against the Jewish God. This is no crime in Roman law. Jesus is brought to Pilate and questioned by him, but Jesus does not respond to the charges "they" (not Pilate) are bringing against him. Mark informs us Pilate asked the people, "'Do you wish me to release for you the king of the Jews?' For he knew it was out of malice that they had brought Jesus before him" (15:9–10). Pilate asks, "What harm has he done?" but receives no answer (15:14). Finally, Pilate "in order to satisfy the mob" (15:15), orders the execution.

Mark's account presents an image of Pilate as so weak and vacillating that he executes a man against whom he knows he has no evidence, simply to satisfy a mob. Some find this, and similar gospel accounts, anti-Semitic, for they place blame on the Jewish people for Jesus' execution, but it is likely the evangelists were motivated more by the need to shift responsibility *away* from the Roman procurator than to shift it *toward* the Jewish people. Unfortunately, apart from Romans, the only other people present were Jewish.

In historical fact, Pilate was brutally repressive and cared little about the desires and wishes of the Jewish people and their leadership. Far from granting them favors and following their urging, he despised them. Rather than giving in to the urging of a Jewish mob, he more likely would have brought in soldiers to attack the mob. Pilate was so hated by the people over whom he had authority that eventually his superiors removed him from office.

The Ending of the Gospel

The conclusion of the Gospel of Mark raises several interesting questions. The first and perhaps most interesting is, what is its ending? The answer is that the Gospel of Mark has five different endings. One is usually printed in Bibles as chapter 16, verses 9 through 20. It begins, "When he had risen from the dead early on Sunday morning he appeared first to Mary of Magdala. . . ." A second, very short ending, is also usually printed in Bibles, but without verse numbers, and it begins, "And they delivered all these instructions briefly to Peter and his companions. . . ." The third is the ending of the Gospel of Matthew, for, remember, Matthew is an extensively rewritten version of Mark. The fourth ending, that of the Gospel of Luke, includes the entire book of Acts. The fifth, though, is the authentic ending. It is Mark 16:8: "They said nothing to anybody, for they were afraid."

How do we now Mark 16:8 is the real ending? There are two excellent reasons. The first is derived from source criticism (see chapter 4, "Gospel Sources"). Since Matthew and Luke used Mark as a source, and since Matthew and Luke differ completely in their accounts of Jesus' resurrection appearances, it is impossible that both used Mark as a source for their accounts. Further, it is unlikely only one did; the accounts in Matthew's and Luke's gospels are written entirely in their own styles and not at all in the style of Mark. Apparently neither had a version of resurrection appearances written by Mark to copy or to adapt.

Text Criticism

Text criticism, or text analysis, is the study of various ancient manuscripts of the New Testament to determine which words, phrases, and passages are original and which are the results of changes in the original. In the ancient world the only way copies of books could be made was to have copies written out by hand. There were no printing presses, no photocopiers, no laser printers, no movable type, no mechanical printing of any kind. All copies were hand-written on scrolls of papyrus, or possibly booklets of papyrus, by scribes who often took down what they wrote from verbal dictation.

Handwritten copies of manuscripts are never absolutely the same as their originals, especially if (as was often the case in the ancient world) they are based on verbal dictation instead of sight reading. All kinds of mistakes occur: letters may be omitted, words left out, sentences copied twice or not at all, and so on. Copyists may choose to make changes, to correct or delete phrases with which they disagree, to add explanations for difficult passages, to improve grammar, or to add stories or sayings where they seem appropriate. This means every single manuscript of the New Testament is different in many small ways, and in some greater ways, from every other manuscript.

More than 1,500 different manuscripts exist which contain New Testament texts, some complete, some fragmentary. Most of these derive from the centuries after CE 400, although we have some fragments of copies of New Testament texts written on papyrus and dated from the middle of the third century (ca. CE 250). Not even fragments remain from the first century. More complete texts exist from the fourth century. The later the date of copies, the more likely it is that errors have occurred in transmission.

Clear connections exist between many different copies, because errors were perpetuated. A mistake made in a second-century copy may consistently occur in later copies of that copy, and in copies of the later copies. Text analysts seek to sort out the history of copies and to trace them back to earlier and earlier versions by grouping related copies into categories and developing family histories of the copies. The hundreds of later versions derive from four basic families of copies: the Alexandrian text (probably the most accurate), the Byzantine text (less accurate and the basis for the King

James Version), the Western text, and the Caesarean text. None of these four texts now exists in a pure form; all must be re-created by careful comparison of their many surviving various copies.

Any particular modern version of the New Testament is a single collection of choices made from the many options the ancient manuscripts make available. Text analysts use both external and internal evidence to make their choices. External evidence is primarily the result of the past century's scholarly efforts to decide preferable readings from the many existing manuscripts. It is often easy to determine preferable readings. Nonsense words, obvious later theologizing, doubled phrases, and so forth can be corrected without difficulty. But some questions simply cannot be precisely answered, and different text analysts will make different decisions about what to accept and what to reject.

Internal evidence comes from comparison between what a particular variant reading (a phrase or passage different from most versions) says and the general perspective and literary style of a particular author. It is reasonable to prefer passages that match an author's general opinions and usual style of writing and to reject those that do not. Also reasonable is the principle that a more difficult variant reading ("difficult" either because it is grammatically clumsy or because it does not fit the theologies of later centuries) is likely to be more accurate than an easy reading. This principle derives from the common-sense observation that copyists tend to make the reading of their copy polished and precise, not awkward and careless.

The earliest and best manuscripts of the Gospel of Mark end with verse 16:8; only later and inferior manuscripts include verses 16:9–20 or the other, shorter ending. From a text analytical perspective, this is not a difficult problem. Mark's ending at 16:8 is a more difficult reading (for

Christians came to expect an account of resurrection appearances), and it is supported by superior manuscripts.

From a theological perspective, the other endings of Mark are canonical, but they are not therefore considered to have been written by Mark. Such problems as this have led fundamentalist Christians to declare that the Bible is "inerrant in the original autograph." They mean by this that they believe the original authors produced texts that were without error, but errors may have crept in later through scribal inattention or deliberate efforts by scribes to improve the original. Many translations contain, as footnotes throughout the Bible, comments like "other manuscripts have . . ." or "some witnesses give . . ." followed by variants on the verse in the text. This is simply honest admission that while a text analytical choice has been made, the reader should be aware that other possibilities exist and that they could be original.

The end of the Gospel of Mark is unique. There alone the resurrection of Jesus is not followed by an appearance to any of his followers. The easiest way to explain this is that Mark believed Jesus would shortly reappear on earth in Galilee, this time "coming in the clouds with great power and glory" (13:26), but this event had not yet happened. Judging by the end of chapter 13 (verses 33–37), Mark assumed Jesus' reappearance would take place soon, certainly within a few years, and "the present generation will live to see it all" (13:30). But other passages in chapter 13 (verses 7–8 and 24–27, for example) indicate that Mark did not think it would take place immediately. Indeed, it is from Mark that we are told that "About that day or that hour no one knows, not even the angels in heaven, not even the Son; only the Father" (13:32). What Mark seems to regard as one event, Jesus' appearances upon his return, other sources regard as two: Jesus' resurrection appearances followed by his "second coming."

Organization of the Gospel

1. An introductory section wherein Jesus travels through the countryside and performs many miracles (1:1–8:21)
2. A central section wherein Jesus reveals the true mission of the Son of Man (8:22–10:52)
3. A section reporting several areas of controversy between Jesus and Jewish authorities in Jerusalem (11:1–12:44)
4. An extended apocalyptic discourse (13:1–37)
5. A passion narrative (14:1–16:8)

Throughout the first half of the gospel, Jesus repeatedly commands people not to tell about him, not to announce his miracles, not to spread the word about his healings. People and demons alike must keep silent. Demons are not weird, red creatures with tails; the term "demon" refers to a person who believes himself or herself to be possessed by an evil spirit. "Demon" here is shorthand for "a person supposedly possessed by a demon." When Jesus speaks to a demon or a demon speaks to Jesus, two people are in conversation. Mark, it may be presumed, did not doubt such people were possessed.

Jesus' requests for silence in Mark's gospel have come to be known as the *Messianic Secret*, although exactly what was to be kept secret, and why, are still subject to dispute among scholars. One theory is that only after Jesus' crucifixion did his disciples begin to believe him to be the Messiah. Mark, realizing it was not clear in the traditions that Jesus claimed to be Messiah, and yet believing Jesus was the Messiah, decided Jesus must have wished it kept secret until after his resurrection. This theory emphasizes Mark 9:9, when after the transfiguration Jesus "enjoined them not to tell anyone what they had seen until the Son of Man had risen from the dead."

Repeated requests for silence in Mark seem especially curious because they so obviously were ignored. Mark reports that people spoke about Jesus' exorcisms and healings whether he wanted them to or not. No other source suggests Jesus wanted this miraculous aspect of his ministry to be kept silent, and the existence of miracles sources demonstrate that proclamation of Jesus' miracles was a main interest of at least some early Christians. Why, then, might Mark have depicted Jesus as seeking to maintain secrecy regarding miracles? We shall return to this question shortly.

Those Who Misunderstood Jesus

REREAD WITH AN OPEN MIND THE PASSAGES YOU HAVE UNDERLINED REGARDING THE DISCIPLES; you will almost certainly be in for a surprise. The disciples are depicted as failing to understand Jesus at all. Twelve are selected (early and apparently at random) and given every opportunity to understand. They are present at his miracles, listen to him speak, and receive special information not available to others (4:10–12; 7:17–18; 9:2; 9:30–32; 14:33). James, Peter, and John are especially singled out for attention, the same men whom Paul somewhat sarcastically calls the three "pillars" of the church in Jerusalem (Gal 2:9). These three disciples witness such scenes as the transfiguration and Jesus' prayers in the Garden of Gethsemene, but to no avail. They continue to misunderstand Jesus and his message.

Many who read Mark assume this situation is temporary, that while the disciples may have had trouble understanding what they witnessed and heard, eventually they managed to overcome doubt and skepticism and came to follow Jesus correctly. Maybe so, but this is not Mark's idea. At the end of Mark, one disciple has betrayed him and the other eleven have run off, one of whom publicly denies knowing him. The women who discover the empty tomb do not tell the disciples about it or about what they heard from the young person (not the angel) at the tomb.

Jesus' family does not come off much better. In chapter 3, Mark reports, "He entered a house; and once more such a crowd collected round them that they had no chance to eat. When his family heard of this, they set out to take charge of him; for people were saying that he was out of his mind" (3:20–21). There is some doubt about the meaning of "he was out of his mind," but the prevailing idea in the first century would have been that one "out of his mind" was one possessed by a demonic or unclean spirit. There follow in Mark several passages regarding demon possession, including the startling passage stating that anyone who declares Jesus possessed of an unclean spirit, rather than the Holy Spirit, has slandered the Holy Spirit and cannot be forgiven. Then Jesus' mother and brothers arrive and send a message in to him. They receive the response, "'Who is my mother? Who are my brothers?' And looking round at those who were sitting in the circle about him he said, 'Here are my mother and my brothers. Whoever does the will of God is my brother, my sister, my mother'" (3:31–35). A charitable interpretation of this is that Jesus includes his family in the category of those who do the will of God, but the passage is more easily seen to contrast the former family (outside) with the new family (inside). Mark 3 implies that his family believed those who said, "He is out of his mind."

In chapter 6, Jesus returns home, teaches in the synagogue, and the crowd is amazed. "'Is not this the carpenter, the son of Mary, the brother of James and Joseph and Judas and Simon? And are not his sisters here with us?' So they fell foul of him . . . [Jesus] could work no miracle there, except that he put his hands on a few sick people and healed them; and he was taken aback by their want of faith." This passage surprises many Christians who have been taught that Jesus had no brothers or sisters. The words translated "brothers" and "sisters" can occasionally mean cousins, or step-brother and step-sister. However, the reports of Paul, Luke, Mark, Matthew, and John indicate that the Christians of the first century had no problem with the tradition that Jesus did have brothers. (Only Mark and Matthew [13:56] specifically mention sisters.) The later development of a doctrine of the perpetual virginity of Mary led to the conclusion that Jesus must not have had any siblings. The New Testament authors knew nothing of this doctrine.

Jesus' brother James became the leader of the church in Jerusalem after the crucifixion. Paul mentions "James, the Lord's brother" in Galatians 1:19 and later gives evidence for his high position when he refers to "those reputed pillars of our society James, Peter and John" (Gal 2:9). James is prominent in Acts. The Letter of James in the New Testament is thought by some scholars to have been attributed to Jesus' brother James, and the letter of Judas (commonly called Jude to avoid confusion with Judas Iscariot) is attributed to Judas the brother of James and, presumably, also the brother of Jesus.

In analyzing Mark 6, we can also utilize information beyond that given by Mark. We have two first-century reactions to the passage produced by the authors of Luke and Matthew. Further, a first-century version of Jesus' saying about a prophet exists in the Gospel of Thomas. Let us consider this information below.

Matthew takes the version of the saying in Mark 6:4 and presents it as, "A prophet will always be held in honour, except in his home town, and in his own family" (Matt 13:57). This slightly tones down Mark's doubly stressed "kinsmen and family." Luke goes further, retaining only, "No prophet is recognized in his own country" (4:24). We can presume, then, that Matthew and Luke, the two earliest biblical analysts we know of, both thought the saying in Mark was too critical of the family of Jesus; Luke deleted all the implied criticism.

Should we assume that Jesus implied that his family did not hold him in honor, or did Mark introduce that idea? If we check our other source of information, Thomas, we find saying 31, "No prophet is accepted in his own village. No physician heals those who know him well." This has the appearance of being a proverb generally applicable to prophets and healers in peasant societies, not a biographical statement. Apparently Mark added the clauses critical of family and relatives, and Luke, recognizing this, deleted them.

But perhaps Mark did more than this. Perhaps he had in front of him a saying in the Thomas version, "No prophet is accepted in his own village. No physician heals those who know him well." and wondered what caused Jesus to say this. Most of the sayings of Jesus now in the New Testament were passed down originally by oral tradition and then in written lists without any narrative to place them in biographical context. Mark may have assumed Jesus could have said such a thing only when he returned to his village, was not accepted there, and could heal few people there. Moreover, Mark had no particular interest in the inhabitants of Nazareth but was interested in Jesus' family, whom he did not think were supportive of Jesus.

What Mark may have done is taken the original saying, added clauses critical of "family and kinsmen," created a logical biographical context for the saying, and then written the account found in 6:1–6. Matthew and Luke, in turn, came across Mark's passage and revised those elements they found inappropriate, Matthew revising a little in 13:54–58 and Luke much more in 4:16–24.

The disciples of Jesus and the family of Jesus became the leaders of the new church and, from their base in Jerusalem, sought to spread the gospel as they understood it throughout first the Jewish and then the Gentile world. Mark's unflattering portrayal of both disciples and family certainly does not come from reports traceable back to Peter or James, since we may be confident they thought they understood Jesus well enough. The failure of disciples and family, then, is an opinion of Mark's.

At the climax of Mark's first section, 1:1 to 8:21, Jesus reacts with anger to his disciples' inability to understand him:

> "Have you no inkling yet? Do you still not understand? Are your minds closed? You have eyes: can you not see? You have ears: can you not hear? Have you forgotten? When I broke the five loaves among five thousand, how many basketfuls of scraps did you pick up?" "Twelve," they said, "And how many when I broke the seven loaves among four thousand?" They answered, "Seven." He said, "Do you still not understand?"

Here, midway in the gospel, the disciples evidently understand nothing. But they have been with Jesus from the gospel's beginning, have heard his teaching and received special instruction. What purpose might Mark have had in portraying them as so obtuse? One major clue to the solution of the problems of the Messianic Secret and of Mark's desire to show the disciples in a bad light may be found by close analysis of Mark 8:27–34:

> Jesus and his disciples set out for the villages of Caesarea Philippi. On the way he asked his disciples, "Who do men say I am?" They answered, "Some say John the Baptist, others Elijah, others one of the prophets." "And you," he asked, "who do you say I am?" Peter replied: "You are the Christ." Then he gave them strict orders not to tell anyone about him; and he began to teach them that the Son of Man had to undergo great sufferings, and to be rejected by the elders, chief priests, and doctors of the law; to be put

to death, and to rise again three days afterwards. He spoke about it plainly. At this Peter took him by the arm and began to rebuke him. But Jesus turned round, and, looking at his disciples, rebuked Peter. "Away with you, Satan," he said; "you think as men think, not as God thinks."

This passage is a turning-point in Mark's gospel. In the chapters preceding it, Jesus speaks publicly in parables and performs miraculous works. After this passage, Jesus instead teaches his disciples plainly, journeys to Jerusalem, is executed, and rises from the dead. Public parable-preaching and miracle-working rarely occur in the later chapters. This passage contains both Mark's assessment of Jesus' central purpose and a major clue to the reason for the disciples' difficulties.

Jesus asks, "Who do men say I am?" His question sets up all that follows. In Mark's opinion there are two perspectives on Jesus: human and divine. The human perspective is misguided. It is that Jesus is a prophet, probably a prophet who formerly lived and died and now has come back to life. People do not seem clear on which prophet he is: John the Baptist? Elijah? Another one altogether? Their answers repeat the opinion of Herod and those about him that Jesus was John come back or Elijah or at least that he was like the old prophets (6:14–16). These opinions are based on the idea that "miraculous powers are at work in him" (6:14).

Peter declares that Jesus is Christ. This, in some sense, is the right answer, but do not be misled. Mark, like any good teacher, is clever enough to know the right word may be a correct or an incorrect answer depending on what the word is thought to mean. What did Peter mean by "Christ"? The Son of Man who was to suffer and die and rise again? A miracle-working prophet? A political messiah destined to overthrow Roman rule?

Mark does not believe Jesus primarily to be either a miracle worker or a political revolutionary. From the Gospel of John we learn that the term "prophet" sometimes implied both ideas. At the conclusion of John's account of the miraculous feeding of the five thousand, "When the people saw the sign [miracle] Jesus had performed, the word went round, 'Surely this must be the prophet that was to come into the world'" (John 6:14). The passage continues with a sentence probably added by the author of John's gospel indicating that the term "prophet" may sometimes have implied a political claim: "Jesus, aware that [those who called him the prophet] meant to come and seize him to proclaim him king, withdrew again to the hills by himself." In Mark's gospel, Jesus does not claim earthly kingship. Mark takes the political term "Son of David" (implying that Jesus is a descendant of the royal house and therefore technically eligible for the kingship) and in one instance puts it in the mouth of a man who is blind (Mark 10:47–48) and in another instance quotes Jesus as denying the Messiah is the Son of David at all, basing the denial on an interpretation of Psalm 110:1 (Mark 12:35–37). So for Mark, the term "Christ" means neither a prophet nor an earthly king.

What does Mark think Peter means by "Christ"? Peter hears from Jesus that the Son of Man has come to suffer, die, and rise again. Peter's initial reaction to this is to "rebuke" Jesus. The word rebuke is the same term used by Mark to describe Jesus' response to demons (1:25; 9:25). In response, Jesus immediately "rebukes" Peter, calls him Satan, sends him away, and states that Peter thinks as humans think, not as God thinks. We know both what people think (that Jesus is a prophet come back to life or a prophet like the old prophets) and what God thinks (that Jesus is the suffering Son of Man). Whatever Peter meant by his statement "you are the Christ" is not what Jesus and God mean, according to Mark.

Mark distinguishes between using correct terms and understanding terms correctly. To proclaim Jesus the "Son of God" and the "Christ" is correct, from Mark's perspective, only if the meaning of the terms is properly understood. Jesus' response to Peter above shows that Peter misunderstands the term. The demons (possessed people) that Jesus has previously encountered state who he is—"Son of God"—but "he insist[s] that they should not make him known" (3:12). Demons get the terms right, but their knowledge is necessarily inadequate, based solely on their experience of Jesus' power to cast them out, to exorcise, and to heal. Mark believes Jesus is more than a miracle worker, and so in his gospel the demons are instructed not to proclaim their inadequate knowledge.

The disciples, too, throughout the first seven chapters of Mark, have witnessed Jesus' public speaking in parables and performing miraculous works. It appears that Peter, like people generally and Herod particularly, understands Jesus to be a prophet, probably a miracle-working prophet. The miracle story most likely to have been derived from an Old Testament prophetic model (2 Kings 4:42–44), the miraculous feedings, is used twice leading up to Peter's confession.

Mark's Central Section

In a tightly organized segment of his gospel, Mark gives three versions of what he believes the correct interpretation of Jesus to be. READ MARK 8:22 THROUGH 10:52 CAREFULLY, NOTING THE FOLLOWING:

1. The section begins with a story of a blind man who is given sight, 8:22–26, and ends with a story of a blind man who is given sight, 10:46–52. These stories form a frame around the section. Mark is using stories about gaining sight to symbolize the idea of gaining understanding.

2. Three separate sections begin with the mention of a journey. These soon are followed by the key passages about the suffering Son of Man (8:27–33; 9:31; 10:35–40).
3. These three sections are followed by passages critical of disciples (8:33; 9:32–34; 10:35–40). The criticism leads to passages insisting that Christians, especially Christian leaders, should be self-sacrificing, show humility, and serve others. The disciples, according to Mark, were too eager to put themselves forward and to inhibit those not in their particular group (9:38–41).

Mark's central section is very carefully constructed, so carefully that an appreciation of its construction is the best evidence that Mark did not primarily intend to write down accurate, factual sequences of historical events. Rather, he designed narratives to dramatize his own opinion of what Jesus did. The central section repeatedly highlights Mark's main point: that people should, first and foremost, think of Jesus in terms of his suffering, death and resurrection. The blindness of the disciples evidently leads them to misunderstand this. Because they misunderstand, they are shown repeatedly to strive for power among themselves as insiders (9:34), or for themselves against outsiders (9:38–41), or for themselves as individuals (10:27–40). Jesus insists that such quests for personal power are completely inappropriate: "anyone who wishes to be a follower of mine must leave self behind" (8:34), "whoever does not accept the kingdom of God like a child will never enter it," (9:15), and "whoever wants to be great must be your servant, and whoever wants to be first must be the willing slave of all" (10:43–44). Jesus presents himself as an example of proper leadership "for even the Son of Man did not come to be served but to serve, and to surrender his life as a ransom for many" (10:45).

The gospel's first section 1:1–8:21 seems to declare Jesus' principal role to be a divinely empowered man. This would encourage his followers, should they wish to be like him, to seek to exercise power. But the second section 8:22–10:52 is designed, quite deliberately, to contradict this impression. Mark is an extraordinarily clever author. He doesn't write simply to say "this is the right view, that is the wrong view," he writes to explain through narrative how people came to hold the wrong view (the gospel's first section) and then, through narrative, how people should come to hold the right view (the remainder of the gospel).

Mark thinks Jesus is misunderstood even by some of those who use correct terms about him, possessed people and even Peter. It is likely that Mark thinks the misunderstandings come from focusing on Jesus' miracle-working powers instead of his suffering and death. Mark's is sometimes called a "corrective Christology," (a *Christology* is a theory of the nature and significance of Christ) because he seems to introduce false impressions of Jesus, as a miracle worker or a resurrected prophet, and then to cancel these impressions by repeatedly having Jesus declare what the correct impression should have been. Mark's own Christology is quite explicit in his gospel. Jesus is made to repeat the same point four separate times in 8:31, 9:12, 9:31, and 10:33–34, the last of which reads, "the Son of Man will be given up to the chief priests and the doctors of the law; they will condemn him to death and hand him over to the foreign power. He will be mocked and spat upon, flogged and killed; and three days afterwards, he will rise again."

Having shown Jesus insisting repeatedly that he must be understood in light of his suffering, death and resurrection, Mark concludes his gospel with a long sustained narrative that portrays those very events (14:1–16:8). Mark is quite good at transferring abstract points into narrated stories. For example, he shows Jesus concluding chapter 13's apocalyptic discourse with the admonition to "stay awake!" (13:37) because the Son of Man will return at any moment. Shortly thereafter, Mark relates the story of Gethsemane (14:32–42) which portrays Peter, James and John as being instructed to stay awake but, three times, failing to do so. Mark here, as elsewhere, uses the disciples as examples of people who do just the wrong thing.

In one interesting passage, Mark cancels what was earlier a strong claim to authority found in both Q and John: "Whoever receives a messenger of mine receives me, whoever receives me receives the One who sent me." Q people would have identified themselves as disciples and messengers of Jesus and would have used the saying above to justify themselves as persons of significance. So, presumably, did Jesus' disciples. However, Mark alters the saying to "Whoever receives one of these children in my name receives me; and whoever receives me, receives not me but the One who sent me" (9:37). This is not the same meaning at all. Mark has changed a claim to status as a special messenger of God into a general statement applicable even to children.

It is likely that Mark was aware of the preaching of Jesus' disciples (and of such leading family members as James) and thought it misguided. He did not believe them entitled to leading positions in the church and felt they were entirely too prone to seek power. They (or their successors who lived during Mark's time) claimed position and authority because they (or their predecessors) had been with Jesus during his lifetime.

If Mark wished to counteract the claims to authority of such people, he faced a serious dilemma. He could not deny that Jesus' disciples accompanied Jesus, were taught by him, and witnessed his miracles. But Mark can deny that these privileges did them any good. Mark purposefully presents Jesus' teachings in his gospel in such a way that the reader of the gospel understands Jesus (as suffering Son of Man) better than the disciples did. At the same time, the reader can see how it was the disciples came to be mistaken (through excessive interest in Jesus' miracles). Mark probably knows (as Paul did, 1 Cor 15:3–9) that witnesses to the resurrection had special claim to status in the church and, to counteract any such claims, ends his gospel denying that the disciples were even aware of the resurrection, much less that they witnessed it.

As odd as it may seem, Mark informs us that Jesus deliberately spoke in enigmatic parables to keep people from understanding him. He says to the disciples, "To you the secret of the kingdom of God has been given; but to those who are outside everything comes by way of parables, so that [as Scripture says] they may look and look, but see nothing; they may hear and hear, but understand nothing; otherwise they might turn to God and be forgiven" (4:11–12). However, the fact that the disciples are given the secret does not necessarily mean they understood it. Perhaps Mark's gospel is motivated not only by the author's desire to explain the true nature of Jesus' mission as he understands it, but also to discuss why, during Jesus' life, people in general and the disciples in particular failed to understand his mission correctly. Mark may have regarded Jesus' parables as obscure riddles and concluded that Jesus must have deliberately made them difficult, which would account in part for people's misunderstanding of Jesus. Mark's judgment is harsher on the disciples. To them "the secret of the kingdom of God has been given" (4:11), and, unlike the common people, they were expected to understand Jesus' parables.

Four important themes come together in the central segment of Mark: the Messianic Secret, Mark's critical appraisal of the disciples, the requirement that Christians behave with humility, and the concept of the suffering Son of Man. Mark probably portrays Jesus as eager to have demons and people healed of illness keep silent because Mark conceives of the people as having been misled by Jesus' miracles. Jesus is seeking to avoid misconceptions about his mission. Jesus' efforts fail. People do not keep silent. The disciples, with special knowledge unavailable to outsiders, are nevertheless failures. Mark shows Jesus revealing "plainly" (8:32) to his disciples that he is to suffer and die and rise in contrast to his previous custom of speaking in "parables" (4:2) to outsiders, but the disciples never do understand Jesus as Mark's gospel tells the story.

Those Who Understand Jesus

Some do understand Jesus correctly, or possibly only one person—an unnamed woman (14:3–9). While Jesus is still alive, she anoints his body for burial and by doing this she shows that she anticipates his death and his resurrection, for, since he will rise again, his body cannot receive the customary anointing. The disciples, typically for Mark, do not understand what she is doing; "They turned upon her with fury." In the greatest praise bestowed on anyone in the Gospel of Mark, Jesus says, "I tell you this: wherever in the world the gospel is proclaimed, what she has done will be told as her memorial."

The Roman centurion (an officer equivalent in rank to an American army captain) who is mentioned in 15:39 directed, and therefore was immediately responsible for, the crucifixion of Jesus; an officer is responsible for the orders he gives his men. Mark probably intended his readers to believe that this man correctly understood Jesus. This centurion, when he saw how Jesus died, declared, "Truly this man was a son of God." From Mark's perspective a declaration that Jesus is a Son of God because of his death (not, for instance, because of his miracles) is correct. Joseph of Arimathaea may also have understood Jesus correctly (15:43), for he is praised as "a man who looked forward to the kingdom of God." He received Jesus' corpse from Pilate and, as "a respected member of the council," had presumably joined in the unanimous council vote declaring that Jesus should be put to death (14:64).

The woman who anoints Jesus, the centurion who proclaims Jesus a Son of God, and Joseph, who eagerly awaits the Kingdom of God—together these three have voted to condemn Jesus, directed his execution, anointed his body for burial, and buried him. But from Mark's perspective they have done the opposite of rebuking Jesus for declaring that the Son of Man must suffer and die; they have willingly participated in those events.

Mark's Apocalypse

Special attention must be paid to Mark 13. Here, Jesus gives a lengthy speech in response to a question put privately by Peter, James, John, and Andrew. "'Tell us,' they said, 'when will this [destruction of the temple] happen? What will be the sign when the fulfillment of all this is at hand?'" This speech can be categorized as apocalyptic, as it foretells in some detail the ominous events scheduled by God to take place before the end of this world and its replacement or renewal by the Kingdom of God. The speech in chapter 13 alternates between the cosmic scale and the local scale, between events to occur in the world at large and events to occur in the lives of local Christians, presumably those living in Mark's community. Scholars think that such local events reflect real social conditions in the early Christian community and, therefore, that they serve as a valuable source of evidence about Mark's community and the events that led to him writing his gospel.

These "local" events are found in 13:5–6, 9–13, and 21–23. They reflect a time of persecution both on the level of the state and on the level of the family. People (probably Christians) come, claiming Jesus' name, with "signs and wonders" (probably healing miracles and exorcisms), who may mislead "God's chosen." Threats arise from within and outside the Christian movement. Significantly, here, as in the first section of Mark's gospel, signs and wonders tend to mislead.

Cosmic apocalyptic material is found in the following verses: 7–8, 14–20, 24–27, 32. They state the end of this world is to come and will be introduced by terrible disasters. This may provide one answer to the obvious question raised by Mark's perspective: why did the Son of Man have to suffer and die? The answer could be that Jesus' tragic death was a part of a whole sequence of tragic events taking place before the end, and it, like the suffering taking place in Mark's community and the suffering and death of John the Baptist, was planned by God.

Mark's little apocalypse, as it is sometimes called in scholarship, seems designed to reinterpret the idea of the imitation of Christ. To be like Christ seemed, evidently, to some Christians to require them to be prophets, to do signs and wonders, or even to come in Jesus' name claiming "I am he!" But Mark believes, and emphasizes, that the imitation of Christ is done by those who are submissive, who are persecuted, who, like the Son of Man, may be required to suffer, to die, and ultimately to rise again.

In Mark's gospel only two phrases, obscure but highly important, serve as clues to the author's interpretation of the significance of Jesus' death. The first is, "The Son of Man did not come to be served but to serve, and to give his life as a ransom for many" (10:45). This is the final sentence of Mark's crucial central section and plays, in literary terms, the role of a climax. It is supplemented by a statement at the Last Supper when Jesus announces, "This is my blood, the blood of the covenant, shed for many" (14:24). These two clues support speculation that for Mark Jesus' death began a new covenant with people (the old covenant being the establishment of a special relationship between God and the Jewish people who kept the Law of the Torah), and that people were ransomed by Jesus' death. We are told little of what the new covenant involves in terms of the relationship between people and God except that people should be servants of one another. We are told nothing of what "many" are ransomed from, and nothing of why Jesus' death for ransom was necessary. These two clues, insufficient as they stand, do not allow us to state with certainty what Mark believed the purpose of the death of Jesus was. A theologian will recognize in those sentences echoes of Paul's way of thinking and use Paul to help explain Mark's meaning. This is perhaps a valid procedure, as Mark seems in several respects to agree with Paul's view of Jesus. But, even though use of Paul's ideas to interpret Mark may be valid, it is good to remember that as it stands, in and of itself, Mark gives only two difficult clues to his idea of the purpose of Jesus' death. Mark assumes his audience understands the purpose of Jesus' death. Thus, he does not tell them that purpose.

For many years scholars casually reasoned that as Mark was the first gospel, at least a decade earlier than the other three, it must therefore be the most historically reliable. This is not necessarily true. Mark's particular perspectives, especially his antagonism to Jesus' disciples, render suspect his accounts of Jesus' interactions with his closest associates. Further, Mark's careful structuring of his gospel, from early stories of miracle working to his central section focusing on the suffering Son of Man to his lengthy account of Jesus' betrayal, trial, and execution, reflects his own organization of Jesus' life more so than research into the actual events in Jesus' life. Mark must be judged as an *evangelist*, not a biographer; evangelists set forth the meaning of Jesus life as they see it within a narrative framework, while biographers seek as nearly as possible to render a factual account of a life. The two are not the same, and the common assumption that the evangelists were biographers has led to much misunderstanding of the nature of the New Testament.

Recurring Themes

Sources

It is impossible to be certain what Mark's sources were, but intelligent guesses can be made. As Mark's version of Jesus' trial and death is quite similar to John's, it is likely both derive from a common source. Since Jesus' death was of supreme importance to some branches of the early Christian church, it is likely that accounts of it were written down before anyone wrote a longer biography. Mark, therefore, probably adapted a previously written passion narrative to his gospel.

In addition, Mark seems to have used two small written collections of miracles in the first half of his book (see chapter 4, "Gospel Sources"). Along with these, Mark may have made use of short written collections of Jesus' parables. Some scholars think Mark 4 comes from such a collection.

Otherwise, Mark seems to be working from an oral tradition he edits, revises, and interprets in his own fashion.

Jesus

In Mark's gospel Jesus' life is not an uninterrupted story of success. He comes to reveal himself as the suffering Son of Man who is also Christ and Son of the Most High God, yet those closest to him fail to understand this correctly. Neither his miracles nor his teachings were of major importance, for, when Jesus gives the central point of his life, they are not mentioned (8:31; 9:12; 9:31; 10:33). Fully half of Mark's short book (chapters 8–16) depict a passion narrative: Jesus speaks of his approaching death, travels to Jerusalem where it will take place, and undergoes the legal prosecution and eventual execution he had predicted. A cliché in the study of the Gospel of Mark defines the book as a passion narrative with an extended introduction.

The Son of Man has power on earth to exorcise, heal, and forgive sins—all somewhat synonymous—but his great power will come later. Perhaps it would be best to think of Jesus in Mark's gospel as the Son of Man come in disguise, and only those who see through the disguise and are not misled will be privileged to live eternally with him when he comes in the future (10:29–31). Eternal life will, apparently, be given to those who repent (1:15, but see also 4:12), who behave in a moral fashion (7:21–23; 10:19), who sell all they have and give the proceeds to the poor (10:21), who follow Jesus despite personal sacrifices of many kinds (10:29–31), and above all who recognize the importance of Jesus' death (10:45; 14:24).

Jesus' death is a crucial part of his mission from God. It is toward death that the gospel is directed, in both a literary and a christological sense. Jesus, the Son of Man, was to suffer and die and rise. Any other interpretation of him showed ignorance and misunderstanding. But why was Jesus' death of such importance? Only Mark 10:45 and 14:24 hint at answers, but those short, puzzling comments do not let a reader see very deeply into Mark's conception. Presumably those for whom his gospel was written understood the purpose of Jesus' death, so Mark feels no need to discuss the matter at length. This means it would be wrong to say Mark wrote his gospel to explain the meaning and nature of Jesus' life and death. Rather, Mark is writing for an audience who believe they know this and are puzzled why others do not.

Although Mark clearly believes Jesus Christ can be understood only from the perspective of his death and resurrection, no resurrection appearances are given; Mark believes Jesus will appear in the future, in Galilee (14:28; 16:7), when he returns as the Son of Man "in the clouds with great power and glory" and "sends out the angels and gathers his chosen from the four winds, from the farthest bounds of earth to the farthest bounds of heaven" (13:26–27). Then those who do understand him correctly will live eternally with him.

Eschatology

Chapter 13 is a self-contained unit outlining the events taking place leading up to the catastrophic end of this world and the glorious return of the Son of Man. Mark insists, on the one hand, that the end is still some time away and, on the other hand, that it will soon come. This can be seen, for example, in verses 7 and 8:

> When you hear the noise of battle near at hand and the news of battles far away, do not be alarmed. Such things are bound to happen; but the end is still to come. For nation will make war upon nation, kingdom upon kingdom; there will be earthquakes in many places; there will be famines. With these things the birthpangs of the new age begin.

The events leading up to the end are occurring in his own time, Mark believes, but this does not mean that in a matter of months all will be over. In times to come, "the sun will be darkened, the moon will not give her light; the stars will come falling from the sky, the celestial powers will be shaken" (13:24–25), but those things have not yet happened.

Mark believes he and his community are living in the midst of eschatological events. God knows when they will finally end, but no one else does, not even the angels in heaven or the Son (13:32). "The present generation will live to see it all" (13:30), but they have not seen it all yet. The events of the end time are terrible; nothing good is mentioned in chapter 13 until finally the Son of Man comes in power and glory. The events of Jesus' life were, similarly, terrible. He was misunderstood, rejected, betrayed, tried, convicted, and executed. Mark's gospel must be understood in terms of this bleak but hopeful perspective. If members of Mark's community were being persecuted, handed over to the courts, flogged in synagogues, summoned to appear before governors and kings, arrested and taken away, betrayed by family members, and generally hated (13:9–13), it probably was part of his intention in writing to show that such terrible occurrences were predicted by Jesus and essential to God's plan. What happened to the Son of Man and to John the Baptist would happen to faithful Christians, and they ought not to be in despair when this occurred.

For Mark, eschatology provides an explanation for otherwise incomprehensible events. If his Christian community is approved by God, how could it be that it was being brutally victimized? Mark's answers that this is the way God planned it for the community and also for John the Baptist and also for Jesus. Those seeking signs and wonders (rather than faithfully enduring persecution) make the same mistake as the disciples did during Jesus' life when they failed to understand his statements about the necessity of his persecution and his death.

Torah Law

Mark's attitude toward Torah Law is somewhat casual. He does not have the passionate concern with it that Paul had. "Commandments" are quoted in Mark: "Do not murder; do not commit adultery; do not steal; do not give false evidence; do not defraud; honor your father and mother" (10:19), to which he adds, "Sell what you have and give to the poor" (10:21), but the laws of Moses here are general moral guidelines to which others can be added. "Do not defraud" is not one of the ten commandments, and neither, of course, is the command to sell what you have. Only half of the ten commandments are quoted. In Mark 12:30–31, Jesus quotes two passages from the Hebrew Scriptures as the two greatest commandments: "Hear, O Israel: the Lord our

God is the only Lord; love the Lord your God with all your heart, with all your soul, with all your mind, and with all your strength" (Deuteronomy 6:4–3) and "Love your neighbour as yourself" (Leviticus 19:18). Both are general admonitions, not specific rules for behavior, and the Pharisees and rabbis would have agreed that these are great and essential commandments.

When it comes to ethnic Jewish commandments such as the complex detailed requirements of food selection, preparation, and purity that developed later into "kosher" practices, Mark's gospel shows Jesus to have eliminated them all: "Thus he declared all foods clean" (7:20). What defiles people is not impure foods but "evil thoughts, acts of fornication, of theft, murder, adultery, ruthless greed, and malice; fraud, indecency, envy, slander, arrogance, and folly" (7:22–23). It is hard to imagine a teacher in any religious tradition disagreeing with this checklist of moral "defilements." The commandments in Mark derive from universal human social standards. They are neither specifically Jewish nor specifically Roman nor Greek. When it comes to ethnic Jewish commandments, Jesus declares them no longer to be in effect.

Paul is deeply concerned about the Torah Law; Mark is not. Mark uses it as a point of reference, but commandments are added and deleted by Jesus in brief statements. Mark's audience was not predominately composed of Jewish people, for Jews would have had no need to be told "the Pharisees and the Jews in general never eat without washing the hands, in obedience to an old established tradition" (7:3). Probably neither Mark nor his audience regarded the laws of Moses as more than general moral guidelines to which various ethnic Jewish customs (like the food laws) had been added. The perspective on Law found in Mark's gospel is that of a Gentile who is sympathetic to Judaism but who does not advocate detailed obedience to specifically Jewish laws and customs.

Community

If we assume that chapter 13 reflects something of the conditions in Mark's community when he wrote his gospel, then that community was in a situation of great danger. The Jewish religious courts were sources of persecution, and some Christians known to Mark had been "flogged in synagogues" (13:9). Others were brought to trial before Roman-supported "governors and kings" and faced the death penalty. It is not clear why Christians might have been in so much legal danger in or about the year CE 70, but Mark's gospel certainly conveys the impression they were.

Not only were external forces (synagogues, government officers) inimical to Mark's Christians, but so also were some members of their families. "Brother will betray brother to death, and the father his child; children will turn against their parents and send them to their death. All will hate you for your allegiance to me" (13:12). A dreadful situation is outlined here. Parents betray children to the courts and to their deaths; children do the same to parents. "All will hate you"—a terrible thing to think or say. But it is from this context (or at least from a situation perceived to be this terrible) that Mark writes.

Controversy

Mark's is a gospel filled with controversies. With few exceptions Jesus is opposed, misunderstood, or forsaken. His family and his neighbors at Nazareth show no understanding in chapters 3 and 6. Throughout the gospel the leaders of Jewish groups oppose him: Pharisees, Sadducees, Chief Priests, elders, Herodians. The Roman authorities eventually execute him. The common people, though they support him nearly to the end, at the last cry out, "Crucify him!" His disciples, given both secret and public evidence of his special status, understand nothing. By the time of the crucifixion, all have abandoned him. The women who were with him remain most loyal, but the gospel's last sentence depicts even them as failing to carry out the only mission assigned to them. Those who understand him—the woman with anointing oils, Joseph of Arimathaea, the centurion—perceive him (however correctly) as a corpse. And God? In Mark, Jesus' last words are "'*Eli, Eli, lema sabachthani?*' meaning 'My God, my God why have you forsaken me?'" That sentence, the longest in the New Testament quoted in either Hebrew or Aramaic, comes from the first stanza of Psalm 22, a cry of desolation, for at the end Jesus is alone.

Do the obtuse, self-important disciples of Mark's gospel represent the people of Mark's community? Some scholars believe so, arguing that Mark presents the disciples as weak and inadequate at first while knowing in the end the disciples showed both courage and understanding. So, the argument goes, did Mark regard his community—as a group who at present feel weak and inadequate and yet, like the disciples, can hope to come through well in the end—but this argument is based not on Mark but on other New Testament books in which the disciples do at last understand. In analyzing Mark, all we can conscientiously use for evidence is Mark. And in Mark the disciples do not come through well in the end at all.

It is more likely that Mark portrays the disciples in such a negative light because Mark was personally in direct conflict with the disciples (or their successors). He thought they did not emphasize the suffering and death of the Son of Man as he thought they should and that they improperly overemphasized Jesus' miraculous powers. To counteract their claims to authority (time spent with Jesus, family relationship with him, perception of him risen from the dead), Mark denies either that these things were the case or that they did the disciples any good.

Interactions

Miracles Sources

Mark's interaction with the sources he used for stories of Jesus' miracles is most interesting. While using them as sources, and as far as we can tell rewriting them little, he does not support their underlying idea. After all, if Mark's idea of Jesus is of a servant destined by God to suffer (10:45), and if the compilers of miracle stories believe he was an extremely powerful and compelling worker of wonders, conflict would inevitably be present. Mark at first allows his readers to assume Jesus did the miracles attributed to him and that they did, as the sources wished, encourage faith that he was a prophet, Christ, or even Son of God. But the miracle stories are placed in his gospel in such a way that doubt is cast on the wisdom of those who take them too seriously. Those who based faith on miracles are like the demons who claim Jesus is Son of God because of his exorcisms, or like Peter, who says Jesus is Christ but does not approve of the suffering Son of Man and is treated like a demon by Jesus. Thus, Mark uses the miracles sources, apparently believes them reliable, but offers a subtle reinterpretation of them. The faith that the miracles sources wish to call forth seems inadequate or even demonic in Mark's narrative, and their perspective is presented as "what people think" and not "what God thinks."

Q Source

Mark did not use the Q document as a source, but, as most sayings in the Q source circulated independently of the written document containing them, it is not surprising Mark knows and uses some of them. He does not always do so without revision, however. Sometimes he alters them in ways appropriate to his general perspective, such as his softening of "Whoever receives a messenger of mine receives me" to

"Whoever receives a child in my name receives me" as discussed above. In another instance, the startling saying,

> If anyone comes to me and does not hate his father and mother, wife and children, brothers and sisters, even his own life, he cannot be a disciple of mine. No one who does not carry his cross and come with me can be a disciple of mine (Luke 14:26–27).

is softened to read, "Anyone who wishes to be a follower of mine must leave self behind; he must take up his cross, and come with me" (8:34). Mark's perspective on Christian life is founded largely on the expectation of imminent disasters accompanying the end of this world and the arrival of the Kingdom of God. But unlike Q's perspective, Mark does not have a bleak view of family and of social life. Disruption of family may occur, but Mark regards such disruption as tragic (13:12) and temporary (10:30). In Q disruptions are expected, if not required (Luke 9:59–62).

Mark and Q differ on the Torah Law, the Q people apparently wishing it to be kept strictly in the traditional way: "It is easier for heaven and earth to come to an end than for one dot or stroke of the law to lose its force" (Luke 16:17). Mark does not regard the Law as crucially important. The food laws are suspended, the laws of Moses are hastily summarized and altered.

Paul

Did Mark receive his central ideas through Paul's influence, or do both Mark and Paul receive their ideas from even earlier levels of Christian tradition? Scholars have argued that question for decades. On the one hand it looks as if Mark's focus on Jesus' death derives from Paul's similar focus on his death. On the other hand, Paul is eager to interpret Jesus' death in terms of his own Christology, while Mark barely interprets it at all. Death "for the ransom of many" sounds like it has Paul's ideas behind it, but it is difficult to say for sure what that phrase means.

Perhaps Mark's casual approach to Jewish legal matters derives from Paul's passionate attempt to free Christians from the obligation of following that Law. On the other hand, Christianity, in moving away from the Jewish world of Palestine into the Gentile world, may have been destined to reject the particular customs of Judaism with or without Paul's influence.

Mark does not use any of Paul's characteristic language, nor does Mark reflect any substantial and thoroughgoing understanding of Paul's complex theology. One might list a dozen Pauline themes missing in Mark, from the idea of justification to the concept of the church as the body of Christ. This convinces many that Mark is not a follower of Paul. Others argue that conversion of Christianity from a Jewish movement of repentance and renewed legal obedience focused on the miracles and teaching of its founder, to a mainly Gentile movement free from the Law and focused on the death of its founder could have come only through the work of a single genius—Paul—and that therefore Mark reflects Paul's influence.

Perhaps a compromise perspective is best. Paul personally established many communities, and his associates established more. Some kept and studied Paul's letters, while most simply remembered him and his teachings as best they could. As with the teachings of Jesus, the teachings of Paul were communicated by word of mouth and gradually were altered over the years. Mark may have grown up in a community founded by Paul, or by one of Paul's associates, retaining Paul's emphasis on the death of Christ and respecting Torah Law only as a general moral code. Many Gentiles throughout the ancient world respected the Torah in this way. Such an image of Mark would allow many of his ideas to come, ultimately, from Paul and would also explain why Mark shows no signs of having studied Paul's letters or the technicalities of his philosophy.

End-of-Chapter Exercises

1. Define *text criticism*. What kinds of information can textual criticism provide you? Why can it be challenging for textual analysts to determine which manuscript is the most accurate?
2. Identify one key feature of Mark's depiction of each of the following: John the Baptist, Pontius Pilate, and Jesus. In future chapters, you will be asked to compare/contrast each gospel writer's depictions of these individuals.
3. Were you surprised by Mark's relatively negative depiction of Jesus' disciples and family? Why do you think Mark portrayed them in this way? Give quotations from Mark to support your answer.

Bibliography

Edwards, James R. *The Gospel According to Mark*. Grand Rapids MI: Eerdmans, 2002.

France, R. T. *The Gospel of Mark: New International Commentary on the Greek Testament*. Grand Rapids MI: Eerdmans, 2002.

Horsley, Richard. *Hearing the Whole Story: The Politics of Plot in Mark's Gospel*. Louisville: Westminster John Knox, 2001.

Kealy, Sean P. *Mark's Gospel: A History of Its Interpretation*. New York: Paulist Press, 1982.

Kelber, Werner, ed. *The Passion in Mark*. Philadelphia: Fortress Press, 1976.

Kingsbury, Jack Dean. *The Christology of Mark's Gospel.* Philadelphia: Fortress Press, 1983.

Marcus, Joel. *Mark: Anchor Bible—Two Volumes.* New York NY: Doubleday, 2000, 2009.

Moloney, Francis J. *The Gospel of Mark: A Commentary.* Peabody MA: Hendrickson Publishers, 2002.

Perrin, Norman. *The Resurrection According to Matthew, Mark, and Luke.* Philadelphia: Fortress Press, 1977.

Rhoads, David. *Mark as Story.* Philadelphia: Fortress Press, 1999.

Taylor, Vincent. *The Gospel According to Mark.* London: Macmillan and Co., 1959.

Weeden, Theodore J. *Mark, Traditions in Conflict.* Philadelphia: Fortress Press, 1979.

The Gospel of Matthew

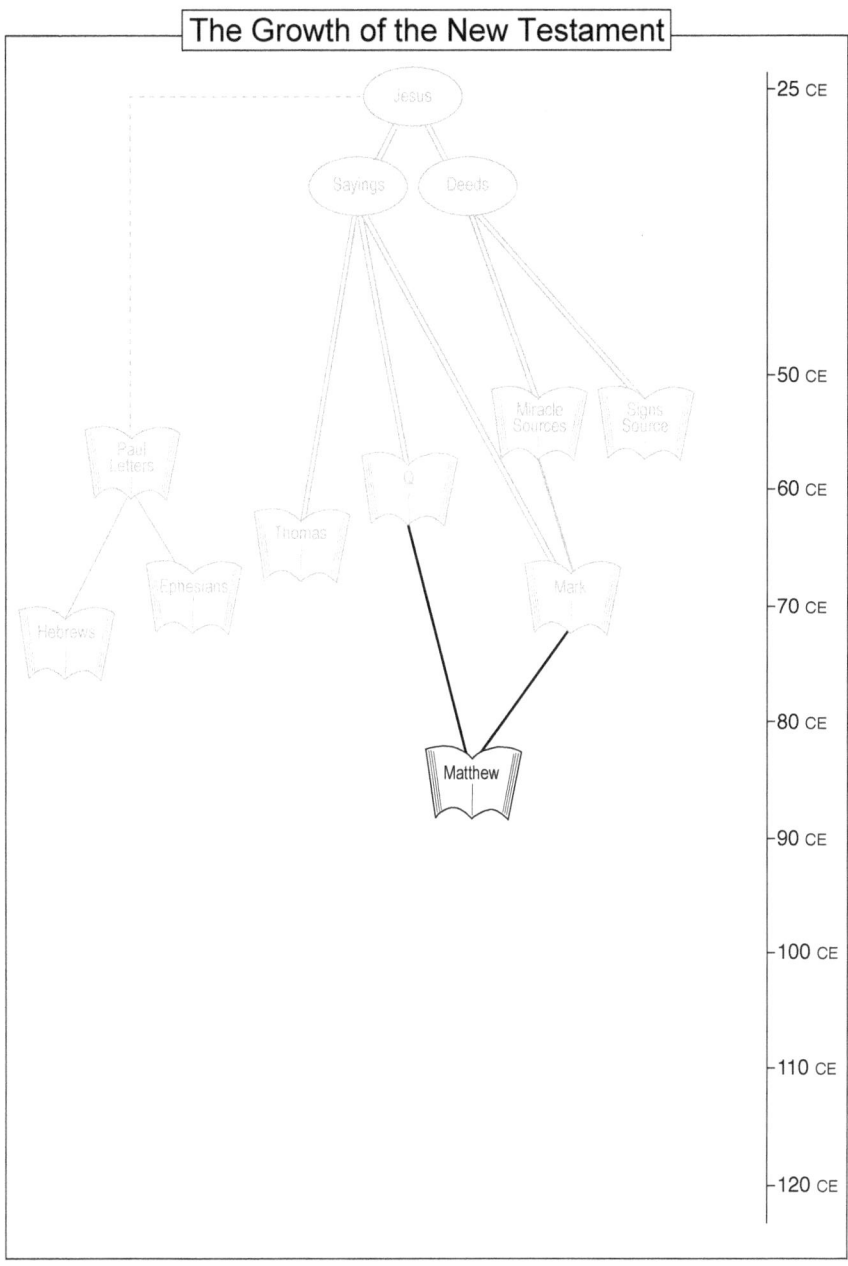

Dashed lines: indirect influence
Double lines: oral transmission
Single thick lines: use of written source
Thin lines: followers, admirers & imitators

CHAPTER 6

The Gospel of Matthew

OBJECTIVES
- Probe Matthew's interests in portraying Jesus' life as a fulfillment of prophesy
- Learn how how scholars use *redaction criticism* to pinpoint alterations that an author (e.g. Matthew) made to his or her sources (e.g. Q source)
- Contrast Matthew with other NT writers in his treatment of Jesus' disciples and his Jewish rivals such as the Pharisees

The Gospel of Matthew is the most popular of the four gospels. It begins with the Christmas story; it contains the Sermon on the Mount, which many regard as the principal statement of Jesus' message; it is more concerned with church order than is any other gospel. Matthew presents Jesus as a miracle worker who came both to fulfill prophecy and to fulfill the Law of God, as one whose disciples struggled but were eventually successful in understanding him. This is a more comfortable perspective than Mark's, and it contributes to Matthew's popularity.

READ THE GOSPEL OF MATTHEW AND UNDERLINE REFERENCES TO PROPHETS AND THE FULFILLMENT OF PROPHECY. Although all the evangelists believe Jesus' life often fulfilled prophecy, this theme is most prominent in Matthew's gospel, and we will investigate it with some care.

Author, Date, and Place of Origin

We do not know who Matthew was. An early report claims he originally wrote his gospel in Hebrew and was a disciple of Jesus, possibly "Matthew the tax collector." But this is not true; Matthew's use of Mark as a source proves both that he wrote in Greek (as Mark did) and that he is not relying on his own memory for an account of the events of Jesus' life. He never claims to be an eyewitness. His references to the Hebrew Bible are taken from the Greek translation of it rather than from the original Hebrew; no author writing in Hebrew would have done that. Jesus is repeatedly said to have dined "with tax collectors and sinners," probably a true report, but to Matthew tax collectors are examples of people who should not be allowed into his church. Matthew, showing his concern for church order, writes that Jesus instructed church members to treat a member who will not reform as they would "a pagan or a tax gatherer" (18:15–17) or, in other words, to expel him or her.

His sympathetic interest in Torah Law and his frequent use of the Hebrew Scriptures indicates that Matthew considered himself Jewish. Whether he was born to a Jewish family or whether he was a Gentile convert to Judaism is debated by scholars. On the one hand he defends the validity of the Law more than any other evangelist does; on the other hand his knowledge of the Torah is limited. For example, "hate your enemy" (Matt 5:43), is not in the Torah.

Matthew may have written his gospel in the Roman province of Syria. That is the guess of many scholars, although there is no firm evidence for it. His use of Mark and Q, and the evidence in his gospel that the church of his day was becoming rather well-organized, indicate a date well after the year CE 70. The year CE 85 is frequently given for Matthew and is a reasonable guess; but it may be off by up to a decade either way.

The Beginning of the Gospel

The Gospel of Matthew prefaces Jesus' baptism with an account of his birth. This account is entirely composed by Matthew and shows his own style as an author in contrast to most of the remainder of his gospel, where he revises and reorganizes the Gospel of Mark. After presenting his version of Jesus' genealogy, which is quite different from the one found in Luke 3:23–38, Matthew argues in three ways that Jesus is Messiah. He argues that Jesus is Messiah because God's angel instructed Joseph in dreams. In the ancient world, dreams were commonly believed to be messages from a deity. He argues that Jesus is Messiah because the prophets of the Hebrew Scriptures announced in advance events of his life. Finally, he argues that the magi (Persian astrologers held in high esteem throughout the empire) found evidence of Jesus' special status in the stars.

Matthew's story begins with the statement that Mary, who is engaged to be married to Joseph, is found to be pregnant through the Holy Spirit. In a dream, an angel tells Joseph to accept the child because it is of the Holy Spirit, and Joseph does so. Magi come from the east, following a star, and King Herod asks them to tell him where the baby is located, but an angel warns them in a dream to go back home another way, and they do so. King Herod orders babies of Bethlehem two years of age and less to be killed, but an angel warns Joseph in a dream to flee. Accordingly, Joseph leads Mary and Jesus into Egypt so as to fulfill a passage from the prophet Hosea (11:1) that, in the original, refers to the people of Israel. After Herod's death, Joseph is told in one dream to return from Egypt and Joseph hears, in a subsequent dream, that he is to settle in Nazareth of Galilee to fulfill a prophecy "he will be called a Nazarene;" no such prophecy is to be found in the Hebrew Scriptures.

Matthew's birth story is a fascinating collection of arguments that provide good insight into the mindset of the people who lived two thousand years ago. It is a carefully constructed legend. Some people today hold to the idea that the story is historically factual and that its biographical accuracy is the most important thing about it, but they are applying modern categories to a piece of writing that came from a culture quite different from our own, one that did not share our modern values.

John the Baptist

John the Baptist plays a role at the beginning of Jesus' ministry, as he does in Mark. More than in Mark, John is shown to know he is inferior to Jesus. We are not told that those who came to John did so as a token of repentance for forgiveness of sins. Rather, while Matthew notes that people who were baptized did so confessing sins (3:6), Jesus' baptism is separated from theirs. When Jesus came to be baptized, "John tried to dissuade him. 'Do you come to me?' he said; 'I need rather to be baptized by you.' Jesus replied, 'Let it be so for the present; we do well to conform in this way with all that God requires'" (3:14–15). This passage is found only in Matthew. The baptism here is said to occur because of the mysterious will of God and not even implicitly because of any need on Jesus' part for forgiveness.

The Ending of the Gospel

Matthew concludes, like Mark, with an account of Jesus' trial, but, unlike Mark, Matthew also gives a brief account of a resurrection appearance. At the end of Matthew's gospel the risen Jesus appears to his disciples (28:2–20), but in a surprisingly short passage. Much of the passage is concerned with dispelling a rumor, present in Matthew's day (28:1), that Jesus' body was stolen by his disciples. The women at the tomb meet the risen Jesus, who tells them the same thing the youth in white clothes told them in Mark's account. In Mark the women told no one what they heard and saw; in

Matthew they "hurried away from the tomb in awe and great joy, and ran to tell the disciples." When the disciples saw Jesus on a mountain in Galilee,

> they fell prostrate before him, though some were doubtful. . . . He said: "Full authority in heaven and on earth has been committed to me. Go forth therefore and make all nations my disciples; baptize men everywhere in the name of the Father and the Son and the Holy Spirit, and teach them to observe all that I have commanded you. And be assured, I am with you always to the end of time" (28:17–20).

This passage is often taken to be a good clue to Matthew's understanding of Jesus and Christianity, for it concludes his gospel and, presumably, states what Matthew believes to be his own mission in life. The mission Jesus conducted during his life in Israel among Jews is now to expand to "all nations." Jesus' followers are to baptize and teach observance of commandments, confident that Jesus remains with them.

Pontius Pilate

More than Mark's, Matthew's gospel insists that Pilate believed Jesus to be innocent. Only in Matthew do we find the story that Pilate's wife had Jesus' innocence revealed to her in a dream (27:19). The story of Pilate literally and symbolically washing his hands of the matter saying, "my hands are clean of this man's blood" (27:25), is, likewise, found only in Matthew. This graphic scene heightens the impression given in Mark's gospel that Pilate believed Jesus to be innocent. It is not to Matthew's credit that he further inserts into Mark's account a passage designed to demonstrate that the Jewish people deserve responsibility for Jesus' execution. Matthew's gospel quotes them as saying, "His blood be on us and on our children" (27:25). This passage has been used to justify much persecution of Jewish people by Christians.

The Organization of the Gospel

From Mark's organization Matthew retains (with additions) only Mark's concluding parts: the apocalyptic discourse and the passion narrative. After the story of Jesus' birth, Matthew divides Jesus' ministry into five central speeches or discourses, each concluding with the phrase "when Jesus had finished this discourse." The five discourses are separated by narratives of travel, teaching, and miraculous actions, which three times conclude with a description of Jesus' great popularity. Matthew's five sections of narrative and discourse are as follows:

1. Jesus' ministry begins: 3:1–4:25 (narrative) concluding, "He went round the whole of Galilee, teaching in the synagogues, preaching the gospel of the Kingdom, and curing whatever illness or infirmity there was among the people. His fame reached the whole of Syria; and sufferers from every kind of illness, racked with pain, possessed by devils, epileptic, or paralyzed, were all brought to him, and he cured them. Great crowds also followed him, from Galilee and the Ten Towns, from Jerusalem and Judaea, and from Transjordan."

1a. This narrative section is followed by the Sermon on the Mount, concluding, "When Jesus had finished this discourse the people were astounded at his teaching; unlike their own teachers he taught with a note of authority" (5:1–7:29).

2. Jesus displays his power, concluding, "So Jesus went round all the towns and villages teaching in their synagogues, announcing the good news of the Kingdom, and curing every kind of ailment and disease" (8:1–9:35).

2a. Next comes a discourse directed to his disciples, explaining how they are to conduct their missions, concluding,

"When Jesus had finished giving his twelve disciples their instructions, he left that place and went to teach and preach in the neighboring towns" (9:36–11:1).

2b. Announcement of the kingdom's coming, concluding, "That same day Jesus went out and sat by the lakeside, where so many people gathered round him that he had to get into a boat" (11:2–13:1).

3. Matthew's chapter of parables follows, concluding, "When he had finished these parables Jesus left that place, and came to his home town" (13:2–53).

3a. The disciples see wonders (13:54–17:27, no conclusion).

4. This is followed by a discourse on discipleship and community order, concluding, "When Jesus had finished this discourse he left Galilee and came into the region of Judaea across Jordan. Great crowds followed him, and he healed them there" (18:1–19:1).

4a. Conflicts with Jewish authorities (19:2–24:2, no conclusion).

5. The final discourse (revised from Mark 13) is apocalyptic, revealing the events to take place at the end of this world, and concludes, "When Jesus had finished this discourse he said to his disciples, 'You know that in two days' time it will be Passover, and the Son of Man is to be handed over for crucifixion'" (24:3–26:1). This serves as the introductory passage to the remainder of Matthew's gospel: his version of the passion narrative.

Some scholars believe that by this fivefold organizational scheme Matthew intends his readers to think of the five books of the Torah. A few go so far as to believe Matthew intends his gospel to be a new Torah. Most scholars, however, are content simply to acknowledge there are five discourses set apart by Matthew and to draw no conclusion from that fact.

While each of the five is largely composed out of traditional sayings of Jesus, the structure and organization of each of them is Matthew's creation.

In the following pages, we will first survey a scholarly technique called redaction criticism helpful in analyzing Matthew. Then a useful tool called gospel parallels will be introduced and used to analyze an important passage in Matthew's gospel. After that we will analyze several of Matthew's main themes.

Redaction Criticism

The Two Document Hypothesis, discussed previously, is the single most important factor in twentieth-century study of the Gospels of Matthew and Luke. To summarize that hypothesis: both Matthew and Luke used two documents, as well as their own insights and oral tradition, to write their gospels. One was a list of sayings attributed to Jesus now called the Q document, and the other was a short narrative document called the Gospel of Mark. This hypothesis, accepted by the majority of scholars today, is a valuable insight into the history of the New Testament. In addition, it allows the reconstruction of a Q source, which can then be considered a separate element in the New Testament, one giving information about an early and influential variety of Christianity (see chapter 4, "Gospel Sources"). The Two Document Hypothesis gave rise to the scholarly approach called redaction criticism.

Redaction criticism (or redaction analysis) refers to analysis of the editorial work of New Testament authors. This textbook contains redaction analysis throughout, and so does some of the work you have been doing if you have completed the exercises provided. Redaction analysis pinpoints changes that an author made in the sources he or she was using. If we know the source an author used and can see how the author changed the source in preparing the text, we can make intelligent guesses about why the author made those changes. We then have a window into the editorial perspective of the author; we know something about the author's motivation to make certain changes. This may sound trivial, but you will see it is not.

When we do have a source, an author's editing is easily seen. For example, the little Letter of Jude found toward the end of the New Testament seems to have been a source for the New Testament letter called 2 Peter. We can learn more about 2 Peter's author by comparing what he wrote with the Letter of Jude than by reading his letter alone; we see what he found important in what he expanded, what he found unimportant or inaccurate in what he left out, and what some of his thoughts were by what he changed.

Redaction analysis presupposes the New Testament writers were creative authors rather than people who just wrote down traditional material. Luke's introductory paragraph (Luke 1:1–4) indicates he thought the "many writers" who preceded him had not done an adequate job. Hence, he tells us, he has decided to write an accurate account. Redaction analysis assumes that is true for all the evangelists; to convey what they thought was true, they felt compelled to revise their sources.

Matthew revised Mark. We have the original of Mark in the New Testament, and the two can be compared easily. To compare Matthew's version of Mark 8:27–33 with the original, you flip pages back and forth from Matthew 16:13–23 to the passage in Mark. Nothing could be simpler. Well, yes, something could: a tool called gospel parallels.

Gospel Parallels

In books of gospel parallels, the three synoptic gospels are set side by side in columns on the page, or they can be set one under the other so that the eye may follow each across the page from left to right. Some students of the New Testament prefer the one, some the other method. The three-column method is probably most widely used. Every library should have a copy of *Gospel Parallels* by Burton H. Throckmorton, Jr. It is an essential tool for serious study and is something a novice will have no trouble using.

TO BEGIN CONSIDERATION OF THE GOSPEL OF MATTHEW, THE FOLLOWING PAGE CONTAINS TWO REVISED VERSIONS OF MARK 8:27–33 AND THE ORIGINAL. READ THROUGH THEM CAREFULLY, MAKING NOTE OF EVERY SINGLE CHANGE YOU CAN FIND.

Matthew 16:13–23

When he came to the territory of Caesarea Philippi, Jesus asked his disciples, "Who do men say that the Son of Man is?" They answered, "Some say John the Baptist, others Elijah, others Jeremiah, or one of the prophets." "And you," he asked, "who do you say I am?" Simon Peter answered: "You are the Messiah, the Son of the living God." Then Jesus said, "Simon son of Jonah, you are favoured indeed! You did not learn that from mortal man; it was revealed to you by my heavenly Father. And I say this to you: You are Peter, the Rock; and on this rock I will build my church, and the powers of death shall never conquer it. I will give you the keys of the kingdom of Heaven; what you forbid on earth shall be forbidden in heaven, and what you allow on earth shall be allowed in heaven." He then gave his disciples strict orders not to tell anyone that he was the Messiah. From that time Jesus began to make it clear to his disciples that he had to go to Jerusalem, and there to suffer much from the elders, chief priests, and doctors of the law; to be put to death and to be raised again on the third day. At this Peter took him by the arm and began to rebuke him: "Heaven forbid!" he said. "No, Lord, this shall never happen to you." Then Jesus turned and said to Peter, "Away with you, Satan; you are a stumbling block to me. You think as men think, not as God thinks."

Mark 8:27–33

Jesus and his disciples set out for the villages of Caesarea Philippi. On the way he asked his disciples, "Who do men say I am?" They answered, "Some say John the Baptist, others Elijah, others one of the prophets." "And you," he asked, "who do you say I am?" Peter replied: "You are the Messiah." Then he gave them strict orders not to tell anyone about him; and he began to teach them that the Son of Man had to undergo great sufferings, and to be rejected by the elders, chief priests, and doctors of the law; to be put to death, and to rise again three days afterwards. He spoke about it plainly. At this Peter took him by the arm and began to rebuke him. But Jesus turned around and, looking at his disciples, rebuked Peter. "Away with you, Satan," he said; "you think as men think, not as God thinks."

Luke 9:18–22

One day when he was praying alone in the presence of his disciples, he asked them, "Who do the people say I am?" They answered, "Some say John the Baptist, others Elijah, others that one of the old prophets has come back to life." "And you," he said, "who do you say I am?" Peter answered, "God's Messiah." Then he gave them strict orders not to tell this to anyone. And he said, "The Son of Man has to undergo great sufferings, and to be rejected by the elders, chief priests, and doctors of the law, to be put to death and to be raised again on the third day."

Many observations could be made. Here are a few:

1. Luke does not mention the location of the event. It is characteristic of Luke to organize the travels of Jesus into a reasonably straight line from Galilee to Jerusalem, and he tends to omit location references conflicting with this pattern. Matthew makes the location slightly more vague, "territory" rather than "villages."

2. Matthew tries to spell out passages he regards as ambiguous. For example, he changes "Who do men say I am?"

to "Who do men say the Son of Man is?" and he goes on to add Jeremiah to the short list of prophets. Luke 9:7–8, probably influenced by Mark 6:14–15, adds that people believe Jesus was a prophet raised from the dead.

3. Both Matthew and Luke expand Peter's answer. Both are convinced that Peter's answer is absolutely correct. Here they differ from Mark where, although Peter replies with the correct term, he does not show correct understanding.

4. Matthew continues with a lengthy passage of substantial significance to the later development of the Christian church. It is on this passage that the Catholic church bases its belief in the primacy of the pope (Peter is believed to have been the first bishop of Rome). Since Matthew wants it clearly understood that Peter's answer is correct, his revision of Mark states both that God revealed Peter's answer to him and that Jesus awarded Peter authority on the basis of it.

5. Luke omits the section of Mark that is critical of Peter. Matthew revises it slightly by telling us what he believes Peter said to Jesus. In Mark, Jesus' severe reaction implies that Peter repudiated Jesus' interpretation of the Son of Man. In Matthew, we hear that Peter, as any friend would, hopes aloud that Jesus would not have to suffer. Further, in Matthew, Jesus does not simply rebuke Peter and call him Satan; his version adds to Jesus' words the phrase, "You are a stumbling block to me." Matthew retains the criticism of Peter found in Mark but softens it; Peter is wrong, but out of friendship rather than out of misunderstanding. Further, Peter has been highly praised in the preceding passage, and so Jesus' comments to him are made in a very different context than they are in Mark where they follow upon Mark 8:14–21, a passage declaring the disciples' utter ignorance.

Matthew as a Redaction Critic

This example of the use of gospel parallels shows the kinds of judgments one can make regarding the evangelists' redactional work. Every passage in Mark was omitted, expanded, condensed, or left unchanged by Matthew and Luke, and they had reasons for taking each of those actions. Often their motivations for their revisions can be inferred. What this demonstrates is that modern scholars are not the only ones who use redaction analysis; Matthew and Luke were *also* redaction analysts. They believed Mark had acted as an author, editing his sources and sometimes adding perspectives that were not always correct. Both, for example, disagreed with Mark's view of the disciples as failures. Luke in his way (largely by editing out what he thought excessive criticism) and Matthew in his way (by revising critical passages to make the disciples more admirable) sought to change Mark to make it acceptable to people who respected the disciples. Their understanding of Mark is not unlike that of scholars today; they believed Mark had access to some historically reliable information which he altered to suit his own perspective. Both Matthew and Luke sought to correct that perspective by revising Mark's gospel. Mark had done something similar; through his gospel he sought to correct the perspective of Jesus' disciples or their successors by criticizing what he believed to have been their understanding of Jesus and supplementing theirs with his own perspective on the suffering Son of Man.

It is unlikely that Matthew knew as much about Jesus as we know by our reading of his gospel and of Mark's, John's, Luke's and Thomas' gospels—three of which Matthew had never read. After all, his main source for Jesus' life, Mark's gospel, was a book with which he somewhat disagreed. He also used, and occasionally revised, a collection of Jesus' sayings we do not have but can reconstruct (the Q source). Finally, he had oral traditions, received from persons in his community, which he used to supplement his other two sources. People may think that the evangelists had immense amounts of knowledge about Jesus' life and teachings that they never committed to writing. But it is more likely that they told us most of what they knew.

Special Matthew

<u>UNDERLINE THE MATERIAL IN MATTHEW WHICH IS NEITHER IN Q NOR IN MARK.</u> This material is called Special Matthew. He may have taken some of the parables in chapter 13 from a short written list, but most of Special Matthew was either composed by Matthew to express what he believed Jesus taught or derived from Oral Tradition.

- Matthew 1:1–2:23
- Matthew 3:14–15
- Matthew 4:13–16
- Matthew 5:5, 7–10
- Matthew 5:19–24
- Matthew 5:27–30
- Matthew 5:31, 33–37, 38
- Matthew 6:1–8
- Matthew 6:16–18
- Matthew 7:6
- Matthew 8:17
- Matthew 7:28
- Matthew 9:27–34
- Matthew 10:5–6
- Matthew 11:28–30
- Matthew 12:17–21
- Matthew 12:36–37
- Matthew 13:14–15
- Matthew 13:24–30
- Matthew 13:35–52
- Matthew 14:28–31
- Matthew 15:23–24
- Matthew 16:11–12
- Matthew 17:13

- Matthew 17:24–27
- Matthew 18:16–20
- Matthew 18:23–35
- Matthew 19:10–12
- Matthew 20:1–16
- Matthew 21:10–11
- Matthew 21:14–16
- Matthew 21:28–32
- Matthew 21:43
- Matthew 22:11–14
- Matthew 23:2–3, 5
- Matthew 23:8–11
- Matthew 23:15–22
- Matthew 23:28, 31
- Matthew 24:10–12, 14
- Matthew 24:30
- Matthew 25:1–13
- Matthew 25:31–46
- Matthew 26:52–54
- Matthew 27:3–10
- Matthew 27:19
- Matthew 27:24–25
- Matthew 27:52–53
- Matthew 27:62–66
- Matthew 28:2–24
- Matthew 28:9–20

<u>READ THE SPECIAL MATTHEW PASSAGES CAREFULLY AND IDENTIFY THE IDEAS THAT OCCUR MOST FREQUENTLY.</u>

The Sermon on the Mount

Probably the key passage for understanding Matthew is 5:17–20. It occurs in the Sermon on the Mount (5:1–7:29), which was composed by Matthew on the basis of sayings found in his sources. The Sermon on the Mount begins with a list of Beatitudes, or blessings (5:1–12). Two passages of praise follow (5:13–16): "You are salt to the world," and "You are light for all the world." These statements introduce the main thesis (5:17–20), which is followed by extensive discussion of the implications of that thesis (5:21–7:20), and finally by a conclusion referring back to the main thesis (7:21–29). That main thesis is as follows:

> Do not suppose that I have come to abolish the Law and the prophets; I did not come to abolish, but to complete. I tell you this: so long as heaven and earth endure, not a letter, not a stroke, will disappear from the Law until all that must happen has happened. If any man therefore sets aside even the least of the Law's demands, and teaches others to do the same, he will have the lowest place in the kingdom of Heaven, whereas anyone who keeps the Law, and teaches others to do so, will stand high in the kingdom of Heaven. I tell you, unless you show yourselves far better men than the Pharisees and the doctors of the Law, you can never enter the kingdom of Heaven.

Matthew certainly must have thought of himself as one who attempted to keep the Law and to teach others to do so. He believed Jesus came to complete the Law and the prophets, and that the Torah Law remains completely in force as long as heaven and earth endure. Furthermore, Matthew, and Jesus as Matthew presents him, certainly believed that people could keep God's Law to a satisfactory degree if they tried to. We will discuss Matthew's understanding of "completing the prophets" shortly, but by "completing the Law" Matthew means that Jesus came to give directions for behavior in accord with God's Law, so that anyone with sufficient dedication may follow the Law successfully.

Matthew's Christian Rivals

We must presume that one group of Matthew's rivals is Christian because they evidently have led people to believe that Jesus came to abolish the Law and the prophets. At a minimum, in accord with that teaching, they tend to relax some commandments. Oddly enough, Matthew, despite his profound disagreement with them, still believes they have a place, however low, in the Kingdom of Heaven. Who were Matthew's rivals? Paul is a name that should spring to mind. It was Paul, after all, who wrote in Galatians, "No man is ever justified by doing what the law demands" (2:16), "Christ bought us freedom from the curse of the law" (3:13), and other similar things. Matthew may have had Paul in mind, but there is no way we can be sure he did. We do know for certain that he had Mark in mind. In Mark's gospel we find the short but important sentence whereby Jesus supposedly cancels the Law regarding pure and impure foods: "Thus he made all foods clean" (Mark 7:19). Mark's gospel teaches that Jesus came to abolish at least that portion of the Law. Matthew, however, would never claim Jesus "made all foods clean"; he omits the passage in his revision of Mark. Presumably Matthew, acting as a redaction analyst, regarded this as Mark's teaching, not Jesus'.

Matthew may concede that the faith in Jesus Christ of people such as Paul and Mark allows them to enter a low place in the Kingdom of Heaven, but he does not believe anyone who would cancel any or all of the Law could have understood Jesus correctly. The fulfillment or completion of the Law is the opposite of its abolition or reduction.

Matthew's Jewish Rivals

Matthew is also in conflict with the Pharisees, and it was a rather bitter conflict, judging from the vehement language in 23:1–39.

REREAD 23:1–39 NOW.

Matthew quotes Jesus calling the Pharisees hypocrites, blind guides, snakes, viper's brood. But the first thing you read is most important, the topic sentence of what will follow: "The doctors of the Law and the Pharisees sit in the chair of Moses; therefore do what they tell you; pay attention to their words" (23:2).

Matthew thought of Jesus as one who came to complete the Law and who instructed his disciples to teach all people "to observe all that I have commanded you" (28:20). Thus in 23:2 he portrays the Pharisees as similar in one respect to Jesus. Matthew urges his audience to be obedient both to the Pharisees and to Jesus. How can such commendation of the Pharisees coexist with condemnation of them?

The key term is "hypocrite," and it is found fifteen times in Matthew but only five times in the rest of the New Testament. The word "hypocrite" is the Greek word for "actor" and, by extension, anyone who pretends to be someone or something he or she is not. Matthew, on the one hand, agrees with the Law as understood by the Pharisees who are divinely appointed to give God's Law, and so they "sit in the chair of Moses." On the other hand, he does not believe they keep the Law fully. That is why they are hypocrites; they teach others but do not follow their own teaching. They are more concerned with appearing pious than they are with true piety. Or so Matthew believed.

Matthew does not criticize the teaching of Jewish legal authorities, only their performance. Only through guidance from Jesus the Messiah, Matthew believes, could these leaders fulfill their own ideals. Jesus is not portrayed as opposing the Pharisees' theories, but as trying to assist them in attaining a shared goal, the fulfillment of God's Law. The Pharisees, on the other hand, are depicted as opposing Jesus during his lifetime and eventually bringing about his death. From Matthew's point of view they are more intent on maintaining their hypocrisy than on supporting God's Messiah.

How then, should people seek to fulfill God's Law? How should they live to ensure they are "far better men than the

Pharisees and the doctors of the Law" (5:20)? The next two portions of the Sermon on the Mount provide some answers.

The Antitheses

The first of these sections (5:21–48) is called the antitheses because in six consecutive passages Jesus quotes the Torah and then, seemingly, alters it: "You have learned that they were told . . . But what I tell you is this. . . ." The first clause quotes Torah ("told" to Moses and the Jewish people at Mount Sinai); the passages following this clause seem to be new Law from Jesus.

REREAD 5:21–6:18 NOW.

The meaning of the antitheses is still debated among scholars. Do they cancel Torah, add to Torah, show that Matthew felt Jesus was a new Moses, that Matthew regarded Jesus as a divine Lawgiver? "You have learned that our forefathers were told, 'Do not commit murder; anyone who commits murder must be brought to judgment.' But what I tell you is this: Anyone who nurses anger against his brother must be brought to judgment. If he abuses his brother he must answer for it to the court; if he sneers at him he will have to answer for it in the fires of hell" (5:21–22). It is impossible never to be angry. If anger is equivalent to murder, then righteousness through obedience is impossible. Perhaps Matthew intends, therefore, to support Paul's contention that righteousness cannot come by Law. Perhaps Matthew seeks to show there is a higher Law than Torah and Jesus came to reveal it for the few people who can keep it. The possibilities are many.

To put the problem in context is perhaps to find an answer. Matthew quotes Jesus as saying, "I tell you, unless you show yourselves to be far better men than the Pharisees and the doctors of the Law, you can never enter the kingdom of Heaven" (5:20). We can assume Matthew does not wish to argue with the theories of Law taught by the Pharisees who "sit in the chair of Moses"; he only wishes Christians to follow the Law more thoroughly than the Pharisees do. Understanding a Pharisaic theory of Law may help clarify the antitheses.

The Antitheses as a Hedge
Rabbinic Judaism evolved from Pharisaic Judaism and taught it was wise to establish a "hedge around the Torah." This phrase derives from imagery of a garden. Suppose a Law exists forbidding one to eat the fruit of a certain tree. It would be possible to live in the garden and not eat that fruit, but temptations might arise if the tree were always right nearby and always easy to reach. Suppose a gardener, determined not to eat that fruit, plants a thick hedge, bush by bush, all around the tree to wall himself away from it so that, even to come near the tree, he would have to push and hack his way through the hedge. Once the gardener plants the hedge, he has decreased the possibility of eating the forbidden fruit; he is no longer anywhere near it. He has made a hedge he chooses not to cross, but if he crosses it, he has not broken the Law he is determined not to break. Rather, he has broken through a hedge he created by himself.

This is, essentially, what the hedge around the Torah means. Regulations are established by Jewish teachers—Pharisees and, later, rabbis—to ensure that none of the laws of God, the Torah, are broken. One well-known example can be found in the rules of kosher. The Torah Law not to be broken is "Do not boil a baby goat in its mother's milk." Regulations came into being to hedge that Law. Do not boil the meat of any baby goat in the milk of any mother goat. Do not boil the meat of any animal in the milk of any animal. Do not cook milk and meat together in any way. Do not mix milk and meat in any way. Today many Jewish families have separate dishes, separate sinks, and separate refrigerators for milk and meat. Their likelihood of breaking God's Law approaches zero. These kosher practices developed after the time of the New Testament, but the theory of a "hedge around the Torah" was present then.

Mark 7:9–12 gives an example of the controversy caused by the hedge around the Torah. Here Jesus is said to argue, rather technically, that the donation of all of one's property to the Jerusalem temple (that is, *corban*) might leave one's mother and father penniless, for they would have no legal access to that property. This is said to contradict the commandment "Honor your father and mother." Here a technicality of Law, part of a hedge, is condemned on the basis that the Torah Law always should come first. Another such passage is from Q and can be found in Matthew 23:23–24. Here, the Pharisees are accused of focusing so much on the hedge they have created that they have more concern for tithing mint and dill and cumin than they have for Torah Law requiring justice, mercy, and good faith.

In both instances, the Torah is upheld by Jesus in cases where conflict occurs between it and the traditions (or hedges) created to enforce it. Jesus argues with Pharisees but often does so in a manner agreeable to Pharisees, for the primacy of the written Torah over oral tradition was a commonly accepted principle in Pharisaic circles.

Arguments among Pharisees are the essence of the Pharisaic method of determining truth. To put it more formally, the Pharisees believed that only through dialogue and the exchange of considered opinion could truth be found. The early and important Oral Law text known as the Mishnah was written after the time of Jesus around 220 CE, but it probably represents the style of legal argumentation of his time. It primarily consists of arguments between one legal authority and another. When Jesus argues Law with the Pharisees, he is not contradicting their entire approach to

Law. Rather, he is acting as a Pharisee would act. The principles he invokes in his arguments, such as the primacy of the Torah, are principles most Pharisees would accept.

If we look at the antitheses found in Matthew's Sermon on the Mount and regard them as hedges around the Torah, we have an approach showing Jesus neither "abolishing the Law" nor "setting aside even the least of the Law's demands." Suppose the statements of Jesus introduced by "But what I tell you is this" mean "But I tell you also to work earnestly to do this," where this refers to regulations constituting a hedge around the Torah passage quoted. The antitheses would then mean:

1. If you earnestly strive never to be angry, you will surely never commit murder.
2. If you earnestly strive never to look lustfully, you will surely never commit adultery.
3. If you do not get divorced at all (except in cases of adultery), you will certainly not break any of the Law regarding divorce.
4. If you do not swear any oaths at all, it will be impossible for you to break your oath.
5. If you do not seek revenge, ever, you will not ever try to get more revenge than the Law allows. (Incidentally, the Law does not *require* "an eye for an eye" but sets that as the maximum revenge allowed. The Pharisees would not demand that a person willing to be merciful to one who blinded him should be compelled to take the eye of his adversary.)
6. If you work hard to love everyone, even your enemies, you will be far more able to love your neighbor.
One passage does not fit this theory of the hedge: "love your enemies" is the opposite of "hate your enemies," not a way of fulfilling that demand through the creation of a hedge. But "hate your enemies" is not in the Torah

at all, nor is it in the books of the prophets. The explicit command "hate your enemies" is found nowhere in the authoritative writings of the Jewish religion. Whether Matthew mistakenly believes this is a commandment of Torah, or whether he finds it implied in the Hebrew Scriptures (for instance, in Joshua) and seeks to cancel it out, is unclear. But it is significant that only in this non-Torah passage do the sayings of Jesus contradict a quoted passage rather than establish a hedge around it.

The concept of hedge means that the demands of Jesus can be both impossible and reasonable. The demands are not "never be angry, never look lustfully, never swear," as though these were new Law, but "never be angry, never look lustfully, never swear," as something to strive for (without hope of complete success) in order not to break the old Law. They are impossible as Law; they are reasonable as approaches to Law. When they are overstated—such as, for example, "If one sneers at one's brother, one will answer for it in the fires of hell"—they should be seen as literary devices, not as statements of facts; such statements have never been regarded as facts by the later Christian church.

There is no way of knowing for certain if Jesus himself created the antitheses. Some scholars believe he did, arguing that only a man who believed he came from God could directly alter the commands of Torah. Others, however, believe the antitheses were created by Matthew, and this is probably the more reasonable approach. From the perspective of antitheses as hedge, the antitheses do not alter the Torah. Furthermore, the antitheses are unique to Matthew in the New Testament. No other book or letter mentions anything like them, although many of the sayings of Jesus included in the antitheses are found elsewhere. The Gospel of Thomas also contains no antitheses. It is likely that Matthew, confronted with the need to understand and explain traditional sayings of Jesus to his audience, put them in the context they have in his gospel, and also likely that it was Matthew who sought to instruct his readers how to achieve righteousness greater than that of the Pharisees, through the creation of a hedge. While many of the sayings may belong to Jesus, their context, and therefore the interpretation we find of them in Matthew's gospel, is Matthew's creation.

To Avoid Hypocrisy
Following the antitheses come three passages written with the Pharisees in mind. Like the antitheses they tend to take a principle to an extreme, in this case advocating the avoidance of self-promotion by performing religious activities in complete secrecy. Pharisees, in Matthew's opinion, are hypocrites more interested in making a good show and impressing people with their righteousness than in being obedient and attaining righteousness. Christians should avoid this tendency, and one way to avoid it is to withdraw one's religious activities from the public arena altogether. If one performs one's religious obligations in private, they are just as valid as if performed publicly, but they do not win the admiration of the crowd. From Matthew 6:1 to 6:18, instructions are given for how to do an act of charity, how to pray and how to fast: do these things in secret, quietly, out of the public eye. This will cut down the temptation to do such acts for the purpose of public approval and, thus, will lead one away from hypocrisy.

Like the antitheses, these verses are probably constructions by Matthew based on sayings of Jesus. Matthew's interpretation of sayings, his redaction of them, is his own, even if many of the included sayings are from Jesus himself. These passages have a similar perspective to the antitheses if we assume they are not intended always to be obeyed literally; should one strive earnestly to perform religious activity in secret one may fail on occasion, but one will almost certainly not be guilty of behaving religiously in a flamboyant and hypocritical manner.

Christian Obedience

The Sermon on the Mount concludes with 7:21–29, in which Jesus insists that it is insufficient to call him Lord but fail to do what he commands. This could be a comment regarding Christians who might declare that faith in Jesus as Lord is sufficient and obedience is unnecessary. From Matthew's perspective, obedience is crucial.

Matthew believes that faith not accompanied by obedience will lead to disaster; even the ability to do miracles (which in the first century was thought often to accompany faith) does not validate faith without obedience to Law. Some Christians may say, "Lord, Lord, did we not prophesy in your name, cast out devils in your name, and in your name perform many miracles?" but if they are not obedient, Matthew believes Jesus will say to such people, "I never knew you; out of my sight you and your wicked ways" (7:22–23). Remember, this is directed toward people who call Jesus "Lord"—Christian people. Just as Matthew's early and key passage in the Sermon on the Mount begins with criticism of Christians who believe Jesus came to abolish Law or to set aside some of the Law's demands, so the Sermon on the Mount ends with the repudiation of Christians who, while calling Jesus Lord and doing miracles in his name, do not obey Torah Law.

Fulfilling the Prophets

More frequently than the other evangelists, but in the same manner, Matthew shows Jesus doing things various prophets of the Hebrew Scriptures supposedly predicted the Messiah would do. The logic of this approach is as follows: God, through the prophets, declared what the Messiah would do.

Jesus was the Messiah. Jesus, therefore, did those things. Anyone wishing to know what Jesus did can refer to the prophets to find out, and anyone wishing to know why certain things happened in Jesus' life can safely presume they happened because the prophets declared they would happen. The predictions of the prophets, therefore, are fulfilled when Jesus does what they predicted the Messiah would do.

Matthew used the prophets in two ways in his gospel. First, Matthew evidently used the writings of the prophets as a biographical source for Jesus. If, for example, a prophet declared, "I called my son out of Egypt" (Hosea 11:1) and this referred to the Messiah, then Jesus must at some point have come out of Egypt. Matthew, therefore, writes an account of a childhood journey to Egypt from which Jesus returns in order to "fulfill what the Lord had declared through the prophet" (Matt 2:15). Second, the prophets can explain why Jesus acted as he did. For example, in order to explain why Jesus taught in parables, Matthew writes,

> That is why I speak to them in parables; for they look without seeing, and listen without hearing or understanding. There is a prophecy of Isaiah which is being fulfilled for them: "You may hear and hear, but you will never understand; you may look and look, but you will never see. For this people's mind has become gross; their ears are dulled, and their eyes are closed. Otherwise, their eyes might see, their ears hear, and their mind understand, and then they might turn again, and I would heal them" (13:13–15, referring to Isaiah 6:9–10).

Matthew here revises Mark. Matthew is understandably disturbed by Mark's statement that Scripture (in Isaiah 6:9–10) anticipated that the parables deliberately would be designed to keep people from turning to God and being forgiven (Mark 4:12). Thus, Matthew turned back to the original source (always a commendable idea) and discovered it does not say what Mark believed it did. In Isaiah 6:9–10, the people are to blame for their lack of comprehension; they are not deliberately being kept from comprehending. Accordingly, Matthew changed the meaning of the passage in Mark and quoted the Isaiah passage at greater length. The idea that prophecy provides a key to understanding the activities of Jesus the Messiah is common to Mark and Matthew, but their interpretation of those activities is not the same. Therefore, their use of Scripture to back up their interpretations differs even when using the same passage.

Isaiah and the Virgin Birth

Let us examine the first prophecy Matthew declares that Jesus fulfilled. In the gospel, an angel of the Lord appears to Joseph in a dream and says the following:

> "Joseph son of David do not be afraid to take Mary home with you as your wife. It is by the Holy Spirit that she has conceived this child. She will bear a son; and you shall give him the name Jesus (Saviour), for he will save his people from their sins." All this happened in order to fulfil what the Lord declared through the prophet: "The virgin will conceive and bear a son, and he shall be called Immanuel," a name which means "God is with us" (1:20–23).

Matthew has quoted Isaiah 7:14. Isaiah's prophecy is as follows:

> The Lord himself shall give you a sign: A young woman is with child, and she will bear a son, and will call him Immanuel. By the time that he has learnt to reject evil and choose good, he will be eating curds and honey; before the child has learnt to reject evil and choose good, desolation will come upon the land before whose two kings you cower now (7:14–16).

Some historical background is necessary to understand this. Prophets in the Hebrew Scriptures do not often predict events in the distant future. Most commonly they interpret contemporary political events theologically, and they offer theologically supported political advice. In the passage quoted above, Isaiah is speaking to King Ahaz of Judah in the year 734 BCE. Since the end of the reign of King Solomon in 922 BCE, two states had existed in the region of Palestine: Israel to the north and Judah to the south. Often, they had gone to war against each other; sometimes they made alliances against greater powers threatening them. In 734 BCE, Judah's King Ahaz refused to join an alliance of small states, including Syria and Israel, against the powerful Assyrian Empire. The alliance planned to go to war against Judah to force it to join; King Ahaz intended to call upon the Assyrian Empire for military assistance against the alliance. It is in this context that Isaiah speaks to Ahaz, urging him not to declare his kingdom an ally of the Assyrians.

The child is a sign, a symbol, for a period of time. The time between birth and moral maturity (when the child will have learned to reject evil and choose good) was considered to be twelve or thirteen years. Isaiah predicts that before that time desolation will come to the lands of Israel and Syria, due to Assyrian invasion. Before he is twelve or thirteen years old, the child will "eat curds and honey," the food of people living on a subsistence level, symbolically indicating that Ahaz's kingdom of Judah will be considerably weakened.

The predicted events did occur. Ahaz, against Isaiah's advice, allied Judah with Assyria. Assyria swept through the kingdoms of Syria and Israel in 734 BCE, defeating them completely. The kingdom of Judah, although not devastated, was reduced in power and prestige to the level of a vassal state to Assyria.

This prophecy apparently has little to do with the birth of Jesus of Nazareth to the virgin Mary. In fact the word "virgin," the key term in Matthew's use of the prophecy, does not occur in the Hebrew prophecy at all. Matthew, however, is not using the Hebrew version of Isaiah but a Greek translation known as the *Septuagint*, in which the word "virgin" does appear. To understand the discrepancy, we must trace the translation of Isaiah's passage into Greek. In Isaiah 7:14, the Hebrew word for a young woman, *almah*, is used. If virginity had been specified, the Hebrew term used would have been *bethulah*. In Greek, the term for virgin is *parthenos*, and the term for young woman is *neanis*. In some Greek translations of Isaiah 7:14, *neanis* is used, but one translation, the Septuagint, instead uses *parthenos*. Matthew, therefore, may have read Isaiah in that translation, discovered that "the virgin will bear a child," presumed this refers to Jesus, and entered the passage in his gospel as a prophecy of which the virgin birth of Jesus is the fulfillment. The origin of the story of the virgin birth may be due to this action on Matthew's part, for he did use the writings of the prophets as a biographical source.

In paying no attention to the original historical context of prophecies, Matthew and the other New Testament writers followed the practice of other Jewish interpreters of that time. They presumed the prophets spoke God's words to all people and not to any particular person. Therefore, prophets' words are assumed to be as applicable in the present as they were when first delivered. Christian preachers continue this practice into the present day. The question then is not what a prophet's words meant at a particular time in the past but what they can be understood to mean in the present. If one believes the prophets primarily spoke of a Messiah to come in the future, and Jesus was that Messiah (as the evangelists believed), it stands to reason that most passages in the prophets are open to interpretation as references to Jesus even if, in their own context, they have nothing at all to do with Jesus or the Messiah.

The belief that Jesus fulfilled the prophets is not based on reading the prophets and discovering they refer to Jesus. It is based on beginning with the belief that Jesus is the Messiah and then reading the prophets with the understanding that they must be referring to him.

Jesus the Messiah

Matthew understands the prophets to be foretelling the coming of the Messiah. Jesus, for him, is the Messiah. Therefore the Messiah, Jesus, is the Son of (or descendent of) David (and Matthew supplies a genealogy to demonstrate he is) and the Son of God. Mark's difficulties with the term "Son of David" are not shared by Matthew.

Jesus the Messiah is still present in the church, according to Matthew. He promises to remain with his people until the end of time (28:20) and declares, "Where two or three have met together in my name, I am there among them" (18:20). This saying emphasizes community. The Spirit in other parts of the New Testament is said to come to individuals, but, in this text, Jesus is said to come to people who have met together, not to isolated individuals. To Matthew, therefore, Jesus is more than a historical figure who came to fulfill the Law and the prophets. Having been raised from the dead, he continues to be present in his community, and the community should act accordingly.

Recurring Themes

Sources

Matthew used Mark as his primary source for Jesus' life and death, even though he disagreed with elements of Mark's interpretation. The only portions of Jesus' life story for which Mark was not his source are Jesus' birth and his brief appearance to the disciples after his resurrection.

Matthew's gospel also contains many sayings of Jesus absent in Mark's gospel. He took the majority of them from the Q source and modified them in accordance with his own point of view.

Many of the sayings classified as Special Matthew come from oral tradition. Other sayings, usually the interpretive ones, were composed by Matthew. Finally, the books of the prophets found in the Hebrew Scriptures constitute a kind of source for Matthew, for in some instances he seems to have thought they revealed biographical data; the story of Jesus' family's exile to Egypt and their return is one example.

Jesus

Jesus' life is important to Matthew. He believes Jesus was both a miracle worker and a teacher. Jesus' miracles functioned as evidence for the truth of his teachings, and they were validated by the positive response of multitudes of common Jewish people. The Pharisees and other Jewish leaders were supposedly too concerned with maintaining their own status to support Jesus. Matthew believes Jesus' teaching activities were extremely important, hence his addition of Q sayings and the sayings called Special Matthew to Mark's basic gospel narrative.

Jesus was the Christ, the Messiah of God, for whom Matthew also uses the terms "Son of God" and "Son of Man." There is no clear evidence that Matthew believes these terms to be anything other than synonyms. The main goal of Jesus the Messiah during his life was to teach proper obedience to God's Law, to ensure (through his interpretation of the Law) that both Jews and Gentiles would be able to win God's approval by acting more righteously than the Pharisees.

Matthew does not see Jesus' death and his suffering as the key events in his life, as do Mark and Paul. Matthew expands Mark's section on Jesus' life but not Mark's interpretation of Jesus' death. Nevertheless, he agrees with Mark that the Son of Man was destined to suffer and die and rise, and he agrees that God ordained those events.

Matthew is more prone to blame Jesus' enemies for Jesus' death and to use it as an example of the hardness of the Pharisees' hypocritical hearts than he is to regard it as an element in God's mysterious plan. In Mark's gospel, some of those who contribute to Jesus' death are praised as persons who understand the necessary death of the Son of Man, but in Matthew those who contribute to his death do so because they reject him. While Mark has the centurion declare Jesus a Son of God "because of the way he died," in Matthew that declaration comes from the centurion's subordinate troops as well as the centurion himself, and it is based not on the way he died but on the awe-inspiring, miraculous events accompanying his death: "There was an earthquake, the rocks split and the graves opened, and many of God's saints were raised from sleep; and coming out of their graves after his resurrection they entered the Holy City where many saw them" (27:52–53). For Matthew, the miracles of Jesus and the amazing events at his death are what convince the doubtful he was Son of God.

Eschatology

Matthew believes this world will soon come to an end and be replaced by the Kingdom of God. Here he basically agrees with the other authors we have studied. His concern with the eventual creation of a community from "all nations" indicates he does not expect the end to come immediately. Matthew is convinced that when Jesus the Son of Man returns, he will judge all people, those within the church as well as outside; "the sheep will be separated from the goats," and the goats will be thrown into the place of wailing and gnashing of teeth.

A reading of Special Matthew reveals that Matthew frequently adds to his sources references about the place of wailing and gnashing of teeth. In Mark, imagery of hell is present only once, in 9:42–48. Luke deletes that passage. Q contains no mention of hell. Neither John nor Paul believed in hell. If not for the work of Matthew, it is questionable whether a belief in hell would have become a doctrine of the Christian churches.

Torah Law

In Matthew's opinion, Jesus came to complete the Law and to assist all people in following it. To be a Christian, he believes, is to follow the Law of Moses while accepting the interpretations of Pharisaic Judaism guided by the interpretation brought from God by the Messiah Jesus. The Law for Jews and for Gentiles is identical.

Community

The people of Matthew's community considered themselves Jewish, although many or most of them may formerly have been Gentiles. In the fourth discourse-section of the gospel, some rules and procedures for community discipline are outlined, but in Matthew the church neither functions as a bureaucratic entity nor does it have a tightly controlled structure. Still, the church in Matthew is more structured than the communities evident in Q, Paul, and Mark. Significantly, the only place in the gospels in which the Greek word for "church" occurs is in the Gospel of Matthew.

Matthew's gospel is evidence for a later stage in the evolution of the Christian movement from wandering itinerant preachers to self-contained and organized churches. His revision of the Beatitudes found in Q, to which he added several, tells us something about the social background of his community. Matthew's version of the Beatitudes is probably further from the original than is Luke's version. We know this for three reasons. First, Matthew seems to have rewritten Mark somewhat more extensively than did Luke, and so he probably also did more rewriting of Q. Second, the version of the Beatitudes in Luke corresponds to the social situation of most of the Q sayings wherein people are impoverished and worried about their daily bread. Third, the version of Beatitudes in Luke is similar to the version in the independent source, the Gospel of Thomas. Matthew's versions are not present in Thomas. We can, therefore, safely assume that Matthew made changes in order to make the Beatitudes relevant to the people for whom he was writing, the people of his community.

In Q, references to people in need and to those who weep are directed to poor, hungry, and unhappy people of the lower economic class. Matthew's Beatitudes can be applied to any person regardless of class. The poverty of those financially in need becomes the need to know God, or poverty of Spirit. Hunger for food becomes hunger and thirst for righteousness. Weeping is transformed to sorrowing or mourning, more moderate expression of emotion. Matthew leaves out the clause about hate in the final Beatitude. Evidently, he addresses an audience of people who are not poor or hungry, who do not often find themselves weeping, who do not wish to believe themselves hated. Matthew also adds to the Q list of Beatitudes several others, all applicable to people who are not poor. This indicates Matthew was addressing people of what today would be called the middle class.

Controversy

Matthew 23 and other passages in his gospel prove animosity existed between Matthew (along with, presumably, other members of his community) and the Pharisees who were leaders of the Jewish synagogues of his day. He regards them as hypocrites in the performance of the Law but respects them as authorities in the teaching of the Law.

Matthew is also in conflict with other Christians, some of whom apparently taught that Jesus came to abolish the

Torah or at least to reduce the number of Torah commandments. These people, he claims, have the lowest place in the Kingdom of Heaven. Some Christians known to Matthew held the view that, although Jesus is Lord, they do not need to obey his interpretation of the commands of the Torah; that view is thought by Matthew to be so inadequate that Jesus, upon his return, will repudiate such people completely (Matt 7:23).

Interactions

Miracles Sources

Matthew, unlike Mark, believes that faith based on the evidence of Jesus' miracles is not misleading. In this he is closer to the point of view contained in Mark's miracles sources than he is to Mark. He probably does not know many more miracles than those in Mark, for if he had known others he surely would have included them. While Matthew feels free to modify the stories he receives from tradition, he does not feel free to invent new stories.

Matthew often reduces the miracle stories in length, while at the same time heightening the miraculous elements in them. In Mark 10:46, Jesus brings sight to one blind man; in Matthew's version of that passage (20:29), he brings sight to two blind men. In Mark 5:23, the daughter of Jairus is close to death when Jesus revives her; in Matthew's version (9:18), she is dead and Jesus raises her from the dead. Matthew adds accounts of an earthquake and the resurrection of many dead people to Mark's story of Jesus' death and attributes the proclamation of the centurion (and his soldiers) to those astonishing events.

All of this indicates that Matthew believes Jesus' miracles provide reliable evidence that he is the Christ and that people who believe on the basis of miracles are correct. He would, of course, insist such belief is inadequate if not accompanied by obedience. Matthew knows of people whom he does not believe to be obedient to Jesus' teachings but who do prophesy in Jesus' name, cast out devils in Jesus' name, and call upon Jesus as Lord (7:23). Matthew does not approve of them, for obedience takes precedence over miraculous power. Jesus for him is the perfect example of a miracle worker absolutely obedient to the will of God.

The Q Source

Matthew uses Q extensively, and he generally agrees with its perspectives. Matthew (and also Luke) respect the disciples of Jesus and use the Q source to supplement the reports of Jesus' teaching found in Mark. This indicates that, from their perspective at least, sayings from the Q source were the sort of things taught by Jesus' disciples.

Both the thesis statement and the concluding passage of the Sermon on the Mount (Matt 5:17 and 7:21–27) are derived from Q. Although not addressing people who are from the same social strata as the Q people, Matthew's perspective on obedience and judgment is more like that of Q than is that of any other evangelist. Matthew supplements several Q passages with conclusions saying that Jesus judges the good and the wicked both within and outside the church. This does not contradict Q, for it is difficult to believe the people of the Q community would have insisted that Jesus would not judge all people. Matthew is emphatic about the need to obey Torah, whereas Q generally takes the necessity for obedience for granted; this may not reflect a difference of opinion so much as differences between the communities addressed by the texts. Q was directed toward Jews who would assume obedience to Torah to be required; Matthew's gospel seems to have been directed mainly toward Gentile converts to Judaism who would not necessarily take the need for obedience for granted. Matthew's relatively well-to-do community contrasts with the people revealed in the Q sayings. While Christianity may have originated as a movement among the poor, it soon spread, and as it spread it appealed increasingly to more wealthy individuals, some of whom may have been among the intended audience for Matthew's gospel.

Paul
Matthew cannot be proven to have known Paul's teachings. He possibly has Paul, or Paul's followers, in mind when he writes, "If any man therefore sets aside even the least of the Law's demands, and teaches others to do the same, he will have the lowest place in the kingdom of Heaven." More probably he was thinking of Mark, whose gospel he had in front of him as he wrote. If Matthew had known of Paul's teachings about the Law he would have profoundly disagreed with them. Matthew upholds Torah obedience for Gentiles, unlike Paul who believes not only that it is unnecessary but that it contradicts the spirit of the gospel.

Mark
Matthew both knows and uses the Gospel of Mark. In several respects he disagrees with Mark; we know this by redaction criticism, by comparing the original Mark with Matthew's revision of it. Matthew respects the disciples and regards them as authoritative teachers. While they may have had trouble understanding Jesus at various points, he believes that in the long run they came to understand and were commissioned by the risen Christ to be his apostles. Matthew does not believe that faith based on the evidence of miracles is misleading; he encourages such faith. He believes that all of the Torah, including the Laws respecting clean and unclean foods, is in force. He does not focus on the suffering and death of the Son of Man as the main point of Jesus' life, but he does not

deny its importance as evidence that Jesus would obey God regardless of consequences.

End-of-Chapter Exercises

1. Define *redaction criticism*. What kinds of information can redaction criticism provide you?
2. How do Matthew's depictions of John the Baptist, Pontius Pilate, and Jesus differ from Mark's? Give a couple examples of how Matthew tailors the narrative to bring about these different interpretations.
3. Read the first two chapters of Matthew and the first two chapters of Luke. These are the New Testament's only two accounts of Jesus' birth. Locate common features. List features that you think are significantly different. What special interests do you discover Matthew had that Luke did not have?

Bibliography

Betz, Hans Dieter. *Essays on the Sermon on the Mount*. Philadelphia: Fortress Press, 1984.

Bornkamm, G., G. Barth, and H. Held. *Tradition and Interpretation in Matthew*. Philadelphia: Westminster Press, 1963.

Carson, D. A. *God with Us: Themes from Matthew*. Eugene OR: Wipf and Stock, 2009.

Fortna, Robert. *The Gospel of Matthew: Scholars Bible*. Salem OR: Polebridge Press, 2005.

France, R. T. *The Gospel of Matthew*. Grand Rapids MI: Eerdmans, 2007.

Funk, Robert, ed. *New Gospel Parallels*. 2 vols. Sonoma CA: Polebridge Press, 1990.

Kingsbury, Jack Dean. *Matthew: Structure, Christology*. Kingdom. Philadelphia PA: Fortress Press, 1975.

Osborne, Grant. *Exegetical Commentary on the New Testament—Matthew*. Grand Rapids MI: Zondervan, 2010

Saldarini, Anthony. *Matthew's Christian-Jewish Community*. Chicago IL: University of Chicago Press, 1994

Sim, David. *The Gospel of Matthew and Christian Judaism: The History and Social Setting of the Matthean Community*. Edinburgh: T & T Clark, 1998.

Stanton, G. N. *The Interpretation of Matthew*. Philadelphia: Fortress Press, 1974.

Throckmorton, B. H., ed. *Gospel Parallels*. Nashville: Thomas Nelson Publishers, 1979.

The Gospel of Luke and the Acts of the Apostles

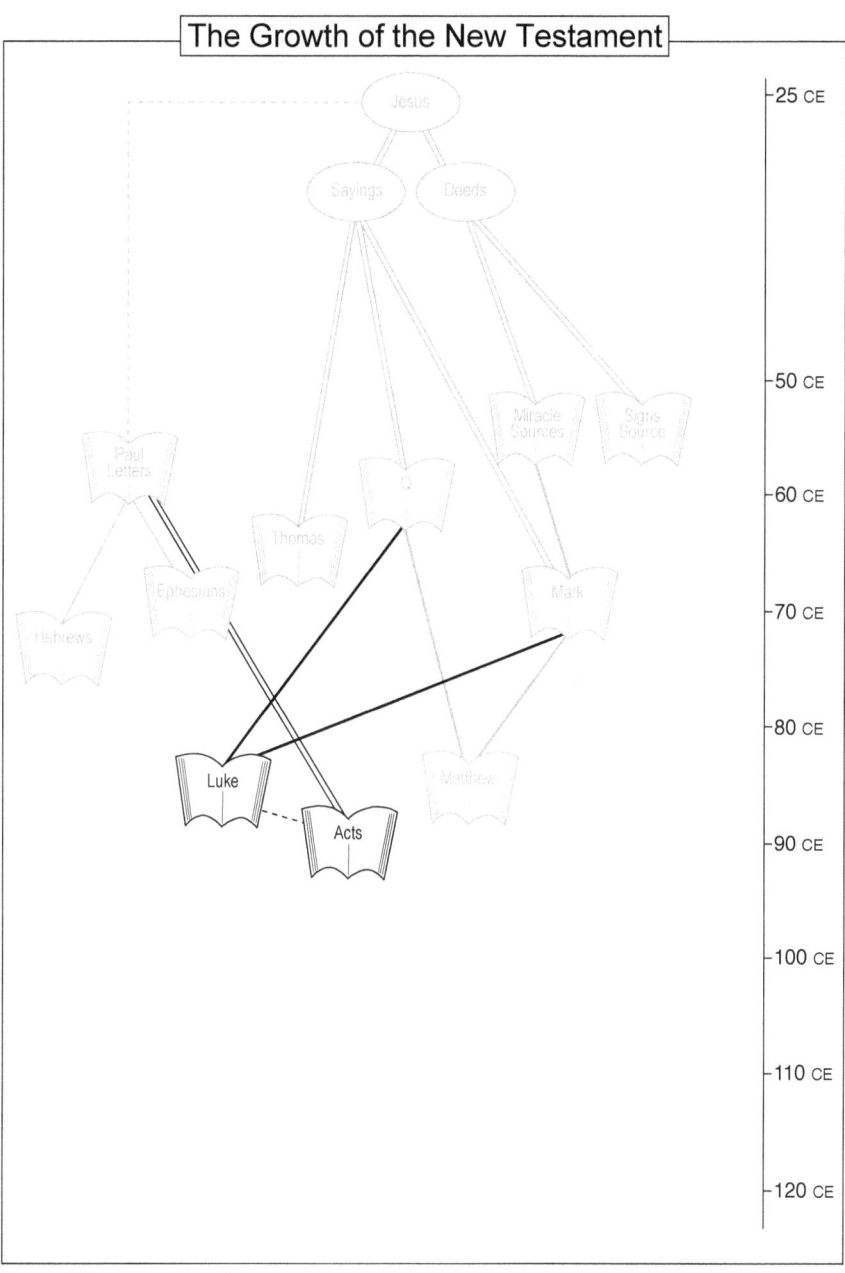

Dashed lines: indirect influence
Double lines: oral transmission
Single thick lines: use of written source
Thin lines: followers, admirers & imitators

CHAPTER 7

The Gospel of Luke and the Acts of the Apostles

OBJECTIVES

- Consider the motivations Luke may have had that led to his writing a history of the early church
- Investigate Luke's unique concern for women & wealthy people
- Analyze Luke's narrative content & structure and consider how Luke portrays Jesus as the paradigm of how a person possessed of the Holy Spirit

More than 25 percent of the New Testament was written by the author known as Luke. His two books, the Gospel of Luke and the Acts of the Apostles, are really one book divided into two sections. The first section tells the story of Jesus' life up to the time of the resurrection. The second section begins with Jesus' ascension, continues through the period of the early church in Jerusalem and the spread of Christianity through the empire, and concludes with Paul's mission to Rome. The books are optimistic in tone; although their principal characters are subject to persecution, they ultimately triumph. The books conclude with Paul in Rome "proclaiming the kingdom of God and teaching the facts about the Lord Jesus Christ quite openly and without hindrance" (Acts 28:30–31). READ THE GOSPEL OF LUKE AND UNDERLINE ANY REFERENCES MADE IN STORIES AND SAYINGS TO WOMEN OR TO PEOPLE OF EVIDENT WEALTH. Luke's gospel is unique in the extent of its concern for women and wealthy people, and later in this chapter many of the passages you will have underlined will be the subject of discussion.

Author, Date, and Place of Origin

We know no more about the identity of the author of these books than we do about the authors of the Gospels of Mark and Matthew. Legend has it Luke was "the beloved physician" who accompanied Paul during some of his journeys. However, the author of Luke/Acts does not seem to have had firsthand knowledge of Paul, nor is there any evidence he was a physician.

Luke/Acts was written late in the first century, somewhere between CE 85 and 100. The date CE 90 is reasonable, although it is only an approximation. We do not know where Luke/Acts was written; somewhere in Asia Minor is a reasonable guess, but it is only a guess.

The Beginning of the Gospel

Luke's first two chapters tell the story of the births of Jesus and John the Baptist. The style of writing in these chapters differs from that of the remainder of Luke/Acts, being more influenced by Hebrew constructions, although still bearing substantial traces of Luke's writing style. It is possible they were written at a different time, but whether they were written earlier or later than the rest of Luke/Acts is difficult to say.

Luke's story of Jesus' birth contrasts significantly with Matthew's. According to Luke, Jesus' family lived in Nazareth and traveled to Bethlehem, where Jesus was born, in contrast to Matthew's account, which describes them as residents of Bethlehem who later resettle to Nazareth. Luke tells us about Mary's experiences and reactions, not Joseph's. In Luke's gospel we hear about the angels and the shepherds of the Christmas story; Matthew's gospel tells about the three magi, the wise-men. These are two quite different versions of the story.

John the Baptist

One can only speculate why John the Baptist has such prominence in the opening chapters of Luke or, indeed, why his birth story is told at all. It is possible Luke's account of John's birth came from stories Luke received from John's followers. John's disciples did not disband after his execution. While some became followers of Jesus, others—probably the majority—remained loyal to John's memory. A small and isolated group of people called the Mandaeans, who live today in the nation of Iraq, are descendants of the followers of John the Baptist. Unfortunately, their extensive literature has become so altered over time that it adds nothing to our historical knowledge of John.

The poem recited by John's father Zechariah in Luke 1:67–69, may have circulated first among disciples of John, for it has no direct connection to specifically Christian teaching. John's followers would have understood the phrase "the Lord's forerunner" to mean that John announced the coming of the Lord God, while followers of Jesus would have thought it referred to the Lord Jesus. Mary's poem (1:46–55) also contains nothing specifically Christian, but this poem, called the Magnificat, has an important place in Catholic devotion to the Virgin Mary. Despite their lack of specifically Christian themes, the two poems in no way contradict Christian teaching. Although both poems are written in Greek, they exhibit the style of, and use language influenced by, ancient Hebrew poetry. They may be Greek translations of Hebrew or Aramaic originals.

Like Mark and Matthew, Luke depicts John as inferior to Jesus. Luke wishes to make it clear that John is not speaking of the future coming of God but of the immediate appearance of the Messiah, Jesus. Therefore, when John says, "I baptize you with water; but there is one to come who is mightier than I" (3:16), the statement is made in the context of people asking him whether or not he is the Messiah.

Matthew and Mark were content to have John play down his own importance before his baptism of Jesus. For Luke this is insufficient; he is also careful not to say John baptized Jesus. Luke moves Mark's account of John's imprisonment to the beginning of his gospel (3:19–20) and subsequently writes about Jesus' baptism. "And when Jesus too had been baptized and was praying, heaven opened, and the Holy Spirit descended on him" (3:21–22). At the time John is presumably in prison. Locating Jesus' baptism after John's arrest is not a mistake on Luke's part but a deliberate decision.

The Ending of the Gospel

Luke's gospel concludes with Jesus' appearances to his disciples in and near Jerusalem. In Matthew his appearance takes place in Galilee. Apparently, the risen Christ did not look the same as he did previously. Matthew informs us "when they saw him, they fell prostrate before him, though some were doubtful" (Matt 28:17), and Luke (24:16) writes that the disciples who first met him did not recognize him until he later broke bread and offered it to them. Then "they recognized him; and he vanished from their sight" (24:31). Later in Jerusalem, suddenly "there he was, standing among them. Startled and terrified, they thought they were seeing a ghost" (24:36–37). John's gospel will repeat the same themes: Jesus' appearance is substantially changed. Mary Magdalene does not recognize him at the tomb (John 20:14), nor do his disciples (John 21:4), and he can appear instantaneously: "Although the doors were latched, he came and stood among them" (John 20:26).

It was after the resurrection that the disciples, in Luke's account, begin to think the Messiah was bound to suffer before entering his glory. The disciples had previously believed "he was the man to liberate Israel" (24:21), but apparently his execution proved to them this was not the case. The risen Jesus, however, "opened their minds to understand the scriptures. 'This,' he said, 'is what is written: that the Messiah is to suffer death and to rise from the dead on the third day, and that in his name repentance bringing the forgiveness of sins is to be proclaimed to all nations'" (24:46–47).

From a historical perspective, the sequence of events in Luke's final chapter gives insight into the earliest development of Christian thought. As Luke implies, Jesus' disciples may have believed that he was a political messiah or a miracle-working prophet destined to liberate Israel from Roman occupation. They did not, Luke indicates, think beforehand that he would rise from the dead. Other gospels' reports that he told them this in advance are probably based on Mark's ideas of what he should have said. Although Jesus is reported to have told his disciples about his resurrection, both Luke's and Mark's final chapters suggest they were unprepared for it. Luke reports that when certain women came from Jesus' tomb to tell his disciples they believed him to be risen from the dead, "the story appeared to them [the apostles] to be nonsense, and they would not believe them" (24:11). Soon, however, rather than assuming that Jesus' mission had been a failure, his followers came to the conclusion that Jesus' death did not contradict the idea of his messiahship, but confirmed it. They then looked for and discovered passages in the Hebrew Bible useful in supporting that claim and believed Jesus had "opened their minds to understand the scriptures."

Finding only limited success in convincing Jews of their point of view, as the book of Acts reports, some of Jesus' followers turned to the Gentile world with greater missionary success.

Pontius Pilate

Luke, like Mark and Matthew, shifts responsibility for Jesus' execution from Pilate to the Jewish people. Pilate first denies there is a case to be made against Jesus (23:4). Luke then includes a paragraph stating that Pilate turned over Jesus' case to Herod Antipas, ruler of Jesus' home region of Galilee, to demonstrate that Pilate had no wish to execute Jesus and to imply Pilate did not even have legal jurisdiction in the matter (23:6–12). After Jesus' return from Herod Antipas, "Pilate called together the chief priests, councillors, and people, and said to them, 'You brought this man before me on a charge of subversion. But, as you see, I have myself examined him in your presence and found nothing in him to support your charges. No more did Herod, for he has referred him back to us. Clearly he has done nothing to deserve death" (23:13–15). In the book of Acts Jews are said to have used Pilate to execute Jesus as though Pilate were acting under their instructions. Responsibility for Jesus' death belongs entirely to the Jews, according to Luke, although ultimately they were carrying out the will of God (Acts 2:23).

Luke's efforts to show that Pilate was not responsible for Jesus' death reflect one of his main themes, that the Christian movement is loyal to and supportive of the Roman Empire. Where official persecution of Christians is mentioned in Acts, from the execution of Jesus to the imprisonment of Paul, persecution is said to have originated with Jews and not with Romans. If anything, the Romans are shown to be defenders of Christians against persecution. Pilate finds Jesus innocent, although he eventually executes him. Later, in Acts, Paul escapes persecution from Jewish opponents by appealing to Caesar, a privilege of his Roman citizenship.

Salvation History

Some scholars believe Luke 16:16 is a key verse for understanding Luke's purpose: "Until John, it was the Law and the prophets: since then, there is the good news of the kingdom of God, and everyone forces his way in." From their perspective, the first third of history, contained in the Hebrew Scriptures, is the period of the Law and the prophets. This period came to an end when the ministry of John the Baptist concluded. The second third of history, related in the Gospel of Luke, is the time of Jesus' ministry. These scholars believe Luke regarded this era as the middle of time, a special period when the Kingdom of God was beginning to break into the world and during which Satan was gone. The Acts of the Apostles is the account of the beginning of the third period of history, the time of the church. Both the gospel and Acts indicate that a time will come when history ends, judgment occurs, and the Kingdom of God arrives on earth. The arrival of the kingdom will be the culmination of history. Stephen's speech in Acts 7:1–53 traces the first period of history and concludes with a prophetic vision of history's eventual end. "Look," Stephen said, "there is a rift in the sky; I can see the Son of Man standing at God's right hand!"

Luke, more than any other evangelist, writes in the style of an ancient historian. His concept of history, however, is focused on history's implications for salvation, which was then a uniquely Jewish idea. Salvation, Luke believes, does not come all at once but as a process stretched out over centuries, a process centered on the time of Jesus' life.

Luke's Teaching about Jesus

READ THE ACTS OF THE APOSTLES. UNDERLINE OR HIGHLIGHT EACH SECTION YOU FIND SUMMARIZING THE LIFE AND SIGNIFICANCE OF JESUS. Most of those sections will appear in speeches or preaching attributed to Peter and Paul. It is in the passages you will have underlined that Luke's ideas and conception of Jesus and his mission are most clearly set forth because Luke wrote the speeches for his heroes as ancient historians almost always did. When you read Acts, do so as you would a novel; Luke intended the book to be full of adventures, conflicts, miracles, arrests and trials and escapes from prison, long journeys, shipwreck and so forth. It's supposed to be fun.

The speeches attributed to Paul in Acts do not contain Paul's particular vocabulary, his style of expression, or his unique ideas. This we know by comparing them to his letters. Therefore, most scholars conclude that while Luke knew something of Paul's life and influence, Luke writes speeches attributed to Paul as a way to give his conception of what Paul *would have said* rather than what Paul actually said. Historians in the ancient world often wrote speeches for the subjects of their books, speeches giving more information about the opinions of the historians than about the opinions of the person who supposedly spoke. Thus, the apostles' speeches in Acts give Luke's opinions, not Paul's or Peter's or the other apostles he quoted. The best source of information about Paul is the letters Paul wrote. Acts is a better source for information about the opinions of Luke than about the opinions of Paul.

Little is known of the teachings of the historical Peter. The style and content of speeches attributed to him in Acts, however, are nearly the same as those attributed to Paul, although we have reason to believe the two were in disagreement (see Gal 2:11–14). But this should not be surprising, as Luke wrote for both Peter and Paul. Except possibly for the lengthy speech of Stephen in Acts 7:1–53, all of the speeches in Acts were created by Luke. Luke's gospel is filled with detail, as are the Gospels of Mark and Matthew, but the speeches Luke wrote in Acts are short, concise summaries. These speeches can save us much intellectual effort, for, rather than going through Luke's gospel and making our own summary of his ideas about Jesus, we can use the summaries Luke himself wrote in Acts.

The Acts of the Apostles was probably written before Luke's gospel was written. Acts contains remarkably few details about Jesus' life. The virgin birth, for example, is never mentioned in Acts. Nor does he quote any miracle stories or any of Jesus' teachings. An author who previously wrote an extensive book about Jesus should be expected to give substantial information about him in any later book written to present the teachings of Jesus' followers about him; Acts, however, does not do this. In contrast, Luke 3:1–3 is an excellent example of how an ancient historian would begin a book by providing a detailed date based on political personages. Another point to consider is that, while Luke did write the self-contained birth narrative in chapters 1 and 2, he never refers to its events again throughout the gospel or Acts. Luke probably wrote Acts, and then wrote a revision of Mark's gospel beginning with what is now his chapter 3, and then finally, some time later, wrote and added his version of the story of Jesus' birth. When Luke paid to have a copy of his work made to be presented to Theophilus, he put a linkage from the first part to the second, which is now Acts 1:1–2. While we tend to think that the gospel writers only had one copy of their works, common sense reveals that it is probable they hired scribes to make several copies to be given away or sold.

Two of the lengthier speeches in Acts are found in 2:22–45 and 10:34–43. They show limited interest in the events of Jesus' life. These events can be summarized quickly:

1. Jesus was anointed by God with the Holy Spirit and with power.
2. After the baptism proclaimed by John, Jesus started from Galilee, went to the Jewish countryside, and, eventually, arrived in Jerusalem.
3. He went about doing good and healing all who were oppressed by the devil, doing miracles, portents, and signs as evidence of the fact he had been chosen by God.

That is about all. Again, no specific miracle stories are told, nor are Jesus' teachings or parables mentioned or discussed. No detailed stories of his life are given. This is true for all of the speeches in Acts.

Jesus' death, on the other hand, is of particular importance in Acts' speeches. In those speeches, claims are made that Jesus' death was planned beforehand by God, announced beforehand by prophets, and brought about by the leaders of the Jewish people. Luke does not want the authorities of the Roman Empire to bear any blame, so he portrays the Jews of Israel as having "used heathen men, [Romans] to crucify and kill him" (2:23). The Romans are only tools in the hands of others. The blame for Jesus' death according to Luke should be borne by Jews and not Romans. The idea of blame, however, is difficult to justify by Luke's own principles, for he states categorically that Jesus' death came about "by the deliberate will and plan of God" (2:23).

Perhaps we should separate the questions of political and final responsibility for Jesus' death. From the perspective of Luke's books, Jewish people are politically responsible, not the Roman authorities. But final responsibility rests with

God, who ordained that those things should happen. If you read Acts' speeches carefully, you can see that Luke is quite definite that everything in Jesus' life, including his death and his resurrection, was empowered by God. God chose Jesus; God sent the Holy Spirit to him; God worked miracles through him; God arranged for his death; God brought him back to life; God exalted him.

The speeches in Acts focus primary attention on Jesus' role after his resurrection. It is as though the purpose of his life was to give evidence that after his death he would receive exalted responsibility. Then God made him both Lord and Messiah, and God designated him judge of the living and the dead. Everything that happens within the church happens through him or is empowered by him, including the power of the apostles to do miracles and, most importantly, the coming of the Holy Spirit to all who have faith. To an extent, Jesus is to the apostles what God was to Jesus.

Luke draws deliberate parallels between the people of the church and Jesus during his life. He received the Holy Spirit; they receive the Holy Spirit. He did signs and wonders; they do signs and wonders. Their regard for money is the same as his; just as he advocated that the wealthy give to the poor, all wealth is equally distributed within the community of the apostles. In the Gospel of Luke, Jesus is the paradigm, or the prime example, of how a person possessed of the Holy Spirit should behave. The way he lived is the way his apostles and other followers should live. The gospel presents Jesus' way of life; Acts shows it being carried out by others.

The Holy Spirit

The factor linking Jesus and his followers is not so much belief, although faith is important, as the Holy Spirit. Luke's two books might be conceived to be a history of the activity of the Holy Spirit, not various histories of the activities of certain famous individuals.

At the time of Jesus' conception, the Holy Spirit brings about Mary's pregnancy. Jesus receives the Holy Spirit at his baptism, and it stays with him throughout his life. Through the Spirit he performs signs and wonders. At his death, the Spirit returns to God and so Jesus' last words are: "Father, into thy hands I commit my Spirit." Risen from the dead, Jesus again receives the Spirit, and through it he speaks to the apostles (Acts 1:2). After his ascension, he sends the Spirit to his followers. Through their ministry the Spirit comes to multitudes of people, Jews and Gentiles alike. Luke is careful throughout his two books to trace the presence of the Spirit from the birth of John the Baptist to the time of the annunciation, through the time of Jesus' ministry, to the time of the early church. Luke believes the Spirit to be the central and crucial link binding all these times together.

The Gospel of Luke

Much of what was said about the origin of the Gospel of Matthew could be said about the origin of the Gospel of Luke. Like Matthew, Luke revised Mark. Like Matthew, Luke used the written sayings source Q. Like Matthew, Luke added to Mark an extended beginning discussing the birth of Jesus and an extended ending discussing Jesus' appearances to his disciples after his death. Finally, like Matthew, Luke added sayings and stories to the gospel found in no other New Testament gospel (some of Luke's, like some of Matthew's, appear in the Gospel of Thomas).

The stories and sayings found only in Luke, thus not in Matthew, Mark, or John, are called Special Luke. Some scholars believe many of these were previously written in a document they call L, which, like Q, was a list of sayings with a particular perspective of its own. But this theory does not convince all scholars; the sayings in Special Luke may have been taken from oral tradition or composed by Luke. Underline each of the following Special Luke passages:

- Luke 1:1–2:52
- Luke 3:1–2, 3b, 5–6
- Luke 4:17–22a, 25–30
- Luke 5:1–11
- Luke 7:11–16
- Luke 7:36–50
- Luke 8:1–3
- Luke 9:51–56
- Luke 10:29–37
- Luke 10:38–42
- Luke 11:2–4
- Luke 11:27–28
- Luke 12:13–15
- Luke 12:16–21
- Luke 12:32–33
- Luke 12:35–38
- Luke 12:47–48
- Luke 13:1–17
- Luke 13:31–33
- Luke 14:1–10
- Luke 14:12–14
- Luke 14:28–33
- Luke 15:11–32
- Luke 16:1–12
- Luke 16:19–31
- Luke 17:12–19
- Luke 17:20–21
- Luke 18:1–8
- Luke 19:2–10
- Luke 19:40
- Luke 19:42–44
- Luke 21:34–36
- Luke 22:31–32
- Luke 22:35–38
- Luke 23:4–16
- Luke 23:27–34
- Luke 23:39–43
- Luke 23:46
- Luke 24:8–53

AFTER YOU HAVE UNDERLINED THESE SPECIAL LUKE PAS‑SAGES, READ THEM CAREFULLY. They should reveal many of Luke's special perspectives and concerns. There will be some overlap between what has been categorized as Special Luke and as Q. This indicates that while there is general agreement among scholars which passages are which, there still remain areas of dispute.

The Responsibilities of Wealth

The author of these books probably received an expensive education, for the gospel is written quite well. For those who assume that Christians of the first century were all poor and needy people, it may come as a surprise to learn Luke categorically states, in Acts, that many worshippers were wealthy. Paul and Silas are said to have converted "a great number of godfearing Gentiles and a good many influential women" (Acts 17:4). "Women of standing as well as men" were converted, Acts says a little later (17:11). Among those who were Christian but fell away were some "women of standing who were worshippers" (13:50). Ananias and his wife Sapphira, who did not give all they possessed to the community, are depicted as well-to-do landowners (5:1–12). Lydia, a Christian woman prominent in Acts 16, is an independent business woman, a dealer in purple fabric, a luxury material. Like these people, Luke came from a wealthy background.

Many passages in Luke, particularly Special Luke, are directed toward wealthy persons.

The Special Luke parable found in 16:1–8 is told from the perspective of a landlord's agent, not from the perspective of the debtors who owe that landlord money. The conclusion Luke composed, "So I say to you, use your worldly wealth to win friends for yourselves, so that when money is a thing of the past you may be received into an eternal home" (16:9), assumes the audience has worldly wealth to use. The parable of the prodigal son in Special Luke (15:11–32) discusses events in a wealthy household; those who hear the parable in 14:7–10 are people who ordinarily *would* take place of honor at a wedding feast; the audience addressed in 14:12–14 is able to invite rich neighbors to a party; those who hear the parable in 17:7–10 are people who have servants to do their plowing and to mind their sheep. The wealthy people addressed in the Special Luke sayings are those who financially controlled the destinies of the people addressed in Q sayings.

And yet Luke uses Q sayings and does not substantially revise them. He does not make them reflect the point of view of the wealthy but allows them to continue to reflect the point of view of the poor. Matthew, on the other hand, seems to have revised some of the Q sayings to make them more acceptable to people who were not poor.

There is nothing contradictory in Luke's approach. One must distinguish between his probable audience and his sympathies. Luke's audience was probably rather well-to-do. Theophilus, for whom this copy of the gospel and Acts was written, is addressed as "Your Excellency" (Luke 1:3, Acts 1:1–2). But Luke's sympathies are with the poor. Jesus, as presented in Luke's gospel, urges the wealthy to share their wealth with the poor, to use worldly wealth to win friends for themselves. Luke creates a compromise in his portrayal of Jesus—not as one who addresses only the poor and hungry, but as one who also addresses wealthy audiences. His primary sympathy, however, remains with the poor.

Women in Luke

Perhaps more striking than Luke's interest in the responsibilities of wealthy Christians is Luke's interest in demonstrating Jesus' concern for women. Remarks favorable to women appear in other gospels (for example, Mark 14:1–9, John 4:1–30), but there we find nothing like the careful, sustained attention paid to women in the Gospel of Luke.

The first two chapters of Luke's gospel tell the story of Jesus' birth and of the birth of John the Baptist. The principal characters in the story are Elizabeth and Mary. Jesus' name occurs only three times in those two chapters. Joseph is mentioned only occasionally and is a minor character. In contrast, Matthew's account gives Joseph more prominence than Mary. Zechariah, the father of John the Baptist, is portrayed negatively by Luke. He is made unable to speak because he does not believe the angel Gabriel. He is directly contrasted with the women who do accept Gabriel's messages.

The stories in Luke 1 and 2 are the stories of Mary and Elizabeth. These women, especially Mary, are portrayed as willing servants of God who happily accept the special roles God gives them. In doing so, they are similar to the apostles whose stories are told in Acts. If Christians can be defined in the Lukan sense as persons who receive the Holy Spirit through their relationship with Jesus, then Mary, to whom the Holy Spirit came, and Elizabeth, who was filled with the Holy Spirit (1:41), are the first Christians mentioned in the Gospel of Luke.

Two others who are filled with the Spirit appear in chapters 1 and 2: Simeon (2:25–35) and Anna (2:36–38). The Holy Spirit is said to have disclosed to Simeon that he would not die until he saw the Messiah. So, guided by the Spirit, he came to the Jerusalem temple and there he circumcised Jesus. Anna was an elderly widow, a prophet guided by the Spirit. She talked about the child Jesus to all who were looking forward to the liberation of Jerusalem.

Anna and Simeon are the first examples in Luke's gospel of his tendency to pair characters and stories so as to ensure stories about men are paired with stories about women. The following list is taken from Mary Rose D'Angelo's article "Women in Luke-Acts: A Redactional View," published in the *Journal of Biblical Literature* (Fall 1990):

- 2 annunciations: to Zechariah (1:5–23) and to Mary (1:26–38)
- 2 songs: of Mary (1:45–56) and of Zechariah (1:67–79)

- 2 prophets: Simeon (2:25–35) and Anna (2:36–38)
- 2 miracles: for a Gentile widow (4:25–26) and a leper (4:25–27)
- 2 first miracles: for a possessed man (4:31–37 [Mark 1:21–38]) and Peter's mother-in-law (4:38–39 [Mark 1:29–31])
- 2 lists of named disciples: male apostles (6:12–19 [Mark 3:12–19]) and female ministers (8:1–3)
- 2 rescues from death: the centurion's servant (7:1–10 [Matt 8:5–13]) and the widow's son (7:11–17)
- 2 penitents: the paralytic (5:19–26 [Mark 2:1–12]) and the penitent woman (7:35–50 [Mark 14:1–11?])
- 3 miracles: the Gerasene demoniac (8:26–39 [Mark 5:1–20]), and the daughter of Jairus and the hemorrhaging woman (8:40–56 [Mark 5:21–43])
- 3 questions about discipleship: the scribe (10:25–37 [Mark 12:28–34]), Martha (10:38–42), and the disciple (11:1–13)
- 2 Gentile accusers of Israel: the Ninevites and the queen of the south (11:29–36 [Matt 12:38–42])
- 2 "releases": the bent-over woman (13:10–17) and the dropsical man (14:1–6 [Mark 3:1–6?])
- 2 parables about hiding something: a man (?) planting mustard (13:18–19 [Matt 13:31–32]) and a woman hiding leaven (13:20–21 [Matt 13: 33])
- 2 parables about finding something: a man with sheep (15:1–7 [Matt 18:12–14]) and a woman with coins (15:8–10)
- 2 people taken: men (?) sleeping and women grinding (17:32–35 [Matt 24:40–41])
- 2 examples of prayer: a widow (18:1–8) and a Pharisee alongside a publican (18:9–17)
- 2 attitudes toward worship: scribes and widow (20:45–21:4 [Mark 12:37–44])

- 2 sets of followers on the road to Calvary: Simon and women (23:26–32 [Mark 15:21])
- 2 audiences at the crucifixion of Jesus: women and all his acquaintances (23:49 [Mark 15:40–41])
- 2 groups of resurrection witnesses: women at the tomb and apostles on the road to Emmaus (24:1–11 [Mark 16:1–8]).

Like Luke, Acts also includes a number of references to women paired with men:
- 2 groups wait in an upper room (1:13–14)
- Menservants and maidservants, sons and daughters prophesy (2:17–18)
- Ananias and Sapphira chastised (5:1–11)
- A crowd of both men and women added as believers (5:14)
- Paul persecutes both men and women (8:3)
- Both men and women added as believers (8:12)
- Paul persecutes both men and women (9:2)
- Peter cures a lame man and Tabitha (9:32–43)
- Worshiping women and first men of the city persecute Paul and Barnabas (13:50)
- Paul is driven from Lystra by his cure of a lame man (14:5–18) then from Philippi by cure of a possessed girl (16:16–34)
- A great crowd of worshiping Greeks and not a few of the first women were persuaded by Paul (17:4)
- Not a few respectable Greek women and men believed (17:12)
- Dionysius and Damaris converted at Athens (17:34)
- Paul received by Priscilla and Aquila (18:1–4)
- Paul persecutes both men and women (22:4)
- Felix arrives with Drusilla (24:24)
- Agrippa and Bernice hear Paul's case (25:13, 23; 26:30)

As you can see, many pairs of stories—one featuring a woman, one featuring a man—are found in the gospel. Sometimes these pairs are found only in Special Luke, but sometimes a story has been added to other sources used by Luke in order to create a pair. For example, one pairing, found only in Special Luke, occurs in Jesus' remarks about widows (4:25) and leprous men (4:28) during his commentary on a passage from Isaiah in the Nazareth synagogue; these are among the first words of his ministry. Another is Luke's pairing of a story taken from Mark (Luke 5:17–20) about Jesus' forgiving the sins of a paralyzed man (and thereby scandalizing Pharisees and teachers of the Law) with a Special Luke story in which Jesus astonishes Pharisees by forgiving the sins of a woman (7:36–50). Luke pairs the Q miracle about Jesus healing the centurion's servant who was near death (7:1–10) with a Special Luke story about Jesus raising the dead son of a widow to life (7:11–17). Luke further pairs Mark's story about Jesus curing a man with a withered arm and receiving criticism for doing that on the Sabbath (6:6–11) with a Special Luke story about a crippled woman cured on the Sabbath, in which Jesus is criticized again for healing on the Sabbath (13:10–17). The parable of the shepherd who sought his lost sheep, taken from Q (15:4–7), is followed immediately by a parable from Special Luke about a woman with a lost silver coin (15:8–10). Significantly, the Q parable is about a man at the bottom of the social order, while the Special Luke parable is about a woman with what was, in those days, considerable wealth. Finally, a parable in 18:1–8, which makes the point that constant crying out to God will bring about God's response, has as its central character a widow; the story paired with it occurs in 11:5–8, and teaches the same point while featuring a man. Almost all of the stories in Luke featuring women are from Special Luke; most of the stories featuring men come from Mark and Q.

These pairs occur too frequently to be coincidences. Luke consciously and deliberately supplements his sources, Q and Mark, by using or composing complementary stories about women.

Perhaps the most significant point Luke's gospel makes about women is the Special Luke passage about Martha and Mary (10:38–42). Martha works at domestic chores while Mary sits and listens to Jesus. The story concludes strongly, "The part that Mary has chosen is best; and it shall not be taken away from her." From Luke's perspective, Christian women are not servants to be kept in the background but should be disciples of Jesus.

Luke distinguishes between "the Twelve" and Jesus' other disciples. Although the Twelve have a special place, they are not his only disciples. To make this very clear, toward the end of his gospel Luke repeatedly asserts women had accompanied Jesus all the way from Galilee to the end. At the crucifixion, "his friends had all been standing at a distance; the women who had accompanied him from Galilee stood with them and watched it all" (23:49). After the crucifixion, "the women who had accompanied him from Galilee followed; they took note of the tomb and observed how his body was laid" (23:55). At Jesus' tomb "Mary of Magdala, Joanna, Mary the mother of James, and the other women" (24:10–11) heard two men in dazzling garments say, "Remember what he told you while he was still in Galilee, about the Son of Man: how he must be given up into the power of sinful men and be crucified, and must rise again on the third day. Then they recalled his words and, returning from the tomb, they reported all this to the Eleven and all the others" (24:6–11).

Luke is following Mark's account here, but has significantly changed it. In Mark, the youth in white clothes tells only "Mary of Magdala, Mary the mother of James, and Salome" (Mark 16:1) to "go and give this message to his disciples and Peter" (16:7). In the first place, the number of women in Luke's account is significantly greater. In the second place, what the women are told is directed to them rather than to the Eleven and Peter; in Luke they are not *ordered* to tell the disciples, they *choose* to do so. Finally, the message they are given, and which they recall Jesus teaching, is the one Mark especially reserved only for Jesus' twelve disciples (Mark 8:31). According to Luke, Jesus previously taught it to the women.

The women go to tell the apostles, but "the story appeared to them [the apostles] to be nonsense, and they would not believe them" (24:11). For a short period, until the apostles finally do believe (24:45), the only Christians with faith in Jesus' resurrection are women, women who act as apostles to the apostles.

From the beginning of the gospel and the stories of Elizabeth and Mary, to the end of the gospel and the story of the women at the tomb, Luke emphasizes the part women played in Jesus' ministry. Jesus' first public words refer to widows (4:25); his last public words are addressed to the women of Jerusalem (23:27–31). Luke emphasizes that women were with Jesus from the beginning of his ministry in Galilee to the end of his ministry in Jerusalem.

It appears odd at first that the one story in Mark's gospel that shows Jesus fulsomely praising a woman (Mark 14:3–9) is missing in Luke's gospel. But one must bear in mind that Mark's point in including this particular story is to make a contrast between that one anonymous woman and the women who accompanied Jesus, the latter of whom went to his tomb to anoint him, ignorant of the fact that he would be risen. The anonymous woman understood Jesus better than the women who accompanied Jesus, from Mark's perspective. Unlike Mark, Luke intends to praise the women who accompanied Jesus, so he deletes Mark's story. Or perhaps Luke transformed it to become the story of the sinful woman who anoints Jesus' feet in 7:36–50. She is favorably contrasted with Pharisees there.

Luke states quite clearly how the ministry of Jesus was financed, and this interesting point links Luke's themes of the responsibilities of wealth and of the discipleship of women. The other gospels leave us to assume he and his followers were supported by donations from the common people and the hospitality of various associates, but Luke's does not. While allowing that Jesus was invited to dine with both friends and opponents, Luke tells us categorically that when Jesus went from town to town, village to village, proclaiming the good news of the Kingdom of God, he was accompanied by "the Twelve and a number of women who had been set free from evil spirits and infirmities: Mary, known as Mary of Magdala, from whom seven devils had come out, Joanna, the wife of Chuza a steward of Herod's, Susanna, and many others. These women provided for them out of their own resources" (8:1–3). This passage naming the women precedes Jesus' parables sermon in Luke just as a passage naming Jesus' male disciples precedes the sermon on the mount (6:12–19).

Luke's theme that the wealthy should contribute their resources to the poor has its high point in 8:1–3, for the wealthy are contributing their resources to the support of Jesus' personal mission. The wealthy in this instance are, all of them, independently wealthy women.

Two theories may account for Luke's emphatic and sustained emphasis on women. The first is conventional, and virtually all analytical scholars are in agreement with it. The second is unconventional, but it also is worthy of attention.

The first is this: Luke was a man who, believing Jesus to be the Messiah for all people, wished to portray him as Messiah for both men and women. Noting that women were not prominently mentioned in his sources, Luke decided to write a gospel emphasizing their presence and their support of Jesus' mission. Luke, then, was a man with great respect for and admiration of Christian women, a man determined to see that Christian women received a place of respect in his church.

The second is this: the anonymous author of the gospel called Luke was a woman. We have reason to believe the author of the Gospel and Acts came from a wealthy background and so may have been either male or female. In many regions of the empire, both the boys and the girls of well-to-do families received education. In some regions women's education was discouraged, but as we do not know where the Gospel was written, it may just as well have been written in a locale where well-to-do girls were educated as in a locale where their education was restricted.

We assume, but do not know, that Luke held a leadership position in a church. Acts tells us some women had churches in their homes (Acts 12:12 and Acts 16:40), and we can assume such women held leadership positions in those churches. Acts also indicates that widowed Christian women sometimes associated, lived, and worked together (9:36–43). In such associations women presumably held leadership positions. It might even be argued that common sense itself supports the thesis that the author of the gospel was a woman, for rarely in the history of the Christian movement have men been known sympathetically and emphatically to argue for the important place of women in the church. But this is exactly what the author of Luke does.

A woman author of a gospel might have resembled Lydia, whose story is told in Acts 16:11–40. Lydia was an independent business woman and, as a seller of luxurious purple cloth, presumably wealthy. She was a "worshipper of God," meaning that although born a Gentile she was sympathetic to Judaism and, even before accepting Christianity, worshiped the Jewish God. Therefore, she knew something of the Greek translation of the Hebrew Scriptures. She was converted to

Christianity by Paul and, through her influence, so was her household. At this time a household would have included the nuclear and extended family, employees, and slaves. A church apparently met in her house, and it surely would have continued to meet after the departure of the apostles responsible for the conversion of its members. Presumably Lydia would have led a church meeting in her house composed in large part of members of her household.

No method exists for conclusively proving the gender of anonymous authors. It is still customary for scholars to presume that all anonymous Christian authors are male. But if, as feminist scholars have argued, women played more important roles in early Christianity than those for which they have received credit, it may well be that we will discover that the custom of assuming male authorship needs to be re-examined and some day a chapter such as this in an introductory textbook will use "she" throughout in reference to the author of the Gospel of Luke and the Acts of the Apostles.

Travel in Luke/Acts

One of Luke's main thematic and organizational structures is based on travel. Evidently Luke does not regard Mark's gospel as a useful guide to Jesus' journeys, because they are substantially reorganized. In Luke's gospel, Jesus is depicted as beginning his mission in Galilee and then journeying through Judea to the city of Jerusalem, where he dies, rises, and appears to his disciples. Luke emphasizes this frequently:

> As the time approached when he was to be taken up to heaven, he set his face resolutely towards Jerusalem, and sent messengers ahead (9:51–52).

> I must be on my way today and tomorrow and the next day, because it is unthinkable for a prophet to meet his death anywhere but in Jerusalem (13:33).

In the course of his journey to Jerusalem he was travelling through the borderlands of Samaria and Galilee (17:11).

For more than half the gospel, Luke depicts Jesus as going toward Jerusalem, traveling exclusively in Jewish territory.

In Acts, Jerusalem serves as the starting point for a pattern of travel that fans out through the regions of Judea and Samaria and beyond into regions increasingly populated by Gentiles. Paul, after his conversion, becomes the prime example of this expansion as he travels throughout the northeastern Mediterranean area devoting himself to a mission predominantly focused on Gentiles.

As Jesus' journey led to Jerusalem, so Paul's journey leads to Rome. At the end of Acts, Paul is preaching the gospel in Rome "quite openly and without hindrance" (28:31). The Gospel of Luke begins its story of Jesus' ministry in the outlying Jewish region of Galilee and concludes in the Jewish capital, Jerusalem; the book of Acts begins in an outlying region of the empire, Jerusalem, and concludes in the empire's capital, Rome. Evidently Luke designed his two books to show the Christian movement continually expanding toward increasingly influential areas.

In Acts, as the Christian movement expands outward, increasingly embracing Gentiles, it seems increasingly alienated from Jewish people. Many passages in Acts show Jews as well as Gentiles becoming Christian: "At Iconium similarly they went into the Jewish synagogue and spoke to such purpose that a large body of Jews and Greeks became believers. But the unconverted Jews stirred up the Gentiles and poisoned their minds against the Christians" (14:1–2). James and the elders in Jerusalem say to Paul, "You see, brother, how many thousands of converts we have among the Jews, all of them staunch upholders of the Law" (21:20). Acts' message is that the mission to the Gentiles followed upon the mission to the

Jews, and Gentiles began to predominate because relatively few Jews chose to become Christians. Neither in Acts nor in history is there a point in the first century when the movement gave up altogether on the conversion of Jewish people and focused exclusively on Gentiles.

Luke's perspective is in agreement with that of modern scholars. At first the Christian movement reached out to Jewish people. This effort was somewhat successful, but limited. The movement then began to attract Gentile converts and, largely through Paul's efforts, began to achieve great success among Gentiles. Luke's two books tell the story of how Gentiles began to predominate in the movement.

Jesus' Mission to the Jews

According to the Gospel of Luke, during his lifetime Jesus spoke virtually only to Jews. Luke is quite careful to show Jesus traveling only within Jewish areas. This may help to answer a problem in Luke's use of Mark for, curiously, Luke omits everything from Mark 6:45 to 8:26. Some scholars believe Luke possessed a copy of Mark from which those passages were missing and so Luke did not know of the passages he did not use. Others look at the passages in Mark and find most of them redundant or not in accord with various of Luke's main themes. They suspect Luke found them to be inappropriate for several reasons:

First, they show Jesus traveling in non-Jewish regions (Tyre and Sidon, the Decapolis) and speaking to Gentile people. Luke sought to portray Jesus as devoting himself to Jewish territory and to Jewish people.

Second, Luke gives an account of the miraculous multiplication of loaves and fishes in 9:10–17 (using Mark 6:30–44) and may have thought it unnecessary to repeat the story as Mark did in 8:1–10. Luke's omissions begin after the first multiplication story and end shortly after the second. He also may have chosen not to repeat Mark's story of the blind man of Bethsaida because he found it to duplicate Mark's account of blind Bartimaeus, which he did use.

Third, Mark 7:1–23 does not support the necessity for Jewish people to follow all the Law of Moses. Luke believes the Jewish people remained obliged to follow the Law. An examination of Luke's use of Mark by means of gospel parallels will reveal that Luke tends to omit material with which he disagrees. Luke is quite seriously concerned with Jews and Gentiles and the different responsibilities of each group.

Fourth, Luke believes Mark went too far in his criticism of Jesus' disciples, and so, like Matthew, Luke modified many of the passages in Mark that were critical of them. One of the harshest criticisms in Mark is found in Mark 8:14–21. Matthew's version tones down this criticism (Matt 16:5–12); Luke omits it altogether.

Compromises in Luke/Acts

Luke accepts the tradition, probably transmitted by the Jerusalem church, that Jesus came to Jewish people and traveled in Jewish territory. The Gospel of Luke takes this point of view. So also does the Gospel of Matthew, in which Jesus is quoted as saying, "Do not take the road to Gentile lands, and do not enter any Samaritan town; but go rather to the lost sheep of the house of Israel" (Matt 10:6).

Luke also accepts the tradition that the gospel should be preached to all nations (to Gentile people), a tradition that, if not begun by Paul, certainly had Paul as a major advocate. The book of Acts takes that point of view, as does the concluding passage in Matthew's gospel. But we should remember that not everyone in the first century agreed with this perspective. First-century Christians disagreed about whether the gospel was for Jews or for everyone. Luke's books present a compromise by turning an apparent conflict into a matter of a change in time and circumstance: in the beginning the gospel came to Jews in Jewish territory; later it came to Gentiles in the whole of the empire. This point of view may or may not be historically valid, but it grew out of an attempt to harmonize two different perspectives. Luke's compromise eventually was accepted throughout the Christian church, but in the first century it was a compromise and not a universally accepted opinion.

Luke was confronted with another problem. Some Christians, and Paul is an example, believed the Law of Moses was no longer in force for Christians. Other Christians, and Matthew is an example, believed the Law of Moses did remain in force for Christians. These are not easily reconcilable positions. Luke sought to reconcile them, believing Peter and James and Paul all taught the true gospel.

Luke reports a compromise in regard to the Law. James and the elders of Jerusalem say the following to Paul:

> "You see, brother, how many thousands of converts we have among the Jews, all of them staunch upholders of the Law. Now they have been given certain information about you: it is said that you teach all the Jews in the gentile world to turn their backs on Moses, telling them to give up circumcising their children and following our way of life. What is the position, then? They are sure to hear that you have arrived. You must therefore do as we tell you. We have four men here who are under a vow; take them with you and go through the ritual of purification with them, paying their expenses, after which they may shave their heads. Then everyone will know that there is nothing in the stories they were told about you but that you are a practising Jew and keep the Law yourself. As for the gentile converts, we sent them our decision that they must abstain from meat that has been offered to idols, from blood, from anything that has been strangled, and from fornication."

So Paul took the four men, and next day, after going through the ritual of purification with them, he went into the temple to give notice of the date when the period of purification would end and the offering be made for each one of them (Act 21:21–26).

In the above passage, the Law is different for Christians of Jewish background and Christians of Gentile background. The Torah Law must to be obeyed by Jewish Christians including Paul himself. Gentile Christians, on the other hand, must obey precisely four of those laws, a decision found also in Acts 15:19 and 15:29. The four may derive from passages in Leviticus chapters 17 and 18, where they are designated for both the non-Jews and the Jews who live in Jewish territory.

According to Acts, this compromise is agreeable to Paul, but would the Paul who wrote Galatians and the other letters have agreed that his Gentile converts must keep a section of the Law? Paul thinks in black-and-white terms; either one seeks salvation through Law or one receives salvation through faith. To seek salvation through faith and a little bit of the Law if you are Gentile and through faith and all the Law if you are Jewish is a compromise Paul could not possibly have accepted. Socially, such a compromise would have led to the division between Jewish and Gentile Christians at meals, and Paul fought against all such sources of division.

Luke seems to have recognized this problem, so he portrays Peter, one of the disciples who usually supported the observance of Law, as having a revelation that changed his mind. Peter, Luke twice informs us, saw a vision from God:

> He saw a rift in the sky, and a thing coming down that looked like a great sheet of sail-cloth. It was slung by the four corners, and was being lowered to the ground. In it he saw creatures of every kind, whatever walks or crawls or flies. Then there was a voice which said to him, "Up,

Peter, kill and eat." But Peter said, "No, Lord, no: I have never eaten anything profane or unclean." The voice came again a second time: "It is not for you to call profane what God counts clean." This happened three times; and then the thing was taken up again into the sky (Acts 10:11–16).

According to Luke, by this means God made all foods clean, and so the social divisions the food laws would bring about, and which so worried Paul, were to be avoided. We know from Paul's eyewitness account of a meeting with Peter (Gal 2:11–14) that although Peter sometimes dined with Gentiles, he agreed to stop when ordered to stop by James, an action Paul regarded as treachery. It is difficult, therefore, to believe Luke's account that Peter received a message from God announcing that all foods are clean.

Luke's books are, in part, compromises made necessary by the various developments of first-century Christianity. Luke conceded to Jewish Christians that Jesus upheld the whole Law. He therefore omitted the portion of Mark in which Jesus is said to have made all foods clean. Instead, he established the principle later by attributing it to Peter's vision. From that point on, the food laws are suspended for Jewish and Gentile Christians alike, while all other laws, apparently, remain in effect for Jewish Christians.

Luke's compromise position—that Gentiles keep only a limited portion of the Law—would not have satisfied either Paul or his opponents. Matthew and James surely would not have agreed that the food laws were no longer in force, and Paul would not have agreed that Christians, especially Gentile Christians, should be required to follow any of the Law.

Luke's compromise did ultimately prevail, but in a different form. Rather than the four laws for Gentiles specified in Acts, most Christians believe ten laws to be required: the Ten Commandments.

Luke, in the later first century, faced some of the problems analytical students of the New Testament face today. How is it that traditions say Jesus came only to Jews and yet the church is composed primarily of non-Jewish people? How can we reconcile Paul's teachings of freedom from the Law with teachings that Law must be obeyed strictly? Luke's answers appear in his books—or, rather, his books are his answer.

Recurring Themes

Sources

Luke's gospel is based on the Gospel of Mark. His gospel begins to follow Mark at Luke 3:3 and ceases to do so at Luke 24:5. He supplements Mark at the beginning with a birth narrative and at the end with an account of Jesus' resurrection appearances. As discussed previously, Luke omits Mark 6:45–8:26. The remainder of Mark he uses in sections. He alternates sections dependent on Mark with sections derived from his other two major sources, Q and Special Luke.

Luke uses Q extensively and evidently regards it as a reliable source for Jesus' teachings, since he seldom revises either its sayings or the order in which the sayings are presented. Matthew, on the other hand, often revises Q sayings and ignores Q's order of sayings, rearranging them into his five sections of discourse.

Many of the passages in Special Luke (meaning material found only in Luke's gospel) probably existed in oral tradition before Luke wrote them down. Some scholars have tried to identify a written collection of sayings, similar to Q, from which much Special Luke material may have come, but their theories have not been widely accepted. Some of the sayings and stories in the Special Luke material may have been composed by the author Luke, as were many transitions, scene settings, and commentaries on sayings in his gospel.

For his story of the births of Jesus and John the Baptist, Luke may have used oral and written traditions from followers of John the Baptist. The two poems in chapter 1 perhaps came from John's followers; they contain no specifically Christian themes.

It is relatively easy to discuss the sources of the Gospel of Luke, because we can compare it with the other synoptic gospels and, to a limited degree, with the Gospel of John. Because Acts is unique, however, our ability to determine what sources Luke used for it is very limited.

Most speeches in Acts were written by Luke and convey his idea of what the apostles would have said; he does not use written speeches of Peter or Paul as sources. There is no evidence Luke was familiar with Paul's letters. The long historical account attributed to Stephen (7:1–53) is written in a style more directly influenced by Hebrew constructions than are other sections of Acts and so was probably not composed by Luke.

Luke probably had a variety of sources of information to work with, some from followers of Peter and James, others from followers of Paul and Paul's associates. No two scholars now agree on which passages came from which sources, with one exception. On one source scholars agree; it is called the "we" source.

Most of Acts is written in the third person: "They did this, they went there," and so forth. But occasionally passages appear written in the first person: "We did this, we went there." Although this may be a literary device used by Luke to make his book more interesting and give it more immediacy, it is more likely Luke had access to the travel diary of someone who journeyed with Paul. The "we" passages contain many details, but few are important in either a theological or a historical sense. The "we" passages are Acts 16:10–18,

20:4–21:18, 27:1–28:16. The details they contain give the "we" passages a definite ring of eyewitness truth. For example, Acts 27:4–8, part of the account of Paul's journey to Rome, reads,

> Leaving Sidon we sailed under the lee of Cyprus because of the head-winds, then across the open sea off the coast of Cilicia and Pamphylia, and so reached Myra in Lycia. There the centurion found an Alexandrian vessel bound for Italy and put us aboard. For a good many days we made little headway, and we were hard put to it to reach Cnidus. Then, as the wind continued against us, off Salmone we began to sail under the lee of Crete, and, hugging the coast, struggled on to a place called Fair Havens, not far from the town of Lasea.

It is difficult to imagine that such interesting but insignificant details were invented.

Jesus

For Luke, Jesus' life is an important introduction to his exalted role as risen Messiah. Jesus' teachings and activities are so significant to Luke that he substantially supplements Mark's account of them. Nevertheless, Acts shows that Luke believes Jesus' primary powers and responsibilities were given him after his death.

Jesus, during his life, was Son of Man and, in Luke's opinion, a prophet capable of doing miracles to provide evidence of his messianic role. His life is a model for the lives of later followers, especially apostles, who are expected to live as he did and do what he did. Acts shows them doing this even to the point of death; Jesus' last words are echoed, with slight alteration, by Stephen's last words (Acts 7:59–60).

Jesus' death does not itself bring salvation, in Luke's opinion. He omits the key element in the crucial Mark passage,

"For even the Son of Man did not come to be served but to serve, and to surrender his life as a ransom for many" (Mark 10:45), altering it to read, "For who is greater, the one who sits at table or the servant who waits on him? Surely the one who sits at the table. Yet here am I among you like a servant" (Luke 22:27). For Luke, Jesus is the servant of God and of humanity; his death is ordained by God and serves as the prologue to his resurrection and exaltation. Jesus is shown by Luke always to be obedient to God. His death is his greatest act of obedience.

Jesus' main role comes after his death. Here Luke's ideas differ from those of Matthew (who believed Jesus' teaching during his life to have been crucial) and Paul (who believed his death to have been of cosmic significance). Although both Matthew and Paul would agree Jesus remained active in the church and present among his people after his ascension, it is in Luke that we find this idea most strongly stressed. Jesus, in Acts, sends the Holy Spirit to all who receive it (Acts 2:33), and Jesus receives it back from those who die (Acts 7:59). Until the ascension, the Holy Spirit had always been sent, and received back, by God. After his death people are healed "in Jesus' name," and sins are forgiven "in Jesus' name." In the future he will return on clouds of glory to usher in the Kingdom of God.

Eschatology

Luke's understanding of the end of this world and its replacement by the Kingdom of God is not very different from that of his sources. He alters Mark's chapter 13 only in details and does not seem to have modified Q sayings about the end very much. But Luke does not expect the end to come immediately. First there will be a time for the church, a period of history when the Christian movement will spread throughout the empire. The very fact that Luke wrote Acts indicates he believes a period of some considerable duration will take place between the crucifixion and the return of the Son of Man. Still, Luke, like Matthew, quotes Mark 13:30 without significant alteration, "Truly, I say to you this generation will not pass away before all these things take place." The two later evangelists apparently did sometimes believe the end to be as immediate as did the Q people, Paul, and Mark, all of whom believed it likely to occur during their own lifetimes.

Torah Law

In Acts, Luke reports that various factions in the early church agreed that the Torah Law was in effect for Christians of Jewish origin. There was one exception, the food laws, which were suspended in accord with a vision supposedly granted to Peter. Christians of Gentile origin, however, were required to obey only four laws: not to eat blood (that is, meat with blood still in it), not to eat the meat of creatures strangled (and which, therefore, would still contain blood), not to eat meat offered to idols, and not to engage in sexual intercourse outside of marriage. Luke depicts these compromises regarding Law arising during the period of the church and depicts Jesus, during his lifetime, as wholly upholding the Law.

Community

By the time of Luke's writing, the Christian church had become a widespread and successful movement. Churches met in private houses in many places. A central authority structure existed in Jerusalem under the leadership of James and his associates. Paul and a host of other apostles successfully spread the message about Jesus to many areas. People as diverse as wealthy Greek women, priests of the Jerusalem temple (Acts 6:7), the treasurer of the kingdom of Ethiopia (8:27), and some leaders of the Jewish community in Rome (28:24) are reported to have joined.

Luke portrays the Christian church as diverse but ultimately united, as a widespread movement capable of finding ways to handle problems arising from differences of background and of belief. Acts indicates that although Hellenistic and Palestinian Jewish Christians initially quarreled about financial support for widowed women, they came to a satisfactory agreement (Acts 6:1–16). Although there was some mutual distrust between the mission to Jews led by James and the mission to Gentiles led by Paul, Acts reports that a compromise regarding the Law was successfully worked out (21:21–26).

These successful compromises may be an ideal vision rather than matters of historical record, but they say something significant about Luke and his books. He was tolerant of diversity and sought pragmatic solutions to conflict rather than demanding that one side give in to the other. Such an attitude was essential if the church was to prosper as an empire-wide social institution. Its eventual success was largely due to the tradition of compromise evidenced in Luke's books.

Controversy

Both the leaders of the Jewish people and multitudes of Jewish people are repeatedly depicted as actively hostile to the Christian movement. The conflict depicted in Luke/Acts is between Jewish authority and Christian teachers. It was, so Luke reports, Jewish people who caused the death of Jesus, who killed Stephen, who sought Paul's death. This attitude has caused some to label Luke as anti-Semitic.

Luke is not anti-Semitic. He is, rather, pro-Roman. He does not want the Roman Empire to believe it has anything to fear from the Christian movement, or that Jesus was in any way a traitor to the empire, or that Paul was anything but a good and loyal citizen of Rome.

Roman authorities did persecute and even execute Christians (the prime case being the execution of Jesus). This demonstrates that Christians were perceived as threats to the empire by various imperial officials. Luke denies the truth of this perception. As he cannot deny the fact of persecution or the fact of the crucifixion, he shifts blame from Roman authority to Jewish authority. His motive may have been that while Jewish antagonism did not endanger the lives of Christians living outside of Palestine, Roman antagonism did. Rather than reveal that some persecution came from Roman and some from Jewish authority, Luke's books portray all persecution as coming from Jews.

Interactions

Miracles Sources

Jesus, Luke writes in one of the speeches in Acts, was a man chosen by God and "made known to you through miracles, portents, and signs, which God worked among you through him" (Acts 2:22). This is the attitude toward miracles held by those who compiled the miracles sources. Throughout the Gospel of Luke and Acts, Jesus—and subsequently his apostles—brings faith to people through miraculous actions. Miracles are evidence of the Holy Spirit's presence in both Luke's and Paul's opinion (see Gal 3:5).

Luke includes a few stories of miracles in addition to those he took from Mark, but he seems to have used no extensive sources. The Special Luke miracle stories are 5:1–6; 7:11–16; 13:10–17; 14:1–6; and 17:12–19. Luke may have had a source for part of Acts listing miracles done by Peter, but this is uncertain (see for example, Acts 3:1–10; 5:1–11; 9:9–25; and 10:36–43).

The Q Source

Luke supplements Mark by extensive use of sayings from the Q source. He modifies them little, as far as we can tell, apparently sympathizing with the impoverished people to whom the sayings are directed. The way of life of the Q people is mirrored in the lives of the apostles in Acts, who are itinerant and dependent upon the conversion of strangers for food and shelter. The apostles in Acts, however, are rarely seen to go hungry and thirsty, to be penniless or without a place to lay their heads and rest. Thus, Luke is less realistic than Q is about the difficulties of the itinerant life. The way of life of those converted in Acts who are not apostles is not radical, and their former social networks remain intact.

Paul

To Luke, Paul is a hero. Although Acts begins with accounts of the ministries of Peter, Philip, and others, it eventually focuses exclusively on the ministry of Paul. As Luke presents it, parallels exist between the careers of Paul and Jesus. Paul began in Jerusalem, and his mission culminated in Rome, the capital of the empire; Jesus began in Galilee and his mission culminated in Jerusalem, the capital of Judea. Both, unlike John the Baptist, received the Holy Spirit as adults, and both performed miracles. Like Jesus, Paul was persecuted by Jewish leaders and, like Jesus, did nothing to offend Roman authority. As Jesus was found innocent by Pilate (Luke 23:13–15), so Paul found protection by appealing to Caesar. As King Herod Antipas found Jesus innocent, so King Herod Agrippa found Paul innocent (Acts 26:31).

Luke does not know Paul's teachings well. What Paul is said to be accused falsely of doing (Acts 21:21), he probably did do, or at least he did something of the sort, but the compromise presented in Acts—that Jews follow all Law but the food laws, and that Gentiles follow four of the laws—would not have satisfied Paul. Paul was not a compromiser: "When you seek to be justified by way of law, your relation with Christ is completely severed: you have fallen out of the domain of God's grace" (Gal 5:4). Although Paul describes a compromise he reached with James in Jerusalem (Gal 2:1–8), it was only in regard to spheres of influence, not matters of central doctrine.

In Paul's letters we read Paul's view of Jesus; in Acts we read Luke's view of Paul's view of Jesus; in this textbook, the author's view of Luke's view, and so forth. This kind of interpretive transmission is inevitable in human communication. Your view of what you read in this book constitutes another step in the same transmission.

Mark

Luke's gospel depends for its biographical outline on the Gospel of Mark. As Matthew does, Luke revises Mark to eliminate perspectives he did not share and to add perspectives he found missing.

Luke's respect for the disciples of Jesus leads him frequently to diminish the criticism of them found in Mark. Although Luke agrees the Son of Man was destined to suffer, die, and rise again, he does not emphasize that suffering and death as strongly as Mark did. For Luke the miracles Jesus did are valid grounds for faith; Mark's gospel seems skeptical of this.

The resurrection appearances in Luke show that before the resurrection Jesus' disciples understood him differently than they did after the resurrection. Before it, they believed "he was the man to liberate Israel" and "a prophet powerful in speech and action" (Luke 24:19–21). Although Luke and Mark seem to agree that the disciples initially misunderstood Jesus, Luke alone indicates that after Jesus' resurrection his followers came to understand correctly. Mark's gospel gives us no reason to think they ever understood.

Luke revises Mark's account of Jesus' travels so that he is shown always to have remained on Jewish territory and usually to have spoken to Jewish people. Mark shows Jesus traveling in Gentile regions and speaking to Gentile people and reports that Jesus canceled the food laws (see especially Mark 7). In Luke's account, Jesus suspends none of the Law. Such differences of opinion seem to have led Luke to omit much of Mark's chapters 6, 7, and 8.

Matthew

Luke's gospel and Matthew's gospel are very similar in their overall structure. Both authors revised Mark by adding Q sayings, adding a resurrection appearance story, adding a birth narrative, and reconfiguring the journeys of Jesus. It seems impossible that they should have done these things just coincidentally. It is most likely that Luke heard Matthew once. Bear in mind that ancient books were read aloud and that Christian gospels were designed to be read aloud to Christian audiences. We know that Luke owned and used written copies of Mark and of Q, and therefore, of course, Luke was very familiar with those texts. When Luke heard Matthew's gospel read aloud, Luke immediately knew what Matthew had done, that he had revised Mark, added Q, added a birth story, and so forth. Luke then decided to do that same thing, producing his own book. Matthew would then have been one of the "many authors" to whom Luke in the first sentences of his gospel. This scenario does not mean that Matthew is a source for Luke's work or that Luke used Matthew, just that Matthew's gospel inspired Luke to write a similar gospel of his own and, one might add, that presumably Luke thought his own version of the story of Jesus would make a better prologue to his book of the Acts of the Apostles than either Matthew's or Mark's version would.

Luke and Matthew agree that the disciples of Jesus were reasonably loyal and reasonably responsive to Jesus' teachings during his life. Both agree that they ultimately understood him. Despite differences of approach, both agree Mark's gospel should be substantially revised.

Luke does not believe, as Matthew does, that one of Jesus principal purposes was to ensure the Torah be followed fully. Luke assumes his readers agree that Jewish Christians should follow Torah Law, so he does not stress obedience.

Luke agrees with Matthew that the miracles of Jesus are good evidence for his special status. Both supplement the miracle stories they find in Mark. Matthew heightens them; Luke adds a few others from his special sources.

Although Luke's and Matthew's gospels are structurally different, conceptually they are similar. In their own ways, both restructure Mark. Both add Q sayings, birth narratives, and stories of resurrection appearances. The differences are matters of emphasis rather than of central opinion. Luke's emphasis on women is missing in Matthew; Matthew's emphasis on the fulfillment of prophecy is greater than that in Luke's gospel (although Luke's emphasis on fulfillment of prophecy is strong in Acts). Matthew revises Q sayings to make them acceptable to middle-class people; Luke does not revise them much but adds several sayings directed toward the wealthy.

Matthew would have disagreed strongly with one important aspect of Acts. The suspension of the food laws through the vision of Peter and the position attributed to both James and Paul that Gentile Christians need keep only a small portion of the Law would absolutely have contradicted the following thesis found in Matthew:

> So long as heaven and earth endure, not a letter, not a stroke, will disappear from the Law until all that must happen has happened. If any man therefore sets aside even the least of the Law's demands, and teaches others to do the same, he will have the lowest place in the kingdom of Heaven (Matt 5:18–19).

Otherwise, however, much of what we read in Acts is summarized in Matthew's quotation of the commandment of the risen Christ:

> Full authority in heaven and on earth has been committed to me. Go forth therefore and make all nations my disciples; baptize men everywhere in the name of the Father and the Son and the Holy Spirit, and teach them to observe all that I have commanded you. And be assured, I am with you always, to the end of time (Matt 28:18–20).

All the apostles in Acts acted accordingly.

End-of-Chapter Exercises

1. Identify 2–3 main principals in Luke's gospel. What influence might his community have had on the way Luke depicted figures like John the Baptist and Pontius Pilate?
2. Why do you think women play such a prominent role in Luke/Acts compared to other gospels?
3. Read Paul's Letter to the Romans, chapter 1 and 2. In those chapters he is discussing the place of Gentiles in God's plan. This he also does in the speech in Acts 17:22–31. Construct an argument either to show the two discussions are saying essentially the same thing or to show they are saying different things.

Bibliography

Barrett, C.K. *Luke the Historian in Recent Study.* Eugene OR: Wipf & Stock Publishers, 2009.

Bock, Darrell. *Acts: Baker Exegetical Commentary on the New Testament.* Grand Rapids MI: Baker Books, 2007.

Conzelmann, Hans. *The Theology of St. Luke.* Philadelphia: Fortress Press, 1982.

Edwards, O. C., Jr. *Luke's Story of Jesus*. Philadelphia: Fortress Press, 1981.

Ellis, E. E. *The Gospel of Luke*. Grand Rapids: Eerdmans, 1981.

Fitzmyer, Joseph A. *The Gospel of Luke*. New York: Doubleday, 1981.

Green, Joel. *The Gospel of Luke: New International Commentary on the Greek Testament*. Grand Rapids MI: Eerdmans, 1997.

Haenchen, E. *The Acts of the Apostles*. Philadelphia: Westminster Press, 1971.

Hengel, Martin. *Acts and the History of Earliest Christianity*. Philadelphia: Fortress Press, 1980.

Jervill, J. *Luke and the People of God*. Minneapolis: Augsburg Publishing House, 1972.

Keck, Leander E., and J. Martyn, eds. *Studies in Luke Acts*. Philadelphia: Fortress Press, 1980.

Pervo, Richard I. *The Mystery of Acts: Unraveling Its Story*. Salem OR: Polebridge Press, 2008.

Parsons, Mikeal, and Richard Pervo. *Rethinking the Unity of Luke and Acts*. Minneapolis MN: Fortress Press, 1993.

Polhill, John. *Acts—The New American Commentary*. Volume 26. Nashville TN: Holman Reference, 1992.

Tiede, David L. *Prophecy and History in Luke Acts*. Philadelphia: Fortress Press, 1980.

The Gospel of John

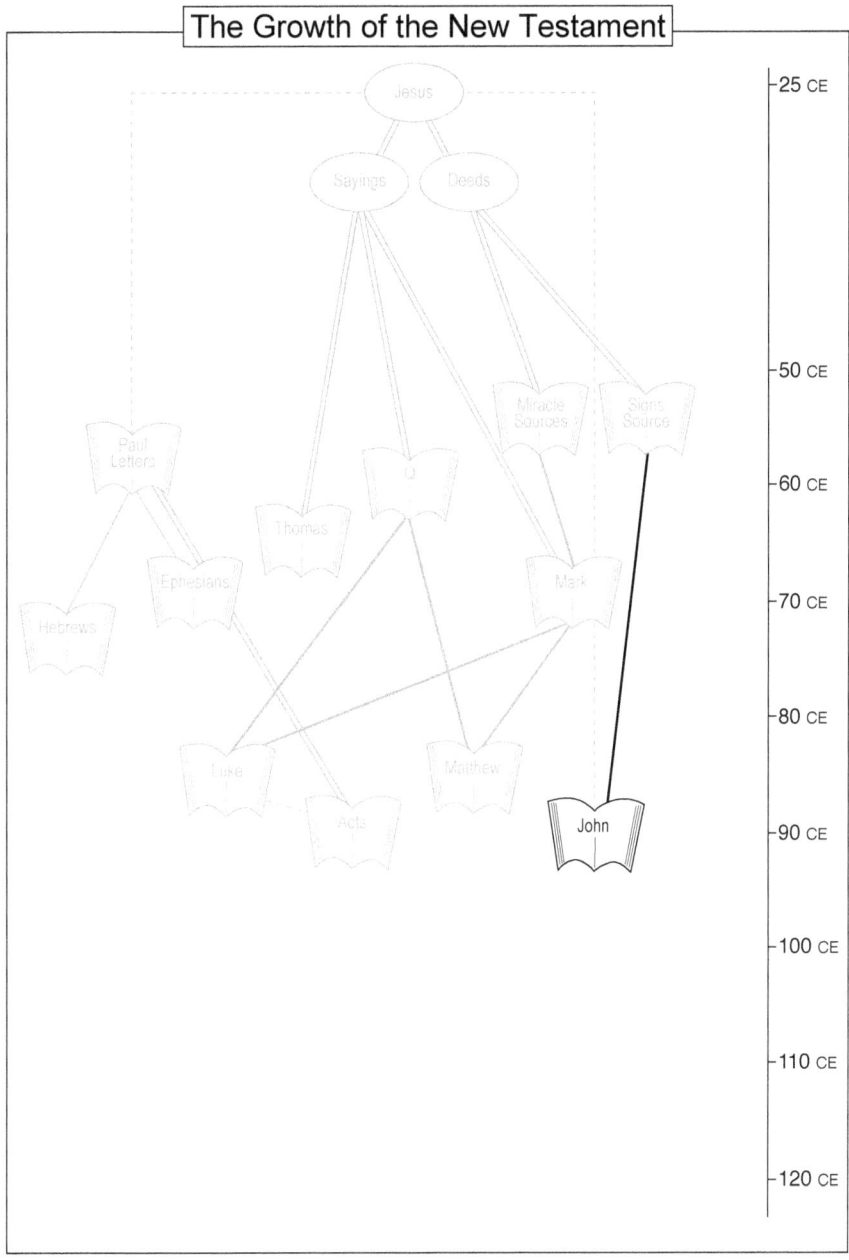

Dashed lines: indirect influence
Double lines: oral transmission
Single thick lines: use of written source
Thin lines: followers, admirers & imitators

CHAPTER 8

The Gospel of John

OBJECTIVES
- Find out what constitutes John's distinctiveness among the gospels in terms of content, structure, and authorship
- Evaluate John's negative depictions of "the Jews" as a collective group
- Investigate the God-world dichotomy that permeates John's narrative and the role this might have played in John's community

The Gospel of John is very different from the synoptic gospels. The ministry of Jesus takes place over a three-year period rather than for only one year. The style of speech attributed to Jesus is not at all the same as it is elsewhere. In John, we frequently find long discourses continuing on for many paragraphs, whereas in the synoptics Jesus' speech (even when collected into discourse sections) consists of short parables, debates, proverbs, and comments. However, while the order of events in Jesus' life differs to some extent from that in the synoptics, the overall biographical outline is the same.

Some scholars divide the gospel into two major parts: a Book of Signs (1:19–12:50) and a Book of Glory (13:1–20:31), preceded by an introductory poem and followed by a chapter of resurrection appearances. In the Book of Signs, Jesus reveals himself primarily through miracles, signs, and wonders. In the Book of Glory, revelation comes primarily through his words and his resurrection.

<u>READ THE GOSPEL OF JOHN. UNDERLINE THE PASSAGES IN WHICH JESUS SAYS "I AM . . ." SUCH AS, "I AM THE LIGHT OF THE WORLD." ALSO UNDERLINE THE PASSAGES IN WHICH JESUS CLAIMS TO HAVE COME FROM ABOVE, OR FROM THE FATHER, AND THOSE IN WHICH JESUS DECLARES HE WILL RETURN</u>

ABOVE, OR TO THE FATHER. The "I am" passages you underline will highlight an important and unique feature of John; the others will enable you to see more clearly the most important themes in John's gospel.

Author, Date, and Place of Origin

After a century or more of study and debate, scholars who analytically study the New Testament have found themselves in general agreement on one point: the Gospel of John is the product of a complex process of creation involving the work of several individuals over a period of years. The gospel seems to have been edited and reedited. Various passages seem to have been shifted from their original location to other locations. For example, it is likely that chapter 7 originally followed chapter 5, for it continues the thought of 5 and takes place in the same region. Chapter 6 seems to have been inserted between them at some later time. Other passages seem to have been written as additions to earlier material. It has been suggested, for example, that John 3:31–36; 5:51–58; 8:1–59; 12:44–50; 15:1–17:26; and 21:1–18, 20–22, were added by a later author to sections he found already in existence. At the end of chapter 14, for example, after delivering several discourses, Jesus says, "So up, let us go forward!" (14:31), but the discourses continue to 18:1 when, "after these words, Jesus went out with his disciples, and crossed the Kedron ravine." Apparently 15:1–17:26 was inserted right after 14:31. Chapter 17, an extended prayer by Jesus, may have been written independently and then added to the end of the section 15:1–16:33. The passage John 7:53–8:11 is out of place in its context, as well, and is written much more in the style of Luke's author than of John's. Today some translations place that passage at the very end of John's gospel.

Some scholars, recognizing John's original order has been altered, have attempted to reorganize the gospel, but they do not agree on what the proper order should be. Many scholars, recognizing the gospel has gone through a complex set of stages to arrive at its present form, have offered theories about what those stages were, but in this matter also there is no agreement.

John's is the only gospel to make any claim to eyewitness evidence. Shortly after Jesus' death, "one of the soldiers stabbed his side with a lance, and at once there was a flow of blood and water. This is vouched for by an eyewitness, whose evidence is to be trusted" (19:34–35). This person is evidently not the author of the gospel. Rather, he is someone whom the author uses to validate his own non-eyewitness account of this particular event. Chapter 21, at the very end of the gospel, may have been written separately, by an individual who had little or nothing to do with writing the other parts of the gospel. In chapter 21, "the disciple whom Jesus loved" is reported to be "this same disciple who attests what has here been written. It is in fact he who wrote it, and we know that his testimony is true" (21:24). The passage is probably meant to refer to chapter 21, rather than to the whole gospel.

"The disciple whom Jesus loved" can also be called "the Beloved Disciple." John's author seats the Beloved Disciple closest to Jesus during the Last Supper (13:23) and is careful to show him arriving at the tomb of Jesus first, beating Peter to the site in a race (20:4). Keeping in mind that we know nothing of him apart from what John's gospel tells us, there are no convincing reasons to believe the Beloved Disciple's name was John, or that he wrote the gospel.

Whoever the man named John was, he was not the same person who is responsible for the New Testament's last book, the Revelation of John, although an author of the Gospel of John may also have written the three Letters of John. Certainly those letters are quite similar to the gospel in their ideas and style, and probably were written by members of the same community as the gospel's author. Because the gospel was written over a period of years by several persons, it is misleading to use one name for its author, but to do otherwise would lead to great confusion. We shall refer to John as the author of the Gospel of John just as we call the unknown author of the Gospel of Matthew "Matthew," but in this case, John refers to more than one person.

The Greek in which John is written seems often to have been influenced by Semitic linguistic constructions. Therefore, most scholars believe it was written in an area where Aramaic was commonly used, perhaps Syria.

The date of John is debated. The earliest fragments of any gospel yet found are fragments of John, and are dated to the first half of the second century, yet the fact that John's gospel came into being through the work of a sequence of editors may indicate it was only toward the end of the first century that it finally was completed. On the one hand, some scholars believe it must have been written a considerable time after the life of Jesus because it contains an exalted view of Jesus as the Word of God come from God. On the other hand, Paul's view of Jesus is quite exalted, and his works are the earliest we have.

The gospel contains few sayings of Jesus from oral tradition, so many scholars assume it was written after the period of oral transmission was nearly over. It could be argued, however, that emphasis on orally transmitted sayings was a later development in Christianity, and sayings of Jesus received through spiritually inspired individuals were found to be satisfactory in the very earliest Christian communities. Paul, for example, depends more on personal inspiration than on oral tradition, a fact he emphasizes in the first part of Galatians. Significantly, the Gospels of Luke and Matthew make much more use of Jesus' sayings than does the earlier Gospel of Mark. The Gospel of Thomas begins by declaring that it contains the words the *living* Jesus spoke, which may be intended to contrast those words with traditions carrying forth words the *risen* Jesus spoke in his followers through the Spirit.

The fact is, we do not know when the gospel was written. Although the date CE 90 is frequently used for John, it is uncertain even in comparison with the inexact dating of the other gospels. Some scholars have argued it may even have been the first gospel written, and, while this is a minority view, it cannot be dismissed out of hand. Even if John's gospel went through a series of revisions, these revisions may have taken far fewer years than the decades many scholars believe were required.

The Beginning of the Gospel

The Gospel of John begins with a poem that probably existed long before the gospel was written. Possibly, it was written before the time of Jesus. As it stands, the poem is divided by inserted passages about John the Baptist. The following passages probably constitute the original: 1:1–5, 10–14, 16–17. The poem begins the gospel, and so we know it was important to the gospel's author, but it is possible to stress its importance too much. Many of the themes of the poem—that Jesus is the Word of God, for example—are never mentioned again.

The Greek term usually translated for "word" is *logos*. Logos is a complex term with broader meaning than the English term word. It can mean "reason," "organizing principle," "saying," or even "philosophical position." Teachings about the nature of life, for example, would be *bios* (life) logos, which gave rise to the word "biology."

The term "logos" was a key word in Greek philosophy of the first century. It is likely, however, that the poem at the beginning of John does not derive from Greek philosophical speculation; rather, it probably stems from Jewish speculations about the nature of the Wisdom of God. In the book of Proverbs, especially in chapter 8, the Wisdom of God is treated as a semi-independent aspect of God who was present at the creation and before creation, and who descends to earth to call human beings to live morally and to seek understanding. Often, as Proverbs reports, Wisdom's call is ignored. Nearly all of the attributes of the Word in the first chapter of John are attributes of Wisdom in Proverbs.

The term for Wisdom in Greek is *sophia*, a noun of feminine gender. "Logos" is a noun of masculine gender. It is possible that because Jesus was male, the masculine term "logos" was substituted for the feminine term, "sophia." If we experimentally substitute "Wisdom" for "Word," and read Proverbs 8, we can see that the following statements from John's introductory poem correspond with pre-Christian Jewish speculations about Wisdom:

> When all things began, Wisdom already was. Wisdom dwelt with God, and what God was, Wisdom was. Wisdom, then, was with God at the beginning, and through her all things came to be; no single thing was created without her. All that came to be was alive with her life, and that life was the light of men. The light shines on in the dark, and the darkness has never mastered it. . . . Wisdom was in the world; but the world, though it owed its being to her, did not recognize her. She entered her own realm, and her own would not receive her (John 1:1–4, 9–11).

The idea that "Wisdom became flesh" is absent from previous speculations. It is not, however, unique to John's gospel, for it is found in the Christian tradition as early as Paul's first letter to the Corinthians, in which he declares Christ is the Wisdom of God (1 Cor 1:24). The concept of Jesus as God's Word is unique to the community of John; the concept of Jesus as God's Wisdom can be found in several other New Testament texts and in the Gospel of Thomas.

Like the Gospel of Mark and the letters of Paul, the Gospel of John contains no story of Jesus' birth. One passage, however, implies he was born in Nazareth instead of Bethlehem and that his father was not a descendent of David (7:41–42); another passage assumes his father was Joseph (1:45). On these matters, John and the synoptic gospels seem to disagree.

Jesus' mission begins during the time of John the Baptist (not after John's arrest as other gospels report) and continues for three years. This number can be derived from the fact that the gospel mentions three Passover festivals.

At its beginning, the gospel takes care to make clear who Jesus is and asserts that at least some individuals recognized him correctly. In 1:29, John the Baptist declares he is "the Lamb of God," and in 1:34, Jesus is "God's Chosen One." Andrew and an unnamed associate call Jesus "Rabbi" (1:38) and then inform Simon Peter he is "Messiah" and "Christ" (1:41). Philip declares he is "the man spoken of by Moses in the Law, and by the prophets" (1:45), and Nathanial says he is "Son of God" and "King of Israel" (1:49). Finally, Jesus publicly implies he is "Son of Man" (1:51). The gradual revelation of the mission of the Son of Man, which characterizes Mark, and the delayed discovery of the testimony of the prophets that Luke reports (24:27) are absent here; Jesus' full complement of titles is announced immediately.

John the Baptist

Like the Gospel of Mark, John's gospel begins its story of Jesus' ministry with an account of his interactions with John the Baptist and even inserts passages referring to John into its introductory poem. More directly than in any other gospel, John the Baptist states his inferiority to Jesus and, indeed, denies that he has any significant purpose other than announcing the coming of Jesus. According to this gospel, John the Baptist was "sent from God; he came as a witness to testify to the light, that all might become believers through him. He was not himself the light; he came to bear witness to the light" (1:6–7). When asked who he was, John the Baptist "confessed without reserve and avowed, 'I am not the Messiah.' 'What then? Are you Elijah?' 'No,' he replied. 'Are you the prophet we await?' He answered, 'No'" (1:19–20). He declares Jesus to be the lamb of God who takes away the sin of the world, that Jesus is God's Chosen One, and that he, John, has seen "the Spirit coming down like a dove and resting upon [Jesus]" (1:29, 32–34).

John does not baptize Jesus, nor is his mission of baptizing given much significance in itself. Instead, his baptizing "in water" seems only to be a prelude to Jesus' baptizing "in Spirit."

The Ending of the Gospel

Like Matthew and Luke, John concludes his gospel with accounts of Jesus' appearances to his followers after his resurrection. The accounts of Jesus' trial, death, and empty tomb in John are sufficiently similar to the accounts in the synoptics to prove that John depends on established tradition for his version of these events.

There appear to be two separate accounts of the appearances of the risen Jesus. One is John 20:14–31; its final passage is a suitable conclusion for the whole gospel. The second, 21:1–25, was written at a different time by a different author.

One of the most interesting aspects of the resurrection appearance stories in John is that they alternate between elements affirming the physical body of Jesus and elements that do not. For example, Jesus mysteriously enters a locked room then immediately gives evidence to Thomas of his solid physical existence (20:26–27). The diverse nature of these accounts testifies to a diversity of opinion in the John community.

Pontius Pilate

In the Gospel of John, Pilate strenuously tried not only to avoid executing Jesus but to declare Jesus innocent. These efforts culminate in Pilate's declaration that Jesus is King of the Jews and imply his belief that his own authority derives from the Jewish God. At first Pilate urges the Jewish leaders to "take [Jesus] away and try him by your own law" (18:31). After their refusal and an interview with Jesus, Pilate declares, "I find no case against him" (18:38). He repeats this two times subsequently (19:4, 19:6). Having heard from Jesus that his (Pilate's) authority derives from God, "from that moment Pilate tried hard to release him" (19:12). This seems to imply Pilate concurs with Jesus' statement.

"The Jews" use political pressure to force Pilate to agree to the execution, arguing they will tell Pilate's superior, Caesar, that Pilate refused to execute someone who defied Caesar. Pilate gives in, supposedly "to satisfy" them. But, at the end, he writes an inscription reading, "Jesus of Nazareth the King of the Jews" and has it fastened to the cross. The Jews protest, wishing it to read "'He claimed to be King of the Jews,'" but Pilate refuses, saying, "What I have written, I have written" (19:19–22). This implies that Pilate concurs with the claim. In writing the account this way, John absolves Pilate of responsibility in Jesus' execution at least as emphatically as any of the other gospels. The abbreviation found at the top of crucifixes—"INRI"—comes from the Latin for "Jesus of Nazareth the King of the Jews," which is *Iesus Nazarenus Rex Iudaeorum*.

Instead of Pilate, "the Jews" are blamed. Only in John are Jesus' opponents called "the Jews." In other gospels, various factions of the Jewish leadership oppose Jesus—Pharisees, Chief Priests, Sadducees—but the inclusive term "the Jews" is not used. It bears repeating that the accounts in the gospels do not give an unbiased historical view of the trial and execution of Jesus. They seek to absolve those who owe their position to Rome (Pilate and Herod) and to shift the blame to others; the only others present are Jewish. While it is conceivable there may have been a kind of grand jury inquiry into Jesus' case by the Sanhedrin, a Jewish court dominated by priests and Sadducees, it is not possible that they or any other Jewish people could have forced Pilate to execute a person whom he declared to be innocent. Pilate, should he have done this, would have been guilty under Roman law of a serious crime and would have been subject to removal from office.

John's Teaching about Jesus

The Gospel of John contains two crucial interrelated statements about Jesus: he came from the Father into the world; he will leave the world and return to the Father (see 13:3, 16:25–30). In a sense, these comprise John's main gospel message. The gospel elaborates on those statements in substantial detail. The elaborations make seemingly complex claims about the nature and mission of Jesus, but they are based on quite a simple system of ideas. Much of the apparent complexity of the gospel derives from two factors: first, the gospel went through various hands in its composition and so contains the perspectives of a number of people; second, its relatively simple underlying ideas are expressed in several ways.

The basic system of ideas in John presupposes two aspects to reality. One is valued positively, the other negatively. These aspects may be thought of in a variety of ways: two realms or two dimensions or two levels or two forms of human existence. The primary image in John is of two levels, one above and one below, but it would be naive to think of them as a heaven up there and a world down here. Rather, the realm above is the place of God, light, life, truth, love, peace, unity, and all other positively valued aspects of existence. The realm below, the world, is the place of the devil, darkness, death, lies, hatred, conflict, disharmony, and all other negatively valued aspects of existence. Initially, human beings are in the realm below and Jesus in the realm above. Jesus comes into this realm, and those who believe in him become members of the realm above. Those who reject him do not. At times the gospel states the distinction between the two realms very directly. Jesus is quoted as having said to "worldly" individuals who oppose him, "You belong to this world below, I to the world above. Your home is in this world, mine is not" (8:23).

The physical world itself is not rejected by God. In John's most famous passage we read (in the often-quoted King James Version), "God so loved the world that he gave his only begotten Son, that whosoever believeth in him should not perish but have everlasting life" (3:16). The world as this physical place is loved, but the world as a realm contradictory to the realm above is repudiated. In most of the passages in John, the second, negative, sense of world is meant.

Even more than Paul, who believes that people made perfect through Christ remain subject to temptations of the flesh, John thinks dualistically, in black and white, without shades of gray. One is either of this world or of the world above; there are no alternatives.

Salvation

Before Jesus came, the people of this lower world were trapped. No transference to the higher world was possible. People remained subject to the devil, death, and darkness. As it was impossible for elements of the lower world to move to the higher world, the alternatives were either for the situation to remain static, with no transference possible, or for elements of the higher world to move to the lower world. Should elements of the higher world enter the lower world, then persons in the lower world might transfer themselves to the higher world through those elements. Jesus is from the higher world.

Although the gospel states that Jesus knows about the elements of the higher world and speaks of them and reveals them, the primary fact is that he *is* those elements. The "I am" sayings in John, found in no other gospel, do not simply speak poetically. When Jesus says, "I am the light of the world" (8:13) or "I am the way; I am the truth; I am the life" (14:6), he does not merely claim to know about those things or to teach about those things; he claims to *be* those things. If one comprehends or "finds" Jesus, one finds the light, way, truth, life. The proposition may also be inverted: if you find the light, way, truth, life, you find Jesus. There are no halfway measures, no people who have a little light and some life and a general grasp of the way.

John's gospel presents Jesus as one from above who has come below and, having gathered people to him, returns above. Those he gathered continue his mission and will join Jesus above. Thus, they have eternal life, light, and truth. Once Jesus has come, the possibility exists for people to come to Jesus. Even though he returned above, a new representative from the higher region has come down: the Holy Spirit, which unites and characterizes those with faith who are still in this world. In John, the Holy Spirit is called the *Paraclete*, meaning "advocate, representative, or helper."

The characteristics of the higher realm are characteristics of the person who has attained it. You cannot gradually attain them. Either you have them or you do not. Those who have life, in this sense, have a different kind of life than those who simply are biologically alive. Their life is eternal, the variety of life appropriate to the higher realm.

Unity

Because unity is a characteristic of the higher realm, those in that realm (including people alive in this world who have attained that realm) are unified with each other and with God. Jesus, because he is that realm and because he presents that realm to us is, therefore, unified with God. Often Jesus' words in John 10:30, "My Father and I are one," are taken to mean Jesus uniquely is God. But, in another place, he said, "If you loved me you would have been glad to hear that I was going to the Father; for the Father is greater than I" (14:28).

Jesus is united with the Father—the gospel leaves no doubt about that—but this unity is not unique to him; it is characteristic of all who have reached the higher realm. Chapter 17 stresses this overriding unity. In verses 20–23, Jesus prays, for those also who through their words put their faith in me; may they all be one: as you, Father, are in me, and I in you, so also may they be in us, that the world may believe that you did send me. The glory which you gave me I have given to them, that they may be one, as we are one; I in them and you in me, may they be perfectly one. Then the world will learn that you did send me, that you did love them as you did me.

Since they are in a state of unity appropriate to the higher realm, they should act accordingly; action in accord with such unity is love.

Jesus is not one thing and his followers another. As he came from above, so they who dwell with him or who have faith in him now come from above. Here, the saying "he who receives any messenger of mine receives me; receiving me, he receives the One who sent me" is interpreted most literally (John 13:20, found also in Q [Luke 10:16 and Matt 10:40]). There is no distinction among those who are of the higher realm; to hear a messenger of Jesus years after his death is still to hear Jesus, and, so, to hear God. The ideas of 13:20 are restated in 16:15 when Jesus addresses his followers and says, "All that the Father has is mine, and that is why I said, 'Everything that he makes known to you he will draw from what is mine.'"

It is hard to imagine that persons born in this world and dwelling in it like everybody else can suddenly achieve the ability to declare they come from above. Yet the logic of John's gospel leads one to believe this can be the case, for when one hears an individual claim to come from above, one does not hear that individual per se, but the Spirit of God speaking through the individual. After Jesus declares in chapter 10, "My Father and I are one" (10:30), the passage goes on to argue that Scripture (Psalm 82:6) demonstrates that those to whom the word of God is delivered, and who accept the word of God, are themselves Gods. Jesus declares in 8:42–47 that only those who listen to the words of God have the right to claim God is their father. Thus, the Gospel of John does not take the concept "children of God" lightly. Jesus is the preeminent child of God; those who have faith in him and continue his work are children of God as well.

Judgment

On the surface, the Gospel of John may seem inconsistent or even contradictory regarding the issue of judgment. Some passages imply that Jesus came to pass judgment on the world and those who hear him:

> It is for judgment that I have come into this world (9:39).

> The Father does not judge anyone, but has given full jurisdiction to the Son . . . As Son of Man, [I have] also been given the right to pass judgment . . . I cannot act by myself; I judge as I am bidden [by the Father] (5:22, 27, 30).

On the other hand, other passages imply he did not come to pass judgment at all:

> It was not to judge the world that God sent his Son into the world, but that through him the world might be saved (3:17).

> I pass judgment on no man, but if I do judge, my judgment is valid because it is not I alone who judge, but I and he who sent me (8:16).

> The man who puts his faith in [the Son] does not come under judgment; but the unbeliever has already been judged in that he has not given his allegiance to God's only Son (3:18).

The key passage is the last one quoted: John does not use the term "judgment" in the same way it is used in other New

Testament books in which "judgment" means "a decision rendered by God or the Son of Man on a person's fitness to receive eternal life." For John, "judgment" refers to the believer's decision.

The Father sends the Son. All inhabitants of the lower realm must then either choose to have faith in him and to believe he came from above, or choose to act against him. The correct choice is eternal life; the incorrect choice leaves one in darkness and in the realm of death. The correct choice does not "lead to" eternal life, or "eventually result in" eternal life. Eternal life is the immediate consequence of belief. The judgment promised or threatened in the future in other gospels and letters occurs in John in the present time. Your choice is your judgment. Eternal life is promised in other sources. In John it is present as soon as the right choice is made.

The Father, then, judges insofar as he sends the Son and thereby requires the judgmental choice to be made. The Son judges insofar as he is the determining factor concerning which choice must be made. But, really, individuals judge themselves, for it is their own choice. Clearly, judgment in John means something quite different than it means elsewhere in the New Testament. It is not judicial. There is no trial and no totaling up of sins, only the requirement that each individual choose to believe or not to believe. We may be reasonably confident that the rather inappropriate term "judgment" would not have been used in John had it not been firmly established in earlier Christian tradition.

Obedience to the Torah is not an important factor in John. Its legal sections are not relevant, although its authority as prophecy remains. Moses is not the lawgiver in John but an important prophet testifying to the coming of Jesus Christ. The most extended discussion of Law occurs in 7:19–

24, where Jesus, with argumentation that would have been acceptable to some Pharisees, contends that the act of healing on the Sabbath is acceptable under Mosaic Law. When it comes to Law in regard to Christians, defined here as those who have attained the higher realm, one new commandment is given: "Love one another" (13:34). As salvation comes instantly with belief, and the only commandment specifically given is to love one another, Torah Law has little significance. Jesus says, "This is the work that God requires: believe in the one whom he has sent" (6:29).

According to the account in John's gospel, Jesus came from the realm above, manifested himself so those who chose to believe might "dwell with him," ascended to the realm above, and, for a brief period, manifested himself to his followers after his death. Afterwards, in Jesus' absence from this lower realm, those dwelling in it can enter the realm above through the work of the Spirit. This term for Spirit, *Paraclete*, has legal connotations and is possibly connected to the idea of the Spirit found in Mark 13:11, that "when you are arrested and taken away [to court], do not worry beforehand about what you will say, but when the time comes say whatever is given you to say; for it is not you who will be speaking, but the Holy Spirit." In John, the presence of the Spirit provides the continuing presence of the higher realm in the lower and, accordingly, the continuing possibility for people to enter that realm.

Baptism and the Last Supper

Only in John is it reported that Jesus baptized anyone, and only in John is Jesus not said to have been baptized: "Jesus went into Judaea with his disciples, stayed there with them, and baptized. John, too, was baptizing at Aenon, near to

Salim, because water was plentiful in that region; and people were constantly coming for baptism. This was before John's imprisonment" (3:22–24). Later, however, the Pharisees hear "Jesus is winning and baptizing more disciples than John: (4:1). The gospel then amends this statement: "although, in fact, it was only the disciples who were baptizing and not Jesus himself." Evidently, at an earlier stage of the gospel, the tradition that Jesus did baptize people was accepted and included to show that even during John's ministry he came to surpass John as a baptizer. Later, the idea that Jesus baptized was retracted.

The passages on baptism are followed by a discussion between Jesus and a Samaritan woman at a well. Jesus declares he will give her "living water," which is "an inner spring always welling up for eternal life" (4:14). From John's perspective, Jesus is the living water (as the Holy Spirit will be later).

It is typical of John's gospel that a discussion of an historical event—the baptisms by John—shifts into a more metaphorical discussion of reception of "water and Spirit" and then into the identification of Jesus with the living water of eternal life. The discussion becomes increasingly abstract, but as it does so it moves increasingly close to the principal themes of the gospel. Recognition that the true water is Jesus, is akin to the recognition that the true air is the Spirit. One must know that *pneuma* is the Greek term for both wind and Spirit to understand 3:8, in which a discussion of Spirit shifts suddenly—but not inappropriately—to quotation of a proverb about wind.

John's account of the Last Supper, 13:1–17:26, is extremely long, yet the incident for which the Last Supper is most famous and which set the precedent for all subsequent communion meals—Jesus' statements "this is my body" and "this is my blood"—do not appear. The most significant action Jesus performs is to wash his disciples' feet and command his followers to do likewise (13:15).

Earlier in the gospel, following the signs source's account of the miraculous feeding of the five thousand (6:1–13), Jesus delivers a long discourse declaring himself to be the food of eternal life and the bread come down from heaven bringing life to the world (6:27, 34). (Recall that the miracles source in John is called the signs source because it uses the word "sign" instead of "miracle.") This discourse occurs in the context of a discussion of the incident when God sent manna from heaven to Moses' people in the desert (see Exodus 16:1–36). The discourse in chapter 6 progresses to a passage probably reflecting speculations about the communion meal:

> Unless you eat the flesh of the Son of Man and drink his blood you can have no life in you. Whoever eats my flesh and drinks my blood possesses eternal life, and I will raise him up on the last day. My flesh is real food; my blood is real drink. Whoever eats my flesh and drinks my blood dwells continually in me and I dwell in him (6:53–56).

Hearing this, many of his disciples exclaimed, "This is more than we can stomach! Why listen to such words?" (6:61). "From that time on, many of his disciples withdrew and no longer went about with him" (6:66). From the perspective of the Gospel of John, literal interpretations of Jesus' words, or of statements in the Hebrew Scriptures, will mislead. Many disciples, so the report goes, were literal in their interpretations and so were offended. The gospel intends Jesus' words instead to be interpreted symbolically. Jesus is the bread of life and living water, and therefore eating and drinking him are the equivalent of recognizing he has come from God.

The Origin of the Discourses of Jesus

There are various ways to think about the question of whose words are being quoted in the majority of the passages in the Gospel of John:

1. Possibly Jesus spoke them in Aramaic during his lifetime, and they were subsequently translated into the Greek versions in John. Few if any analytical scholars accept this alternative. Most of the words attributed to Jesus in John are too far out of accord in style and substance with the words attributed to Jesus in all other sources (the synoptics, Paul, and Thomas) for them to have been produced by the same person. All evidence indicates the style of sayings in the synoptics is basically that of Jesus, even though there is great debate as to exactly which of those sayings originate from Jesus.

2. Perhaps an author or authors wrote the words in Jesus' name. This theory is held, implicitly, by many scholars. The idea that discourses in John's gospel originated as written texts seems attractive at first. The gospel, after all, is a written document. Scholars speak of the sayings of Jesus in John as the products of community speculation and reflection on Christian faith, implying that theologically sophisticated community members wrote down words into the Gospel of John that they believed Jesus would have said. But it is not probable the sayings of Jesus found in John were written down by individuals in the privacy of their studies. Rather, the sayings appear to derive from an oral environment, that is, from spoken words and not from written texts.

3. Persons spoke the words in Jesus' name through the action of the Holy Spirit. This is the most likely origin of the discourses in John. They originally were actual speech presented publicly to actual people, some sympathetic but many unsympathetic. The discourses were then transcribed, either on the spot or from memory, and finally edited into

their present written form. The assumption that speech by later Christians would be the same as the speech of Jesus is inherent in the logic of John's system. To rephrase John 13:20, "He who writes down the words of a messenger of Jesus writes down the words of Jesus; writing down those words he writes down the words of the One who sent Jesus."

How should one in the community of John go about learning what Jesus taught? The writer of the gospel does not recommend researching ancient documents or discussing matters with elderly eyewitnesses. The answer is contained in the following statement attributed to Jesus: "I have told you all this while I am still here with you; but your Advocate, the Holy Spirit whom the Father will send in my name, will teach you everything, and will call to mind all that I have told you" (14:26). Therefore, John's gospel recommends that a person who wishes to determine what Jesus said, can either ask him during his lifetime in the world, or, later, ask one to whom the Holy Spirit has been sent.

The discourses in John derive from a period considerably after the crucifixion, and from individuals who spoke Greek rather than Aramaic. Their origin, therefore, derives from the Holy Spirit rather than from Jesus. Theoretically, this should make no difference, for otherwise it would be senseless for the gospel to declare that Jesus said the Holy Spirit would "teach you everything and call to mind all that I have told you." Insofar as people possessed of the Holy Spirit spoke what they heard from the Spirit, they would speak what Jesus spoke, or so the Johannine community believed.

Could later followers of Jesus, born again through the Spirit and thus united with the higher realm, declare they (not just Jesus personally, in Aramaic, during his life in Palestine) are "the way, the truth, and life?" Yes. John's gospel emphasizes the unity of all those who through Jesus enter the higher realm of God.

Only those who "come from above" can claim to reveal the God whom they have seen "above." All who have faith are united with Jesus (or the Spirit), who "comes from above." They too, therefore, can say they come from above. To have faith has a present-tense aspect, of course. Less obviously it also has a past-tense aspect (one has "come from above") and a future-tense aspect (one has "eternal life" and has passed through "judgment"). The Gospel of John can, without contradiction, switch tenses in midsentence: "I tell you, a time is coming, indeed it is already here, when the dead shall hear the voice of the Son of God, and all who hear shall come to life" (5:25). Events others assumed to be future are made present in this gospel: "Now is the hour of judgment for this world; now shall the Prince of this world be driven out" (12:31). To those who believe, the future is now.

In the community of John there presumably were people who had received the new Advocate, the Holy Spirit. If one accepted such people as messengers of Jesus, essentially one thereby received Jesus, and thus the One who sent Jesus. When such people spoke, their listeners heard God. That is asking a great deal of individuals. For them to claim to speak the words of God, to represent God, would lead inevitably to the kind of misunderstandings repeatedly evidenced in the gospel. Those who are messengers of Jesus, who have received the Holy Spirit and belong to the higher realm and can claim Jesus dwells in them, are revealers of God, as Jesus was. But revealers who say that hearing their words is the same as hearing God will, obviously, be accused of self-glorification and claiming to be God. Time after time the speaker in the gospel demands that his listeners not confuse him with the originator of the words spoken. The words invariably are said to derive from the Father.

Imagine a Christian man of the John community on a street corner declaring that his listeners' eternal fate depends on accepting his words as those of God. He would immediately be accused of extraordinary self-glorification. His response would be that he, personally, did not claim to be God and that he, personally, did not offer private opinions as revelations. Rather, he would insist that what he spoke through the Spirit was delivered to him from above and that he laid no claim to any personal glory at all.

Many discourses in the Gospel of John contain such disclaimers. Here are several examples:

> The teaching that I give is not my own; it is the teaching of him who sent me (7:16).

> I have not come of my own accord. I was sent by the One who truly is, and him you do not know. I know him because I come from him and he it is who sent me (7:28).

> I do nothing on my own authority, but in all that I say, I have been taught by my Father. He who sent me is present with me, and has not left me alone; for I always do what is acceptable to him (8:28–29).

> God is the source of my being, and from him I come. I have not come of my own accord; he sent me. Why do you not understand my language? It is because my revelation is beyond your grasp (8:42–43).

> When a man believes in me, he believes in him who sent me rather than in me; seeing me, he sees him who sent me . . . I do not speak on my own authority, but the Father who sent me has himself commanded me what to say and to speak (12:45, 49).

> I am not myself the source of the words I speak to you; it is the Father who dwells in me doing his own work (14:10).

> The word you hear is not mine; it is the word of the Father who sent me (14:24).

The very repetitiveness of these examples should add up to a solid impression: whoever is responsible for the words in the discourses in John is denying flatly, repeatedly, and emphatically that he is the source of his own words or authority. The discourses in the Gospel of John derive from Jesus, but not from the Jesus whose life story the gospel relates; they derive from Jesus in the sense that Jesus is the source of the Spirit of God in whose name a Spirit-inspired Christian prophet might speak.

Recurring Themes

Sources

The principal source for the sayings and discourses of Jesus in the Gospel of John is probably the transcribed speech of Spirit-inspired prophets of the John community. In addition, the gospel contains a few sayings from the same oral tradition used by the other evangelists. These few are usually edited to reflect the point of view of the gospel.

For the most part, however, John's source for the speech of Jesus appears to be the speech of Christian prophets speaking in the Spirit. If one imagines a Christian speaking in the Spirit, the speech of the Spirit will be about its own self, about its own nature. The Spirit perhaps would say "I come from the Father into the world." A member of the Johannine community might write this down and, quite logically in accordance with the point of view of that community, assume that Jesus had said the same thing in the Spirit. Accordingly, he might write down, "Jesus, speaking in the Spirit, said: 'I come from the Father into the world.'" But as time went on the community simplified this to "Jesus said, 'I come from the Father into the world.'" Johannine Christology does not assume that the Spirit spoke through Jesus but that Jesus should be identified with the Spirit. In later years, the Spirit as Paraclete might come into believers who then could speak in the name of Jesus so that, as Jesus says in John's gospel, "the Holy Spirit whom the Father will send in my name, will teach you everything, and will call to mind all that I have told you" (14:26).

At its beginning the gospel contains a poem focused on the word *logos*, which probably, when first written, was intended to refer to the word *sophia*. Whether the poem is pre-Christian or not is uncertain, but if we assume the ideas it contains refer to the Wisdom of God (identified, in John, with Jesus), then it at least contains ideas circulating prominently in Judaism prior to Christianity.

John apparently used a collection of miracles during one stage of the composition of the gospel. This collection, referring to miracles as "signs," has come to be known as the signs source (see chapter 4, "Gospel Sources").

Despite John's substantial differences from the synoptic gospels, its account of Jesus' trial, execution, and the discovery of his empty tomb is similar in outline, though not in detail, to that of the synoptics. This similarity indicates John used a source in common with the synoptic authors. Possibly he was familiar with one of their versions; more likely both he and they were dependent on a passion narrative written in the early years of the Christian movement before any of the gospels had been written.

Jesus

The phrase "Jesus' life" has two meanings in reference to John. In one sense it is "Life" with a capital letter, an aspect of God's higher realm. As such, Jesus' Life begins before the creation of the world, and it is Life the believer can receive.

In this sense of the word, it is eternal Life, and it is either synonymous with or correlated with Light, Truth, and Unity, which are characteristics of the higher realm.

In the more ordinary sense, Jesus' life is significant in John primarily for the very fact that he came to the world. The particular events of his life testify to the fact of his presence in the world and to the fact he came from God; in themselves, they are of little importance. His life is his presentation of himself to the world with the demand that the world recognize him for what he is. All else is detail.

Jesus' death is not the essential element in salvation for John. Jesus is called "the Lamb of God" who "takes away the sin of the world" only once (1:29). Although the gospel deliberately places Jesus' death on the day of preparation for Passover (in contrast to the synoptic accounts), there are no indications that he was thought to have died as a sacrifice for sin and, in fact, in Judaism the Passover lamb is not a sacrifice for sin. Jesus is called the Lamb of God in the first chapter, in which the whole list of christological titles is systematically employed, and the phrase is never again discussed or defined.

Jesus' death is his return to his original place, the higher realm. Therefore it is not a tragic or even problematic death; it is a journey home. John reports Jesus said, "No one ever went up into heaven except the one who came down from heaven, the Son of Man whose home is in heaven. This Son of Man must be lifted up as the serpent was lifted up by Moses in the wilderness, so that everyone who has faith in him may in him possess eternal life" (3:13–15). Many scholars assume the "lifting up" of the Son of Man refers to his crucifixion, resurrection, and ascension. It seems odd that this should be likened to the raising up of a serpent. The reference is to Numbers 21:4–9, in which the story is told of the Israelite people, disrespectful of God, being punished by a plague of serpents. They come to Moses for help. "And the

Lord told Moses to make a serpent of bronze and erect it as a standard, so that anyone who had been bitten could look at it and recover." The connection between this and John's image of Jesus is clear: Jesus is one sent by God, upon whom anyone in the realm of death might look and subsequently believe and thereby attain life. Understood in this way, the image of the uplifted serpent refers to Jesus' whole mission rather than specifically to his crucifixion, resurrection, and ascension.

Eschatology

The technical term for the variety of belief in the end of this world found in John is realized eschatology. The future has already become present. The end of this world—understood as a world of darkness, lies, and death—has already come because Jesus brought a potential end of the world with his arrival in it. For some people the end has come; they believe that Jesus came from the Father. For others the end has not yet come, but they may begin to believe in the future. In one sense, therefore, the end time is coming; in another sense, it is already here. But in any case the potential for the end is here. Those who believe now have eternal life and now have passed through judgment. In the other texts we have examined, these characteristics are reserved for those who successfully survive the trials of the end and at a future time enter the Kingdom of Heaven.

Torah Law

The system of ideas in John's gospel contains no room for the idea that one must be obedient to detailed Judean laws. Instantaneous salvation comes to those who believe. They are expected subsequently to act in accordance with their belief and thus to obey the command to love one another. This command is not a law in the sense found in Torah, nor is it a revision or alteration of the Mosaic Law such as can be found elsewhere in the New Testament. It is a command along the lines of "live eternally," and as such it is, or should become, a characteristic of those in the higher realm.

Moses' role in the gospel is that of a prophet, the most important of the prophets. "If you believed Moses, you would believe what I tell you, for it was about me that he wrote. But if you do not believe what he wrote, how are you to believe what I saw?" (5:46). Here, the reference is not to Moses the lawgiver but Moses the prophet. When Moses is said to be a lawgiver, no particular implications are drawn from the fact. "Did not Moses give you the Law? Yet you all break it" (7:19); this statement may imply the people's disregard for the Law is not surprising considering their disregard for Moses' testimony to Jesus Christ. It does not imply that obedience to Moses' Law is necessary for salvation or even that one who never breaks it will be saved. From the point of view of John's gospel, the Torah is important as a prophetic document, but as a legal document it has little significance.

On some occasions the Gospel of John interprets Torah stories in reference to Jesus. The story of the bronze serpent that Moses raised up in the desert to protect the people (Numbers 21:4–9) is adapted to Jesus in John 3:14–15. The story of Moses asking for bread, or manna, in the desert (Numbers 11:1–9) seems to underlie the story of Jesus as the bread of life in John 6:26–59, and the theme of Jesus giving Living Water in John 4:1–14 may reflect the theme of miraculous water in Exodus 17:1–6.

Community

Many members of the community of John were probably Jewish by birth. The gospel is oriented significantly to Jewish festivals, concerning which Gentiles would have been ignorant, and the arguments it contains regarding the temple and Mosaic prophecy probably would not have been devised by

Gentile Christians. John is sympathetic to Samaritans, and the gospel's community probably had Samaritan members. The gospel portrays Samaritans as capable of anticipating and recognizing the Messiah, Jesus, even though he comes from the Jews (4:1–42).

Some members of the community were probably Gentile by birth. There is nothing to exclude Gentiles from recognizing that Jesus came from God, and the principle that one must be born again through the Spirit means Jewish birth would be no factor in community membership.

Controversy

The community is in serious conflict with what it calls "the Jews." As the gospel shows substantial numbers of Jewish and Samaritan people correctly recognizing Jesus, the phrase the Jews cannot mean all Jewish people. It must be a subset of some sort, a subset probably including members of the leadership of the synagogues.

Three times, the gospel indicates the members of its community were expelled from synagogues. This expulsion is not depicted as a temporary crisis but as a permanent condition and may mark the beginning of the permanent break between the Jewish and the Christian religions. In 9:22, we are told the parents of the man born blind "were afraid of the Jews; for the Jewish authorities had already agreed that anyone who acknowledged Jesus as Messiah should be banned from the synagogue" (see also 12:42 and 16:2). Conflict between the John community and "the Jews" is emphasized in the gospel.

Interactions

Miracles Sources

John probably used a list of miracle stories to provide a narrative structure for the gospel. It is called the signs source because it uses the term "signs" (in Greek, *semeia*) to indicate the miraculous actions of Jesus (see 20:30). The list was evidently written down to provide evidence Jesus was the Christ.

The Gospel of John retains from the signs source the idea that the signs do lead to belief, but at the same time it denies that those seeking truth should seek signs. Jesus says to the officer in the royal service whose son was ill and who came wishing him to help, "Will none of you ever believe without seeing signs and portents?" (4:48). Later (6:30), when he is asked by the people, "What sign can you give us to see, so that we may believe you?" rather than conjuring manna from heaven (as they seem to expect), he informs them, "I am the bread of life." In another place, however, Jesus is reported to have said, "If I am not acting as my Father would, do not believe me. But if I am, accept the evidence of my deeds, even if you do not believe me, so that you may recognize and know that the Father is in me, and I in the Father" (10:37–38). The ambiguity in John between rejecting the practice of seeking signs and, on the other hand, believing in signs as evidence (along with the use of a source providing stories of signs), arises from the various stages through which the gospel passed. The signs source stems from a period when signs were an important way of communicating about Jesus; the rejection of signs, or their transference into metaphor, as with "the bread of life," is from a later period when asking for signs was regarded as evidence of a lack of faith.

The Q Source

John did not use the Q source and probably did not know of its existence. It is more surprising that both Matthew and Luke had access to two of the same documents (Mark and Q) than it is that John did not have them (or did not choose to use them). John's realized eschatology is in direct contrast with the future-oriented eschatology of Q. Whereas Q tends to regard the judgment at the end time as a judicial trial, John regards it as the event of belief whereby the end of this world is made present.

Q predicts the second coming of the Son of Man, but for John there is no second coming. The Spirit will come after Jesus, but nowhere is it stated Jesus will come again. What Q thought the second coming would produce—the Kingdom of God on earth—John thought had been produced already in the first and only coming of Jesus, which would be sustained forever by the Spirit as Paraclete. Where Q thought Jesus would usher in the Kingdom of God, John believes Jesus to *be* the Kingdom of God.

John seems to have relied upon persons inspired by the Spirit rather than on traditional sources, oral or written, for the sayings of Jesus. If John was an early, or the earliest gospel (as is possible, but not probable), the later gospels may have been written in reaction to its tendency to rely on Spirit-inspired prophetic information. The use of written sayings placed into a narrative context provides some control over the attribution of sayings to Jesus and gives the sayings contextual meaning that they lack in simple lists. The sayings of Christian prophets would have had an unfortunate tendency to vary widely from prophet to prophet, a difficulty discussed in the First Letter of John, in which "false prophets" and "antichrists" seem to be synonymous. They are contrasted with authentic "prophets" who presumably would be authentic "christs."

The Gospel of Thomas, a collection of sayings similar in format to Q, contains many ideas close to those of John. There we find sayings from the perspective of realized eschatology and the statement by Jesus that "I am the light." Thomas, like the poem introducing the Gospel of John, believes Jesus to be the Wisdom of God, who has come to earth to call humanity but who frequently finds rejection. Although Thomas is not a literary source for John, it may well reflect an earlier stage of development in the literature of the community that later produced John.

Paul

There is no evidence that John knew of Paul's letters or was directly influenced by Paul's teachings. Nevertheless, interesting relationships between the two exist. These relationships probably derive more from the working out of common themes than from an historical connection. As John's gospel seems to rely heavily on the speeches of inspired Christian prophets for knowledge of Jesus' teachings, so Paul relied on inspiration for his teachings, as did his communities (see 1 Cor 12:1–14:40). Neither John nor Paul felt obliged to seek what we would call historically accurate quotations.

Most striking is their common conception that, through Jesus, humanity received the ability to be totally transformed. How they speak of the transformation differs, but Paul almost certainly would have agreed with John's emphatic claims that anyone who believes in Jesus has (or will receive) eternal life, walks in light, and enters the realm of God. Paul, however, includes an "eschatological reservation" in nearly all of his comments about transformation: he believes that total transformation must await the return of Christ. John's "realized eschatology" requires no return.

Much that Paul wrote is intended to deny that striving to keep the Law will bring salvation. John never discusses the matter but, implicitly, he agrees with Paul. From John's standpoint, to keep the Law but not to believe Jesus came from the Father and returned to him would not be a successful means of seeking salvation.

The major difference between the two is the difference in their interpretation of Jesus' death. For Paul, Jesus' death was the dividing line between the old order and the new, between the time when people sought salvation through Law and the time when salvation was achieved through faith. For John, Jesus' coming to earth is the dividing line; Jesus' death opened a way to God for people who already had eternal life. For Paul, his death brought the opportunity for eternal life.

Mark

John and Mark seem to agree on the inadequacy of believing that because Jesus could do miracles and signs he was, therefore, Christ. Neither deny the miracles occurred. Both use them in their books, but neither wishes them to be the principal image their readers have of Jesus.

John does not share Mark's focus on the suffering, death, and resurrection of the Son of Man. In John, Jesus is glorified in his death and resurrection. His death and resurrection should be sources of revelation, but not the primary source of revelation; during his life Jesus revealed himself and brought eternal life to those who understood. For Mark the revelation of Jesus the Son of Man through his suffering, death, and resurrection was the essential element of his mission.

At times John, in a style reminiscent of Mark, shows some of Jesus' disciples seriously misunderstanding him. In chapter 6, Jesus' statements about eating flesh and drinking blood alienate some of them permanently. Shortly thereafter, we hear "even his brothers were not believers in him" (7:5), but this is followed by the implicitly optimistic statement to his brothers, "The right time for me has not yet come, but any time is right for you" (7:6).

On the whole, however, John's gospel gives a positive impression of the disciples. At the gospel's very beginning, Andrew tells his brother Simon Peter, "We have found the Messiah" (1:41). Peter's statement in John 6:69 is probably a version of the tradition we find in Mark 8:30 and reads: "We have faith, and we know that you are the Holy One of God," which is correct from John's perspective. At the end, the disciples do encounter him raised from the dead, in contrast to the ending of Mark, where they all have fled and learn nothing of the resurrection.

Matthew

Few of Matthew's primary interests are reflected in John. For Matthew the Law is crucial, and Jesus came, in large part, to interpret it and bring it to completion. There is no good evidence that Christians of John's community were expected to follow the Law. The one command given is "love one another," but even that may be a command with which Matthew would disagree. The saying in Matthew, "love your enemies" (Matt 5:44), includes people inside and outside the Christian community. In John "love one another" refers only to those who believe and have faith. It does not include those who are in the "world" and live in darkness.

In John the Law is prophetic, testifying to the coming of Jesus the Christ. On this point Matthew would agree, while insisting the Law must be obeyed more strictly by Christians than even by the Pharisees themselves.

Luke

Luke's gospel has a "low Christology," which is a technical theological term meaning the humanity of Jesus is more strongly emphasized than his divinity. According to Luke, during his life Jesus revealed what he would be after his death, when God would give him unique and important tasks. He remains, however, a human being whom God chose for these special tasks. There is no implication in Luke that Jesus and God are one. This contrasts, of course, with John's "high Christology," or emphasis on Jesus' divinity. In John, Jesus says, "I and the Father are one," and, according to the logos poem beginning the gospel, Jesus was with God from the beginning and was God.

Luke's gospel has the lowest Christology of any New Testament text we have studied; John's gospel has the highest. The fact that both survive in the New Testament and are equally counted as Scripture is both a testimony to the diversity of interpretations of Jesus in the first century and a cause of the diversity of interpretations of Jesus in this century. The New Testament's diversity of interpretations is the greatest intellectual resource Christianity has.

End-of-Chapter Exercises

1. What did you discover when you underlined the "I am . . ." passages in John as directed on pages 279–80?
2. Compare and contrast John's portrayal of John the Baptist, Pontius Pilate, and Jesus with the synoptic gospels. What makes John unique?
3. What does John's negative depiction of "the Jews" as a group suggest about the context in which this gospel was written? Would you think differently if the Greek word *Ioudaios* was translated in terms of place—"the Judeans"—instead rather than a religion—"the Jews"?
4. Reread the miracle story of the man born blind, John 9:1–41. What interpretations are made of the miracle and of blindness by those sympathetic and those not sympathetic to Jesus? How does Jesus, in John's account, interpret this miracle?

Bibliography

Brown, Raymond. *The Gospel According to John*. Anchor Bible, vols. 29 and 29A. New York: Doubleday, 1966.

Haenchen, Ernst. *The Gospel of John*. Volumes 1 and 2. Philadelphia: Fortress Press, 1984.

Jervell, J. *Jesus in the Gospel of John*. Minneapolis: Augsburg Publishing House, 1984.

Keener, Craig S. *The Gospel of John: A Commentary*. Peabody MA: Hendrickson Publishers, 2003.

Kostenberger, Andreas. *Baker Exegetical Commentary on John*. Grand Rapids, MI: Baker Books, 2004.

Kysar, R. *John's Story of Jesus*. Philadelphia: Fortress Press, 1984.

Lee, Dorothy. *Flesh and Glory: Symbolism, Gender and Theology in the Gospel of John*. New York NY: Crossroad, 2002.

MacRae, G. W. *Invitation to John*. Garden City NY: Doubleday, 1978.

Neyrey, Jerome. *John: New Cambridge Bible Commentary*. New York NY: Cambridge University Press, 2006.

Perkins, Pheme. *The Gospel of John: A Theological Commentary*. Chicago: Franciscan Herald Press, 1978.

Smith, Dwight M. *John*. Philadelphia: Fortress Press, 1976.

Thompson, Marianne Meye. *The God of the Gospel of John*. Grand Rapids MI: Eerdmans, 2001.

Apostolic Letters and the Revelation to John

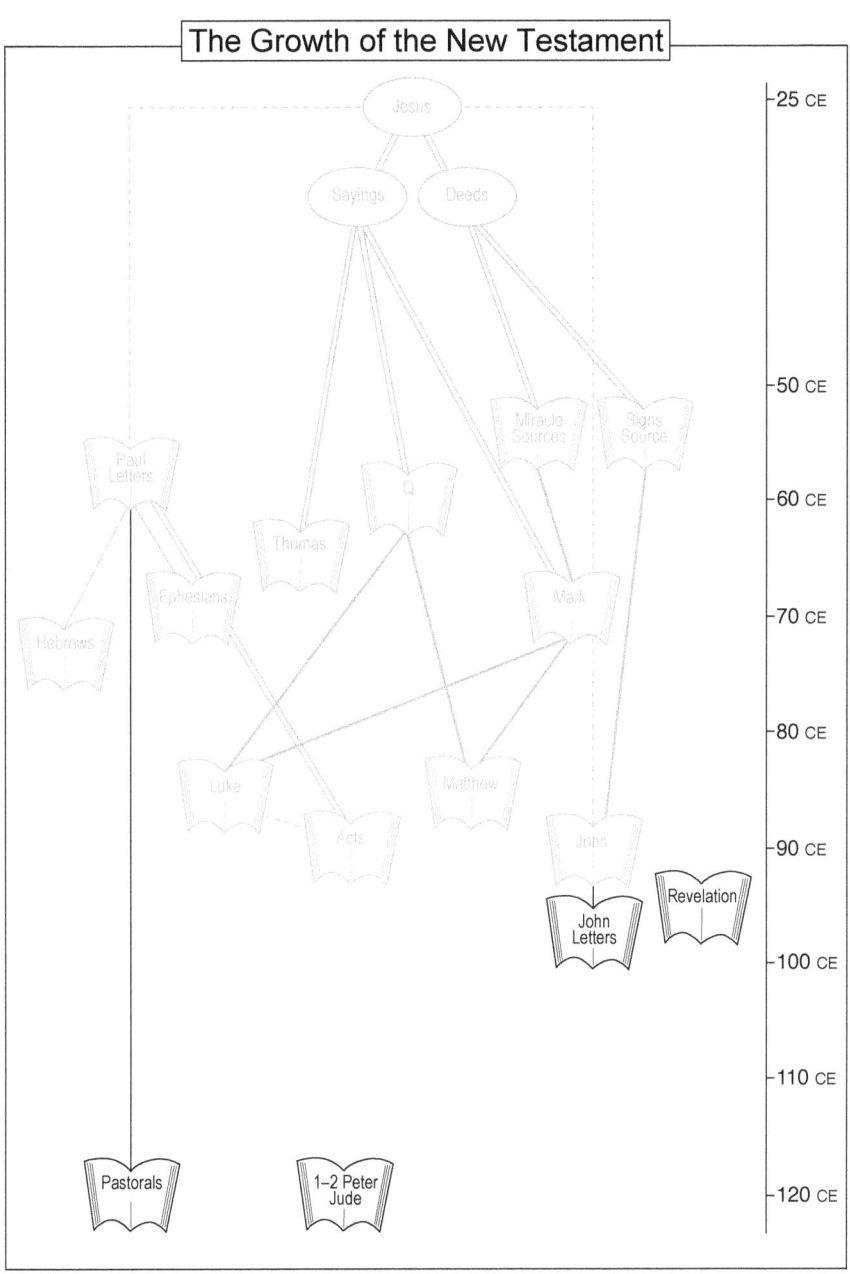

Dashed lines: indirect influence
Double lines: oral transmission
Single thick lines: use of written source
Thin lines: followers, admirers & imitators

CHAPTER 9

Apostolic Letters and the Revelation to John

OBJECTIVES

- Trace the consolidation of Christianity into an organized & structured movement through these later letters
- List the different forms of authority called upon by authors in the NT to defend their claims
- Discuss ancient & modern debates over which books should be included in the NT canon
- Analyze Revelation as representing early Christian & Jewish apocalyptic outlooks instead of a historical record

In this chapter we will survey briefly the New Testament's concluding texts: the letters known as James, 1 John, 2 John, 3 John, Hebrews, Ephesians, 2 Thessalonians, 1 Timothy, 2 Timothy, Titus, 1 Peter, Jude, 2 Peter, and the Revelation to John. All in one way or another present themselves as letters, but some are not letters, as we shall see. The Revelation to John begins as a series of seven letters and then becomes a description of visions. We shall not consider any of the concluding letters with the same amount of detail with which we treated earlier texts, for, with the exception of the Revelation to John, they are relatively straightforward and easy to understand. The consensus of scholars is that they were written toward the end of the first century or during the first part of the second century. They provide us evidence of the consolidation of Christianity into an organized and structured religious movement.

James

READ THE LETTER OF JAMES PAYING ATTENTION TO THE SEPARATE UNITS: 2:1–13; 2:14–26; AND 3:1–12. The Letter of James is written in good Greek by a person familiar with the forms of thought and argument commonly found among educated, Greek-speaking people. Since its author was also thoroughly familiar with the traditions and teachings of Judaism, we may be reasonably confident he was a Hellenistic Jew. Although Jesus' brother James is sometimes said to have written this letter, the letter nowhere claims or implies its author is Jesus' brother, and it is unlikely that James would have been educated in the manner of the letter's author.

Although known as a letter, James is really a collection of teachings or short sermons about how to live and how not to live. Four self-contained short sermons are easily isolated: 1:2–27, 2:1–13, 2:14–26, and 3:1–12. The parts of the letter, while not inconsistent, do not show any logical development of one idea from another. It probably circulated originally as a collection of separated teachings and was later combined into the form we now have.

It is questionable whether the Letter of James was originally Christian. The addition of two phrases (James 1:1, 2:1) could have adapted a collection of Hellenistic Jewish teachings for Christian use. There is nothing in the letter that could not have been accepted by most Jews. "Faith," for example, is not necessarily faith in Christ but faith in God, faith like Abraham's. "The coming of the Lord" (5:7) could refer to the coming of the Lord of Hosts (5:4). The letter insists faith must be accompanied by good works. This has troubled those who most firmly adhere to Paul's gospel of salvation through faith.

In its insistence that action must accompany faith, the letter is reminiscent of Matthew's gospel (Matt 7:21). If the letter was originally Christian it might have been written, as Matthew's gospel might have been written, in part to argue against those Christians who believed they were free from the obligation to follow the Law. James is uncompromising about the Law: "If a man keeps the whole law apart from one single point, he is guilty of breaking all of it" (2:10). Paul would agree with that statement, but would conclude that because everyone will break some point of the Law sooner or later, the Law cannot bring about salvation. James, in contrast, concludes that therefore people must earnestly strive to keep the Law, arguing, "A man is justified by deeds and not by faith in itself" (2:24).

Both Paul and James appeal to Genesis 15:6 to demonstrate their points. James 2:18–24 uses that passage—along with the story in Genesis 22:1–19, which recounts Abraham's obedience to God's command to sacrifice his son Isaac—to prove that faith must be combined with obedience to the Law. For Paul, Genesis 15:6 proves faith alone is essential (see Rom 4:1–25).

While taking a strong stand on a variety of matters, the letter seems most strongly to object to improper behavior by wealthy people. When the Lord comes, their wealth will do them no good, and, insofar as it tempts them to oppress the poor, their wealth will lead to their condemnation (5:1–6). This perspective, like many found in James, can be discovered in other New Testament letters and gospels. The reason for this is not that the author of James used those writings as sources, but that many moral positions taken in James's letters and elsewhere, including the letters of Paul, were moral positions common in the ancient world and were taught by philosophers and religious leaders from many different traditions, including, especially, Judaism.

Hebrews

READ HEBREWS. NOTE THE COMPARISONS MADE BETWEEN CHRISTIAN BELIEFS AND PRACTICES AND JEWISH BELIEFS AND PRACTICES. Scholarly comments on the New Testament document sometimes called "the Letter of Paul to Hebrews" usually contain the quite valid observation that the document is not a letter, is not by Paul, and is not written to Hebrews. It is an essay or sermon written for Christians by a Christian whose name we do not know. The author makes substantial use of the Greek translation of the Hebrew Bible, the Septuagint, rather than the Hebrew-language original text. His discussion of Judaism and of practices in the Jewish temple derive more from his reading of biblical texts than from firsthand experience.

Hebrews has one main purpose, but the many details used to achieve that purpose make it seem complex. The main purpose of Hebrews is to demonstrate through biblical examples that Christianity is superior to Judaism. This does not mean Judaism is totally rejected, only that in the author's opinion it is inferior. By choosing to compare Christian ideas favorably with Jewish ideas, the author adopts Judaism as a fit standard of comparison, but he finds item after item in Judaism and in Jewish priestly practice to have been superseded by Jesus Christ. The following are examples:

> God formerly spoke through prophets; in Jesus, he speaks through a Son who is "heir to the whole universe," who is "the effulgence of God's splendor and the stamp of God's very being and sustains the universe by his word of power" (Heb 1:2–3).

> Moses . . . was faithful in God's household; and Jesus, of whom I speak, has been deemed worthy of greater honor than Moses, as the founder of a house enjoys more honor than his household (3:2–3).

> The high priests made by the Law are men in all their frailty; but the priest appointed by the words of the oath which supersedes the Law is the Son, made perfect now forever (7:28).

> The first covenant indeed had its ordinances of divine service and its sanctuary, but a material sanctuary" (9:1). "But

> now Christ has come, high priest of good things already in being. The tent of his priesthood is a greater and more perfect one, not made by men's hands, that is, not belonging to this created world; the blood of his sacrifice is his own blood, not the blood of goats and calves . . . (9:11–12).

Examples could be multiplied. Hebrews especially stresses the excellence of Jesus' priesthood. Jewish priests were born into a special caste called the Levites, of which Jesus was not a member. Hebrews makes a sustained argument that there is a priesthood, that of Melchizedek, superior to the priesthood of the Levites. This idea is based on a passage in Genesis 14:18–20 in which Abraham encounters Melchizedek, the king of Salem, who is called "priest of God Most High." Melchizedek brings out food and wine and blesses Abraham, who gives Melchizedek a tenth of everything. This passage intrigued Jewish interpreters because Melchizedek is given no genealogy, is not related to Abraham, and is never again mentioned in the Torah. Only once more in the Hebrew Bible is there a reference to him. Psalm 110, written to be sung on the occasion of the enthronement of a king of Israel or Judah, contains the line "The Lord has sworn and will not change his purpose, 'you are a priest forever in the succession of Melchizedek.'" The author of Hebrews comments extensively on Psalm 110 and finds that psalm to be evidence that Jesus is a priest in the succession of Melchizedek and that Jesus' priesthood is superior to Levitical priesthood. Jesus' priestly role takes place in the temple in heaven, not in the temple on earth, and, therefore, Hebrews argues, he is the ideal prototype on which all earthly priests should be modeled. This is the foundational ideology of the Catholic priesthood.

In conceiving of Jesus as sacrificial victim and as high priest of the sacrifice and as the Son of God enthroned with God who receives the sacrifice, Hebrews has had a powerful influence on later Christian theology and liturgy. The Jewish practice of sacrifice ended with the destruction of the temple in 70 CE, but, due largely to the influence of Hebrews, the theory and symbolic practice of sacrifice continue to exist in Christianity to the present day. Because Hebrews discusses the ritual of the Jewish temple in detail, but never mentions its destruction, it may have been written prior to 70 CE.

1 John

READ THE FIRST LETTER OF JOHN. On what issues do the author and the Christians he calls antichrists disagree? Three letters attributed to John appear in the New Testament. All reflect the ideas and the style of language found in the Gospel of John, and some scholars assume the author of the gospel and the author of the letters were the same person. Others believe the letters were written much later than the gospel, probably by someone else, but either way scholars generally agree that the letters and the gospel derive from the same community.

The First Letter of John is not really a letter at all but a sermon directed to the author's congregation. The language of the sermon contrasts realms of life and death in a typically Johannine way. In addition to restating basic principles found in John's gospel, the sermon focuses on other, more specific matters. It repeatedly insists that loving behavior is required of Christians. Those who do not love are metaphorically termed murderers. The sermon does not advocate adherence to the Torah Law but it does argue against the idea that those who have faith are thereby free to behave in a sinful fashion.

First John addresses a disagreement within the Johannine community. Some individuals believe the Spirit of God has revealed to them that Jesus' appearance on earth was more spiritual than physical and that it would be a mistake to believe he came in the flesh. Others believe the Spirit of God has revealed to them that Jesus' appearance on earth was physical and that it is essential to believe he came in the flesh. The sermon's author is a member of the latter group.

Disagreement in John's community over the nature of Jesus' appearance illustrates a problem faced by many early Christian groups. At first the group relies for its direction on verbal information from individuals who are inspired by the Spirit. Eventually, they discover that some persons who believe themselves inspired are saying things others in the group find entirely wrong. The group then must decide how to proceed. The group may stop seeking verbal information from inspired individuals and rely instead on inspired written texts. Precedent for this had been set in Judaism, where reliance on Spirit-inspired prophets had ceased among the official Jewish leadership. Instead of living prophets, written prophetic books such as those of Isaiah and Jeremiah became the principal sources of divine guidance. Among the ordinary Jewish people, however, respect for prophetic books was coupled with continued belief in living prophets. During their lifetimes, John the Baptist and Jesus were considered prophets by many ordinary people but few Jewish leaders.

Similarly, from the beginning of the Christian movement, followers of Jesus used Hebrew Bible texts, including the prophetic books, to support Christian teachings. At the same time, the Christian movement continued to receive information from Christian prophets. As time went on, however, Christian groups had trouble deciding which prophets were reliable and which were not. This difficulty is evident as early as the time of Paul, who condemns those who teach a gospel differing from his own (Gal 1:6–7) and of Mark, who refers to impostors who "will come claiming to be messiahs or prophets, and they will produce signs and wonders to mislead God's chosen" (13:22). We may suspect that any time a Christian called another Christian a false prophet, the accusation was returned in kind. The increasing diversity of teachings coming from people who believed themselves inspired by the Spirit led Christians to begin choosing a canon of written scripture. A canon of scripture is a clearly defined authoritative collection of specific texts. Written texts of scripture may be diversely interpreted, but they at least provide an unchanging set of data from which to start.

Although the Johannine community did not yet possess a canon of scripture, nevertheless it had to confront the problems arising from contradictory information from Spirit-inspired individuals. In this situation, a group may declare that some people who believe themselves inspired by the Spirit of God are, in fact, inspired by another spirit, presumably a demonic spirit. The question then will be how to tell which is which.

In 1 Corinthians 12:10, Paul had suggested a possible solution: appealing to people in the church who have the gift of discernment. That is, some people are possessed by the Spirit of God so that they can tell which people are similarly possessed and which people are possessed by other spirits. This process would lead to difficulty, of course, should two spiritually inspired persons mutually declare the other possessed by a demonic spirit.

In 1 John a different solution is proposed. To determine whether a person is inspired by God's Spirit or another spirit, a doctrinal test is established. The test is whether persons will declare "Jesus Christ has come in the flesh." "Every spirit which acknowledges Jesus Christ as come in the flesh is from God, and every spirit which does not thus acknowledge Jesus is not from God" (1 John 4:2–3).

Over time, of course, more and more doctrinal requirements would be needed to test the validity of spirits, and more and more rival groups would appear, each regarding different doctrines to be true. One solution to the problem of myriad lists of doctrines would be to select a canon of written texts, which could then be used to control the potentially unlimited number of possible doctrines. Doctrines consistent with the texts would be acceptable; those clearly in conflict with the texts would be unacceptable. In the absence of a canon of Christian texts, the author of 1 John must rely upon his own authority to insist his congregation should believe "Jesus came in the flesh."

2 John

READ THE SECOND LETTER OF JOHN. This, the New Testament's shortest text, is a personal letter written in the same style as 1 John, probably by the same person. Here the author takes the title "the Elder," which presumably is a title of authority in the church. As it deals in much the same words with the same problem (rival Christians called "antichrists"), it was probably written at about the same time as 1 John. The purpose of the letter is to tell its recipient not to welcome or even greet anyone who does not "acknowledge Jesus Christ as coming in the flesh" (1:7).

Many scholars of the New Testament declare that the lady referred to in the letter's opening passage and the sister referred to in the letter's close are two churches. This is not likely. That a letter would be addressed both to a church and also to the collectivity of its members, "her children," would be unlikely. First John uses "children" as a favored term for church members. But nowhere in 1 John is the church considered feminine; when the author refers to church members it is to "brothers" (3:13) and "fathers" and "young men" (1:13–14). As 2 John was, more likely than not, written by the same author, it is improbable that that author would think of the church as a lady or a sister. Furthermore, the term "lady" is not used for a church in any other first- or second-century text. It is more reasonable to assume the words "lady" and "sister" mean what they say, that the letter addressed a woman with responsibility for a church, and that she is greeted by her real or metaphorical sister, the author of the letter. Women did on occasion have responsibility for churches, which we infer from texts such as Acts 12:12, where Peter comes to "the house of Mary, the mother of John Mark, where a large company was at prayer." The fact that "Elder" is masculine in gender does not mean necessarily the author was male if the term "Elder" was a technical term for an established church office. Today, for example, the Presbyterian church does not usually distinguish elders from eldresses, and there are instances of female deacons (masculine gender) mentioned in texts of the early church.

3 John

This short personal letter was probably written by the Elder, author of the other two letters of John. Addressed to Gaius, it encourages him to show hospitality to certain itinerant Christian teachers of whom the author approves. It may have been carried by Demetrius (3 John 1:12) as a letter recommending him to Gaius. Gaius and Demetrius are otherwise unknown.

The author is apparently in serious conflict with Diotrephes, who may be the leader of Gaius's congregation (3 John 1:9). Diotrephes is making charges against the author and refuses to receive his representatives. It is unfortunate we know nothing of Diotrephes' charges. For all we know, his charges may have had some foundation.

The three letters of John, taken together, reveal considerable conflict. The author in 1 John encourages love among those who agree with him and despises other Christians with whom he disagrees and whom he calls "the antichrist." It is conceivable that among Diotrephes' "baseless and spiteful charges" against the Elder was the accusation that the Elder is an antichrist, since that seems to have been the preferred term of abuse in that community. In 2 John, the lady is urged not to receive the itinerant representatives of an opposing group, while in 3 John, the author is furious with Diotrephes, who will not receive representatives friendly to him. As both the second and third letters conclude with the comment that the author has much to say that he does not wish to put into writing, there was more to the disputes than the letters reveal. In these letters, as in the letters of Paul and elsewhere in the New Testament, the pleasant vision of the primitive church as a place of love and brotherhood among all Christians can be seen to be false. That was an ideal, perhaps, but not a reality.

Ephesians

READ THE LETTER TO THE EPHESIANS. Few scholars think Ephesians was written by Paul because the language of the letter is rather different from that of letters certainly written by Paul, and because some ideas seem out of accord with Paul's discussion of them elsewhere. For example, Paul usually does not declare that Christians have already attained perfection. He reserves that for the time when the Lord comes. In this letter, however, we read that already "in union with Christ Jesus, [God] raised us up and enthroned us with him in the heavenly realms" (2:6).

Even if this is not Paul's letter, it is certainly a Pauline letter written by a disciple of Paul's who is familiar with Paul's characteristic ideas and concerns. The author repeatedly stresses the Pauline idea of unity and love within the community of Christians (e.g. 4:2–6), stresses the necessity of grace rather than obedience to Law, and reflects Paul's idea of the church as bride of Christ and body of Christ (5:29–33).

You should read Ephesians in two stages because it has two separate sections: one section, from the beginning of the letter to the end of chapter 3, lays out a set of theological ideas about God and Christ, salvation, and the nature of the people of God. The other, beginning with chapter 4 and continuing to the end, describes Christian ethical values and moral principles. For Christians today, the Letter to Ephesians contains no surprises, as it states in reasonably clear terms what the foundational principles of the Christian religion are. It is remarkable that such a short piece of writing, written in the last half of the first century, can so comprehensively state principles for a religion with over one billion adherents two thousand years later. Of all the forms of Christianity that were in competition with one another during the religion's first three hundred years, the form defined in the letter to the Ephesians became normative and foundational.

The first section of the letter stresses human transformation. Having discussed the nature and functions of Jesus Christ in chapter 1, the author turns immediately to questions of transformation. "You he made alive," he writes, "when you were dead" (2:1). Where there once was a separation between the Jewish people, the people of God, and Gentiles, now we hear that the two have become one and that the separation has been ended. This is called "the mystery of Christ," and clearly shows a religious movement that regards itself as the culmination of Judaism through the potential incorporation into Judaism of everyone in the world.

The second section of the letter, beginning at chapter 4:1, explains in more detail what is expected of transformed people. They are not only members of a mystical body of Christ in the abstract, they also need to function within a viable human social organization with leadership roles (4:11) and rules for moral conduct. Sometimes those rules make perfectly good sense; it would be hard to find anyone who would disagree that the world would be a better place if most of the requirements in Ephesians were carried out. Some of the rules seem oppressive, however. For example, the letter's discussion of the relationship of husbands and wives (5:21–33) is "patriarchal" by the standards of today, requiring women to subordinate themselves to their husbands. Yet, in terms of the standards of the first century, the author speaks in defense of the rights and role of women in marriage, and the demand that husbands love their wives is emphatically repeated.

Imagine what it might be like to live in a city in the ancient world, one where people lived jammed together without sanitation or clean water; where people lived short lives punctuated by disease; where slavery, thievery and prostitution were common; where many were separated from their ancestral homelands, their relatives, and families; and where everyone lived in constant uncertainty. Then imagine a local community within that city dedicated to mutual support and respect, open to new members, where people tried to live in accordance with the principles in Ephesians 4–6; you may be able to see why Christianity spread so rapidly. If there were communities like those Ephesians describes, they would have been wonderful refuges for most urban people of Roman times. The principles announced in the letter to the Ephesians would have encouraged mutual assistance within a community while providing self-esteem for all members in accordance with the idea that they are a new and transformed people of God, and the community would have worked to achieve an orderly, mutually loving lifestyle within families. If you ask what it was that Christianity offered that led people to convert and become members of the communities scattered throughout the Roman Empire, it was the *lifestyle* offered in the second part of Ephesians more than the *doctrines* in the first part of Ephesians that brought people in and convinced them to stay.

2 Thessalonians

READ THE SECOND LETTER TO THESSALONIANS. The principal difficulty in ascribing the letter to Paul is that in First Thessalonians, the time of the end—the return of the Lord—is anticipated very soon. But in Second Thessalonians that time is evidently rather far off and will not arrive until a long sequence of events have already taken place. Various rather mysterious beings will have to arrive in the world before Christ comes again. These beings—a man who is the embodiment of wickedness, a restrainer, man of lawlessness—are otherwise unknown from Paul's writing. Oddly enough, such malevolent beings seem to be sent by God, yet it is God who also restrains them. The idea that God puts people into states of delusion (2:11) does not sound like Paul, and Paul generally speaks of the return of the Lord happily, as something Christians should look forward to. Here, however, the author seems rather to dread the occasion, or at least to dread the events that lead up to it. Even though the end is delayed and Christ will supposedly not return quickly, it appears that the timeline for his return is a matter of decades rather than centuries.

This short letter is apocalyptic, at least in its central section from 2:1–2:12, for it reveals the extraordinary events that the author believed would take place at the end of this world. The community has evidently been subjected to a variety of prophetic apocalyptic messages. Some even say that the day of the Lord has already come. Note that there have been several means of communicating this odd message: it comes by Spirit, which means that people speak in a state of possession believing that the words of the Spirit are coming out from them; it also comes by word, which may well mean the preaching of Christian prophets, or even by letters falsely attributed to Paul (2:2). This is rather ironic, since Second Thessalonians itself is probably a letter falsely attributed to Paul. In any event, the principal purpose of this letter is to insist that the "coming of our Lord Jesus Christ" is something that will happen in the relatively distant future.

This letter, like the letters of John, is further proof that early Christian communities were beset with internal conflicts and rivalries. One person's letter attributed to Paul contradicted another's. There appeared to be false spirits, raising the question of how to determine which Spirit-inspired speech is true when two people's speeches disagree with one another. A person could not rely on signs and wonders and miracles as proof because these, too, could be misleading; Second Thessalonians warns against pretended signs and wonders (2:9).

The Pastoral Epistles

READ THE FIRST LETTER TO TIMOTHY, THE SECOND LETTER TO TIMOTHY, AND THE LETTER TO TITUS AND LOCATE THE PLACES WHERE ISSUES OF CHURCH DISCIPLINE, ORGANIZATION AND PERSONNEL ARE DISCUSSED. These letters are attributed to Paul but were written around 120 CE by someone writing in Paul's name. Each letter uses vocabulary Paul is not known to have used; each has a different concept than Paul had of key matters such as faith; and each refers to Paul's close friends Timothy and Titus in formal rather than friendly terms. They are commonly known as the *Pastoral Epistles,* or Pastoral letters. The name comes from their purpose, which was to instruct Christian pastors how to live and what to teach their congregations. The Pastoral Epistles assume that Christian churches are governed by the kind of carefully organized authority structures that developed decades after Paul's time.

They are similar in style, in content, and in the issues they raise, so scholars generally believe that they were written by the same person.

The Pastoral Epistles provide evidence for the evolution of authority structures in Christian churches. At the time Paul wrote his letters (the late 50s), authority in his churches was unstructured. Itinerant Christian teachers and prophets, like Paul and others mentioned in his letters, traveled from town to town establishing churches and preaching to already established churches. The churches had people who worked in them (the Greek word for worker or servant, *diakonos*, is the origin of the term "deacon") and probably were led by more or less informal groups of elders (the Greek word for older man, *presbyteros*, is the origin of the term "presbyter" and is often translated "elder"). In Paul's day such people were probably in charge only of housekeeping, finances, and so forth. The ultimate spiritual authority for doctrine and teaching came, it appears, primarily from Spirit-inspired persons within the congregations and from occasional visits and letters from prophetic itinerants like Paul who felt responsibility for the congregations.

Several decades later the situation had changed. Rather than relying primarily upon the inspiration of the Spirit, fixed principles of doctrine and behavior began to be established. These principles the Pastorals call "the faith," and so they use the term "faith" in a way differently than Paul used it; for Paul, faith is a dynamic and transforming trust in God; it is not simple adherence to correct principles. In the Pastorals, those who are entrusted with teaching "the faith" constitute a church hierarchy. Deacons are subordinate to elders; elders select a general overseer to provide leadership (the Greek word for overseer, *episkopos*, is the origin of the term "bishop"). First Timothy gives instructions for bishops (3:2), elders (5:19), and deacons (3:8). Authority in the Christian church, initially charismatic and based on Spirit inspiration, has become institutional, based on formal elected or appointed positions. Decades after the writing of the Pastorals, bishops assumed almost complete responsibility for churches, and elders became assistants to bishops. Eventually the role of the elder became the role of the priest.

The Pastorals address questions about various subdivisions of Christian congregations. For example, in 1 Timothy, rules are established to specify persons who may be considered destitute Christian widows and thus receive financial support from the church. The letter insists that anyone who could support elderly relatives but does not do so "has denied the faith and is worse than an unbeliever" (5:8). This charge seems to derive less from concern for the commandment to honor father and mother than from concern that church financial resources not be consumed needlessly. The letter does, however, advocate double pay for elders who do a good job (5:17).

Women, according to the Pastorals, are to be subordinate to men. Paul's teaching that in Christ there is no male or female (Gal 3:28) is now laid aside. Directions for women's dress are provided (1 Tim 2:8–9), and then we read, "A woman must be a learner, listening quietly with due submission. I do not permit a woman to be a teacher, nor must woman domineer over man; she must be quiet" (2:10–12). The reason given for these commands is that it was not Adam who first sinned but Eve (2:13–14). Paul himself never blamed Eve separately for the fall.

1 Peter

READ THE FIRST LETTER OF PETER. First Peter is an open letter to several churches located in Asia Minor. The Galilean fisherman named Simon bar-Jonah (Matt 16:17), whom Jesus called Peter, is not the author of the letter. In the conclusion of the letter, the author probably makes a personal reference: "Greetings from her who dwells in Babylon, chosen by God like you, and from my son Mark" (1 Pet 5:13). Although the reference to the lady dwelling in Babylon is usually said to mean the church in Rome, it is entirely possible that the lady here, like the lady in Second John, is a real person, the author of the letter. Babylon is a code word for Rome in the book entitled Revelation and could mean Rome here as well, but it could also mean what it says—Babylon in Mesopotamia, which was the home of a major Jewish community in the late first or early second century CE. In that period, wherever there were major Jewish communities there were also growing Christian communities.

Scholarly opinion is divided as to whether 1 Peter is one or two letters. If it was once two separate letters, the first ends at 4:11 and the second consists of the verses from 4:12 to the end. Even if it was originally two letters, 1 Peter as it stands is consistent and can be read as a single text.

The letter was written to give encouragement to churches in Asia Minor suffering from persecution. It is more likely the persecution was informal, deriving from various groups antagonistic to Christians, than that it was imperially sponsored. The letter supports the authority of the government, as well as that of several seemingly repressive human institutions. It forthrightly condemns rebellious behavior. The letter requires its recipients to "submit yourselves to every human institution for the sake of the Lord, whether to the sovereign as supreme, or to the governor as his deputy for the punishment of criminals and the commendation of those who do right" (2:13–14). Servants are to accept the authority of their masters even when the masters are perverse (2:18). Women must accept the authority of their husbands (3:1), and younger men must be subordinate to their elders

(5:5). Jesus Christ is put forward as a model of obedience and of unresisting acceptance of suffering and injustice. In addition to submissiveness, 1 Peter requires loving and moral behavior and encourages its audience, which apparently was apparently made up of Gentile Christians, to refrain from behavior characteristic of pagans.

Twice this letter refers to Jesus preaching to the dead, the only times in the New Testament where such an idea occurs (3:19–21, 4:6). Here the idea that the gospel should be preached to all people has its most complete application.

Some scholars believe 1 Peter was designed originally as a sermon to be given on the occasion of the baptism of new Christians. This belief is based on a passage in which baptism is likened to the flood in the days of Noah where a few persons "were brought to safety through the water. This water prefigured the water of baptism through which you are now brought to safety" (3:20–21). The common tendency of New Testament writers to claim events recounted in the Hebrew Bible are really symbolic references to Christian beliefs and traditions here finds a peculiar application; the waters of the flood were certainly not sent in order to bring people to safety.

Jude

READ THE LETTER OF JUDE. Mark 6:3 records the names of four brothers of Jesus: James, Joseph, Judas, and Simon. The author of Jude may claim to be James's brother Judas. "Jude" is an alternative spelling for "Judas," used by translators to avoid confusion with Judas Iscariot. The name Judas was very common at the time. Jesus' brother James assumed leadership of the church after the crucifixion, a leadership disputed by such independently minded people as Paul (Gal 2:9). It is possible that, after the death of James, Judas may have claimed authority. Christians who took literally the claim that Jesus was king of the Jews from the House of David may have found it reasonable to assume that the eldest surviving brother, in the absence of male children, should have authority. Be that as it may, the Letter of Jude was actually written by someone living one or two generations later than Jesus' brothers.

The Letter of Jude is written to condemn certain Christians whose behavior the author believes to be scandalous. The language of Jude is so exaggerated it is difficult to tell what exactly his opponents were doing. The letter claims "they pervert the free favor of our God into licentiousness" (1:4), and it is possible "they" are people who took Paul's gospel of freedom from the Law to mean any behavior whatsoever was acceptable.

Jude refers to "the predictions made by the apostles of our Lord Jesus Christ" (1:17), a reference that could have been made only at a time substantially later than that of the apostles, a time when Christians were beginning to look to the teachings of the apostles for authority rather than to the immediate inspiration of the Spirit. The predictions of Jesus' apostles are given the same weight in Jude as the scripture of the Hebrew Bible (1:4), and the author uses both as prophetic sources of evidence that his opponents are to be condemned. The tendency to regard apostolic teachings with the same respect as scripture would culminate eventually with the creation of new scripture based on apostolic authority, a scripture with equal or greater authority than the Hebrew Bible. That new Scripture is, of course, the New Testament. Although there is no evidence in Jude that the creation of a Christian canon of scripture had begun, the principle of apostolic authority that is already advocated in the Letter of Jude came to govern the selection of Christian canonical texts.

It is interesting that Jude considers two documents to be authoritative that do not appear in the present Hebrew Bible. Both are Jewish writings and thus give us good reason to assume Jude's author was a Jewish Christian. The text known as the *Assumption of Moses* is the source for the reported debate between Michael the archangel and the devil over possession of Moses' body (1:9). Jude quotes the text entitled *Enoch* in 1:14–15 and regards Enoch as an inspired prophet. During the first century, Jews generally agreed on the inspired authority of most of the texts the Hebrew Bible would contain. The five books of Torah were certainly considered scriptural then. However, during most of the first century there was no complete agreement upon a canon of Jewish Scripture. Scholars believe the final authorized collection of Hebrew Bible texts began to be established in approximately 90 CE, about the time the Letter of Jude was written.

2 Peter

The letter called 2 Peter was not written by the person who wrote 1 Peter, and it may be the latest of all New Testament writings. It may have been written as late as 130 CE. The author makes a sustained effort to convince his readers he is Jesus' companion Peter. He frames his letter as a sort of "last will and testament." He writes, "I think it right to keep refreshing your memory so long as I still lodge in this body. I know that very soon I must leave it; indeed our Lord Jesus Christ has told me so" (1:13–14). The presentation of teachings in this fashion was rather common in the ancient world, especially by Jewish writers.

Second Peter is similar to Jude in its condemnation of the beliefs and behaviors of Christians with whom the author disagrees. Indeed, much of Jude is incorporated into

2 Peter: Jude 1:4–16 can be found in Second Peter 2:1–18; Jude 1:17–18 appears in 2 Peter 3:1–3.

One interesting passage gives a description of a vision of the Lord. Peter claims to have seen with his own eyes Jesus in majesty when, at the hands of God, Jesus was invested with honor and glory. Upon the sacred mountain, Peter heard the voice of God declare Jesus to be "my Son, my beloved" (1:16–18). This seems at first to be an account of the transfiguration (Mark 9:2–8), but the general Christian belief was that God invested Jesus with honor and glory after his resurrection, and the reference to the sacred mountain is probably to Mount Zion, the location of the Jerusalem temple. Accordingly, some scholars believe the description in 2 Peter is of Jesus' resurrection rather than of the transfiguration and may come from a tradition independent of the four gospels.

In addition to condemning the behavior of his opponents in the manner of Jude, the author of 2 Peter protests against those who have lost faith in the second coming of Jesus: "They will say: 'Where now is the promise of his coming? Our fathers have been laid to their rest, but still everything continues exactly as it has always been since the world began'" (3:4). Christians throughout the New Testament period had eagerly or fearfully awaited the coming of the end of this world and the return of Jesus Christ. As time went on and these events did not take place, their failure to occur seemed to provide evidence that Christian teachings were invalid. The apostles' most emphatic predictions—indeed, perhaps, Jesus' own predictions—were not, apparently, going to come true.

Various solutions were offered to the problem that Jesus failed to come again. Some, such as Luke, believed the end would indeed come, but it would be a long time coming and prior to its coming there would be a period for the church to spread and for the gospel to be preached to all people. Others, such as John (and the Gospel of Thomas), suggested that, in fact, the end had already occurred and the opportunity for eternal life was already present. In the words of the Gospel of Thomas (saying 113), "The Kingdom of the Father is spread out on the earth, and men do not see it." Another solution, one adopted by various writers, including the author of 1 Peter (1 Pet 4:7), was to announce that the delay was over and the end would occur immediately. The author of 2 Peter instead suggests that people have misunderstood the predictions; even if they seem to indicate the end will come in only a few months, "with the Lord one day is like a thousand years and a thousand years is like one day" (3:8). Presumably, therefore, many thousands of years could still pass without invalidating predictions of the end. Furthermore, he writes, the Lord is merciful in not returning for judgment, because, by delaying, he makes it possible for more people to repent.

To avoid an excessive number of interpretations of scripture, the author of 2 Peter insisted that only authorized teachers may interpret scripture: "No one can interpret any prophecy of Scripture by himself. For it was not through any human whim that men prophesied of old; men they were, but, impelled by the Holy Spirit they spoke the words of God" (1:20–21). That said, it is unclear in 2 Peter whether those authorized to interpret Scripture are to use established principles of interpretation or to rely on inspiration from the Holy Spirit.

The Beginning of the Christian Canon

The Pastoral Epistles and the other letters found toward the end of the New Testament are *pseudepigraphal writings*, which means that they were written in the name of revered figures from the past. Individuals chose to write in the name of James or Peter or Paul because they felt that only by using such respected names would their own letters or essays be taken seriously enough. Further, by the end of the first century the Christian churches had developed the principle of apostolic authority, which is the view that doctrinal and moral teaching may be trusted only if it has been transmitted directly from Jesus' apostles. Listed below are the various ways Christian teachers legitimized their teachings:

1. *Personal authority:* Jesus' parables and other sayings were based on his personal authority. Paul's letters usually appeal to his personal authority as a community's founder.
2. *Apostolic authority:* Those people whom the risen Christ supposedly authorized to teach were credited with apostolic authority. Paul writes in this regard that the risen Christ "appeared to Cephas [Peter], and afterwards to the Twelve. Then he appeared to over five hundred of our brothers at once, most of whom are still alive, though some have died. Then he appeared to James, and afterwards to all the apostles. In the end he appeared even to me" (1 Cor 15:5–8). The titles of most New Testament texts appeal to apostolic authority.
3. *Spiritual authority:* Those people who believed themselves to be inspired by the Holy Spirit could claim the Spirit's authority for their teaching and writing. The author of Revelation does this.
4. *Institutional authority:* Those people with institutionalized authority based their claim on their position in the church hierarchy: deacons, elders, or bishops. The Pastorals' author has this kind of authority.

Toward the end of the first century those with a legitimate claim to apostolic authority had nearly all died. Spiritual authority continued to be asserted, but it was increasingly viewed with suspicion. Texts such as 1 John show some of the difficulties that claims to spiritual authority can cause.

Most pseudepigraphal texts derive from attempts by individuals living after the age of the apostles to assert apostolic authority. However, unlimited multiplication of texts bearing the names of revered apostles would lead inevitably to chaos within the church. To counter this tendency, churches began to select texts they regarded as having legitimate apostolic authority and to discard texts they thought did not have such authority. This process of selection was part of the process that led eventually to the creation of the New Testament canon.

We know nothing about how specific texts were chosen to be canonical, nor do we have very much knowledge of many of the rejected texts. Only a handful survive. It is dubious reasoning to argue that canonical New Testament texts were chosen because they contain correct teaching, for, over the centuries, Christians have come to define correct teaching as teaching in accord with the New Testament texts, so the argument becomes circular and invalid: "The New Testament canon was chosen because those documents contain teachings in accord with the teachings of the New Testament canon." It is equally circular to argue that, "The New Testament is divinely inspired because the divinely inspired teachings of the New Testament say the New Testament is inspired." Yet even today such arguments are made.

All of the texts in the New Testament are attributed to figures from the apostolic age, such as John, Peter, Paul, and Matthew. Likewise, many additional texts circulating in the late first and second centuries bore the names of apostles and pretended to have been written by apostles. It is not likely that texts were respected only because they bore the name of an apostle, however. More likely, churches or groups of Christians first thought a text authoritative and then came to believe that it derived from an apostle. The four gospels were not authoritative because it could be historically proven that they derived from Matthew, Mark, Luke, and John. Rather, they were first considered authoritative; *therefore*, they were then assigned to people who lived in the apostolic age.

Toward the end of the first century and for some time thereafter, any respected text, even if respected only by a minority of Christians, received an appropriate apostolic title. The Gospel of Thomas, the Gospel of Mary, the Gospel of Peter, the Secret Book of John, the Apocalypse of Peter, the Acts of John, and the Acts of Peter are examples. These texts still exist, some completely and some in fragmentary form. They provide no historically reliable information about the apostles whose names they bear, but they are significant. They reveal the desires of Christians during the time of the formation of the canon to attribute texts to apostolic persons and they preserve a host of Christian ideas and perspectives from very early times.

Second Peter is the only New Testament text to refer to any other New Testament texts as "Scripture," and so it stands at the beginning of the time when the New Testament canon began to form. The author writes,

> Bear in mind that our Lord's patience with us is our salvation, as Paul, our friend and brother, said when he wrote to you with his inspired wisdom. And so he does in all his other letters, wherever he speaks of this subject, though they contain some obscure passages, which the ignorant and unstable misinterpret to their own ruin, as they do the other scriptures (3:15–16).

Evidently Paul's letters are regarded as scripture similar in authority to the scriptures of the Hebrew Bible. It is interesting that in the early second century, just as they do today, readers of Paul's letters find "obscure passages" that are then misinterpreted.

As death depleted the ranks of apostles and others who were eyewitnesses to Jesus, the motivation to set certain

Christian texts apart as inspired writing increased. Within a generation or so after the writing of 2 Peter, the creation of a Christian canon of scripture was well under way. Toward the end of the second century the four gospels, Acts, and Paul's letters were considered scripture by most churches.

A Christian leader in Rome named Marcion, in about the year 150 CE, established the first "New Testament" separate from the Hebrew Bible. Marcion rejected from his canon the Hebrew Bible and also most of what is now considered to be Christian Scripture. He regarded as scriptural only the Gospel of Luke and certain letters of Paul, and he even edited those to accord with his own ideas.

Marcion's ideas, particularly his notion that the God revealed in the Hebrew Bible was a secondary demonic god, proved unacceptable to most Christians. In response to Marcion's initial "New Testament" canon, churches whose members did respect the Hebrew Bible established canons of their own that were more extensive, canons usually containing all four gospels discussed in this book. In the late second century CE, Irenaeus, the bishop of Lyon in what is now France, writes of the four gospels—Matthew, Mark, Luke and John—as if they were an established, unquestionably authoritative set. Churches continued to disagree, however, whether such texts as Revelation, Jude, and 2 Peter should be included. Some included the Letters of Clement, or the text called The Shepherd of Hermas. It was not until the mid-fourth century that Western Christian churches finally agreed completely on the New Testament canon we now have.

The Revelation to John

As a general rule, the documents in the New Testament occur in the order of the value placed on them by Christian leaders of the third century. The Revelation to John, commonly known simply as Revelation, is the New Testament's final text. The title of the work, in Greek, is the "Apocalypse" of John, and that title is retained in some translations. *Apocalypse* means "to raise the covering," ("apo-calypse"), which in turn implies the uncovering of hidden divine secrets about events in the present and in the future. Revelation purports to show through symbols the events that will take place during the end of this world. Revelation is not unique in its apocalyptic approach. Other, much shorter apocalypses appear in the New Testament: First and Second Thessalonians contain apocalyptic passages; Mark 13 is apocalyptic. Some apocalyptic material may also be found in the Hebrew Bible, and the author of Revelation was probably influenced by this. BEFORE READING REVELATION, YOU SHOULD READ DANIEL 7–8, ZECHARIAH 12–14, AND EZEKIEL 1, 10, & 39, TO UNDERSTAND THE STYLE AND CONTENT OF APOCALYPTIC WRITING.

Revelation's author is said to be named John, but he is not the author of the Gospel of John or of the letters of John. Revelation shares some ideas with the gospel and letters of John—for example, the idea of Jesus as the Lamb of God—but it is written in a very different Greek style and lacks some of John's gospel's principal themes.

Because he was exiled during a period of persecution by Rome, the author lives on the small Greek island of Patmos. He writes, "It was on the Lord's day, and I was caught up by the Spirit; and behind me I heard a loud voice, like the sound of a trumpet, which said to me, 'Write down what you see on a scroll and send it to the seven churches'" (Rev 1:10–11). He claims to be writing what he experienced during an altered state of consciousness that he describes in terms of the Spirit. The seven churches are specified by name; they all are located in cities of Asia Minor, which is modern day

Turkey. Chapters 2 and 3 of Revelation contain letters written to those specific churches and make accusations against members of those churches.

These letters might be contrasted with the letters of Paul in respect to the authority claim of the writer. Paul consistently appeals to his personal authority over churches. Revelation's author does not seem to have personal authority but considers himself to be a means by which the heavenly world can communicate to churches on the earth. Supposedly, we are not hearing John's opinions but, rather, we are to experience and hear through his words what he himself experienced and heard. It is quite possible that he was not known personally in the seven churches. He expects those who read the letters to acknowledge that they are the words of the Spirit, and so, in theory, the author of the letters is the Spirit of God, not John, for we hear repeatedly "Hear, you who have ears to hear, what the Spirit says to the churches!" Each letter contains specific commendations and, more often, condemnations directed toward a particular church. Scholars have sought to determine more specifically what the situations were in those churches, but the evidence in Revelation is so sketchy that opinions vary considerably.

From 4:1–22:21, Revelation reports the author's visions of events in Heaven that are understood to symbolize events on earth. It symbolically details the devastations that will accompany the end of his present age and, with less emphasis, the glories that will accompany the age to come—the "new heaven and the new earth" (21:1).

This overall pattern of movement from extended devastation to predicted glory can be found also in smaller units of Revelation's organization. As any reading of the text will reveal, the author has made sustained use of an organizational pattern oriented around the number seven. There are seven seals, seven trumpets, seven bowls, and so forth. Often within the seven "uncoverings," the "apocalypses" of these units, the first four are forms of catastrophe to come upon the earth. The next two are richly detailed catastrophes to come. The last, the seventh unit, is more affirmative, or at least ambiguous: the seventh seal is a time of silence preceded by a vision of the victory of God's people; the seventh angel gives a scroll as sweet as honey that turns the stomach sour; and the seventh bowl is the final destruction of Babylon the great. The number seven was commonly understood in the ancient world to symbolize completion, which derives from the fact that there are seven visibly moving heavenly bodies: Sun, Moon, Mercury, Venus, Mars, Jupiter and Saturn.

The Organization of Revelation

Although Revelation seems to be very tightly organized around units of seven, scholars disagree on how, exactly, to understand its full structure. The following is one system of organization; it could be far more detailed. This system understands Revelation to be analogous to a dramatic performance.

<u>READ THE REVELATION TO JOHN FOLLOWING THE OUTLINE BELOW:</u>

    The author and his experience:
- Title and introduction (1:1–3)
- First vision (1:9–20)

    The Spirit writes to churches
- Letters to Seven churches (2:1–3:22)

    Prologue to the Drama
- Vision of the Throne of God (4:1–11)

    Dramatic Act One
- Scene One
  - The Seven Seals (5:1–8:1)
- Scene Two
  - The Seven Trumpets (8:2–11:14)

Dramatic Act Two
- Scene One
  - The Attack of the Dragon and Beasts (12:1–14:5)
- Scene Two
  - The Judgment of God (14:6–20:15)
  - The Sickles (14:65–20)
  - The Seven Bowls of Plague (15:1–16:21)
  - The Judgment of Babylon (17:1–19:10)
  - The Judgment on the Beast (19:11–21)
  - The Judgment on Satan (20:1–10)
  - Resurrection and Judgment Day (20:11–15)

Dramatic Act Three
- Scene One
  - The New Creation (21:1–8)
- Scene Two
  - The New Jerusalem (21:9–22:5)

Concluding Comments (22:6–21)

Revelation is divided into several parts and it is probably best, when reading the whole text, to pause between parts to take a breath and think about what you've read. Don't just read with your intellect, read with your imagination; depict in your mind the pictures the author draws.

The first section of Revelation (1:1–3) is a prologue by John, explaining the sequence of communication involved in its creation: God gave Jesus Christ a revelation, which Jesus then communicated to an angel, who then brought it to John, who will now report it to his community and, eventually, to you. There follows (1:4–8) a second prologue in the form of an open letter to the seven churches of Asia. John begins by giving his own name as author but adds Jesus Christ as co-author. John provides a litany of descriptive phrases about Jesus. A third prologue (1:9–20) starts with John's description of his personal situation: he is exiled onto the Greek

Mediterranean island of Patmos. Evidently, he was found guilty of giving testimony in favor of Christ and Christianity, which he probably did in Rome. In Roman legal practice the punishment of exile was generally reserved for people of the upper classes, while people of lower social class might have been scourged, imprisoned, or killed for the same crime. The third prologue gives the first of Revelation's many astonishing visual descriptions: Jesus Christ stands behind John and commands him to act as Jesus' scribe in receiving dictation and transmitting it to seven particular churches.

After the prologues, we read the letters that were supposedly dictated by Jesus Christ. Each reaches out to the people of a separate Christian community. The principal concerns of the letters are with the faithfulness of the communities, or the lack thereof, the tendency of the communities to follow the teachings of people John disagrees with, and so forth. We do not know any more about the "Nicolaitans" or the so-called "synagogues of Satan" than what we read of them in these little letters, which give us practically no information at all.

In Revelation 4 and 5, John, and we along with him, peer through an open door into heaven. Then, as John is taken over by the Holy Spirit, we enter into the throne room of heaven itself. You should read this chapter with an open imagination; it is designed for imagination, not for detailed explanation, although a brief internet search will give you a whole variety of interpretations of aspects of these visions and all the other visions in revelation. There are, for example, twenty-four elders around the throne of God. Are these saints of the church, angels in heaven, righteous kings, prophets, none of the above? We do not know.

To a considerable degree the imagery John uses is found in chapters 1 and 10 of Ezekiel's prophecies in the Hebrew Bible. The living creatures mentioned in Revelation 4:7 (from Ezekiel chapter 1) later became fundamental symbols in Christian art representing the four evangelists: Mark the Lion, Matthew the Ox, Luke the Human, John the Eagle. The lamb with seven eyes and seven horns represents Jesus Christ. While often the symbols in Revelation have been adopted by the Christian religion, sometimes they are not. For example, while the four living creatures are common in Christian symbolism, the symbolic seven eyed lamb and the idea of the seven spirits of God (5:6) are almost never found outside of Revelation.

In Revelation 7, we are introduced to the 144,000 who will be sealed for salvation (12,000 people for each of the 12 tribes of Israel). But this specific number reference is immediately followed by John mentioning a great multitude that cannot even be counted and that stand before the throne of God clothed in white. In Revelation the color symbolism is rather clear: white is for purity, red is for blood, gold is for value, and purple is for royalty.

The idea of the scroll with seven seals has particularly intrigued people. In chapter 6, the first four seals are opened to unleash the famous "four horsemen of the apocalypse" (6:1–8). The fifth seal opens to reveal martyred Christians who hunger for revenge but who are told to wait a little longer until all those who would be killed for the faith are dead. Much of Revelation is about vengeance, anger and slaughter, and, continuing along these lines, the opening of the sixth seal brings divine wrath onto a cosmological level: the sun blackens, the moon turns as red as blood, the sky disappears, mountains vanish, socially elite men, kings, generals, and the rich become desperate to hide from the wrath of the Lamb! The action pauses for moment so that the righteous might be sealed with a protective symbol in the throne room of God, which is described again (7:9–12).

As the narrative continues, we suddenly come to a half-hour of silence (8:1), which should remind the reader that not only has heaven been described with blazing visual images, symbols, colors, and creatures, but also there has been strong emphasis on the sounds of heaven—the praises and thundering and songs. It is a clamorous place; the voices and trumpets are usually described as being very loud. The seventh seal is removed and violent symbols come flooding forth in Revelation's prose. Most of the human race is slaughtered . . . but read on for yourself. Don't follow anyone's summary or explanation of the Revelation to John without first-hand knowledge from your own reading.

Revelation 21 shifts from condemnation and the description of the end of the world of the Roman Empire to a vision of a new world. A heavenly Jerusalem descends and replaces Rome; a demonic city is removed and a divine city appears. John describes heavenly Jerusalem with precise measurements and exact descriptions of the jewels out of which it is constructed. The Lord God will be present in the new city and his light will replace the light of the sun, and all the faithful Christians, the 144,000, and the countless multitude will enter it and live forever.

The concept of God in Revelation is far removed from the common twenty-first century idea that God is, above all else, a loving divine parent. The God of Revelation is enraged with most of humanity, and a great many passages in Revelation describe God's anger, wrath and vengeance. The final peaceful conclusion of the book does, to some degree, modify this picture, but it does so only in reference to the comparatively few faithful Christians. From the point of view of Revelation, the heavenly Jerusalem will arrive only after God has provided for the slaughter of most of humanity.

It needs to be emphasized that when scholars carefully read Revelation, they discover that it does not quite fit any one organizational scheme. The author of Revelation is clearly writing in a symbolic fashion on some occasions, but on most occasions he is letting his imagination fly, and we have no reason to believe that each description is some sort of symbolic code. On a few occasions he gives clues to the interpretation of his symbols (1:20, 4:5, 5:6, 17:9–18, 19:8) but even so, they can remain obscure. There are discontinuities, variations in the meaning of symbols, and elements that do not seem related to the context in which they appear. Some have hypothesized that Revelation was compiled, somewhat crudely, out of a set of originally independent apocalyptic vision texts. Others have devoted years of their lives to composing highly intricate schemes to account for all of Revelation, but no such scheme has been widely accepted.

One widely shared conclusion of scholarship is that Revelation was motivated by John's absolute, unremitting hatred for the Roman Empire and its emperor. This is especially true for chapters 17 through 19, wherein the whole of the Roman Empire and its allies, its merchants, its success, and its wealth all are condemned. Few other New Testament texts share such a violently anti-Roman attitude, and some, like the book of Acts, are intended to show the Roman authorities that Christians do not intend to oppose them. Clearly, Revelation was written after a period of the persecution of Christian people by Roman authority, and the visions written down by the author are a response to this persecution. He declares that Christians, especially the martyrs to persecution, can expect ultimate vengeance and victory. Babylon the great (the Roman Empire) will be overthrown and the beast killed. How do we know Babylon is Rome? Because it is the city of the seven hills (17:9). The author knows of seven emperors of whom five have fallen, one reigns and one is to come and reign for but a little while. The beast that once was alive and is alive no longer is an eighth emperor and yet one of the seven. This sounds simple enough, especially when one understands that there was a popular legend that the emperor Nero would come back to life (so he could be the eighth who was one of the seven). Unfortunately, it is possible to identify the sixth emperor (who is alive at the time of the production of Revelation) with Nero, or with Vespasian, or with Domitian, depending on how you interpret the evidence. It all depends on which emperors one counts; some of them only ruled for a matter of days and so may be ones to whom John refers, or perhaps he ignores them. Be that as it may, most scholars believe that revelation comes from the later part of the reign of emperor Domitian, some time in the 90's CE.

We hear that the number of the (Roman) beast is 666 (13:18) a number value that has been the cause of great speculation, for the number value is said to be the value of the letters of a man's name. In the ancient world, in all languages, letters were used as numbers; our "Arabic" numerals had not been invented yet. In Rome, for example, D = 500, C = 100, L = 50, X = 10, V = 5, I = 1. If one takes the numerical value of the letters of the name Caesar Nero as written in Hebrew, they equate to 666, a fact which is often offered as the solution to the mystery of 666, but one might argue that the number-letters given above, in order, in Roman numerals *also* equate to that mystery number, for DCLXVI = 666, in which case the number of the beast is the numbering system of Rome.

Readers who wish to investigate the structure and symbolism of Revelation further may turn to any of dozens of published interpretations, but you should bear one particular principle in mind: it is dreadfully egocentric to think that Revelation is all about you. It was written for and about people who lived two thousand years ago. For the past two thousand years, in every century, there have been preachers, teachers, leaders and readers who have assumed that Revelation was written for them and their particular time. They concluded that the end of the world would come in their lifetime and in their presence. They were wrong. Revelation was not about them. Revelation is not about you, and it is not about now.

There are three ways interpreters approach the decoding of the Revelation to John:

First, some believe that our evidence is sufficient to determine in some detail the author's view of his own time and situation. Revelation was written in the latter half of the first century and reflects the persecution of Christians by Roman authority. It reflects other social and environmental conditions: famine, earthquake, war, and so forth. It contains clues (the seven emperors, the mystery of 666) that may be decipherable. From this perspective, Revelation is not intended to predict events much further in time than a few decades. The author thought that the new heaven and the new earth would arrive soon; they did not. Nevertheless, we can decipher his text in order to understand his date, his circumstances, and his beliefs about what is to happen. But even if we can do this to a degree, there remain many symbols that we cannot possibly interpret and, indeed, we can reasonably conclude that even Revelation's author didn't understand them all. If Revelation stems from an altered state-of-consciousness visionary experience, as the author says it does, there is no reason to think that the author could tell you what all of the sights and sounds of his experience were supposed to symbolize.

Even if the political situation of the author and the date of his composition cannot be known for certain, we can certainly make progress in understanding Revelation in reference to other apocalyptic works, canonical and non-canonical, Jewish and Christian. This will allow greater understanding of the author's thought, and the thought of Christians and Jews of his time.

Second, one might believe that Revelation speaks to one's own time. This is not an uncommon approach. For centuries, some Christians have thought that the decoding of Revelation should be done in reference to events taking place in the centuries or decades preceding their own date. From this, they have concluded that the arrival of the new heaven and the new earth would take place in a few years or decades. This has sometimes had pernicious effects: David Koresh, who orchestrated the Waco, Texas disaster of 1993, firmly believed that he had the key to Revelation's decoding. Among his conclusions were that law enforcement officials of the United States were agents of the Beast and that he and his followers should die the death of Revelation's martyrs.

Those who regard Revelation as a prophetic text and believe its code to be directed toward their own time and situation are arrogant and self-obsessed. God, they seem to think, did not intend to speak to people one hundred, five hundred, fifteen hundred years ago, or 500 years from now, but meant only to speak to them right now in the early twenty-first century. Over the centuries hundreds of attempts have been made to decode Revelation in light of the events of the decoder's particular period of time. Each attempt has exactly the same validity as all other attempts, for there is no way to determine which, if any, of all their various interpretations are correct. Therein lies the prime difficulty of Revelation. If there is no way to determine whose decoding of the imagery of Revelation is correct; anyone may make it mean anything they want and so claim the authority of the word of God for their opinions. Recently, various symbols in Revelation have been said to represent Franklin Delano Roosevelt, Ronald Reagan, popes of the Roman Catholic church, the European Common Market, the leadership of the Soviet Union, victims of the AIDS epidemic, the United States Alcohol, Tobacco and Firearms authorities, terrorist assaults on symbolic American structures, and dozens of other groups and individuals. No one can prove these identifications are correct. Political prejudices and ideologies can be made to look

Christian by such misreadings of Revelation, for, where no rules apply, anything goes.

Third, one may say in all candor and honesty that Revelation's symbolism cannot be thoroughly understood. We do not have enough evidence to go on, and what evidence we have is too ambiguous. The present author tends to take that perspective. Revelation is an interesting piece of writing and should be understood as such. It can tell us much about the apocalyptic mentality of early Christian and Jewish thinkers. But efforts to decode it in historical detail or in light of present circumstances are not time well spent. Enjoy it! Revelation is one of the most colorful, exciting, bizarre, complicated and just plain weird texts that has ever been written. It is the foundation of much Christian artistic symbolism and it is worth your time to read and read again. But it isn't all about you.

End-of-Chapter Exercises

1. Describe some of the ways in which community concerns seemed to influence the way the author of the letters to Timothy structured his arguments. Suggest some concerns a letter to a modern-day audience would need to address.
2. Reread 2 Timothy. Can you find reasons why analytical scholars came to the conclusion that the author of Romans and Galatians did not write it?
3. Look at the list of various ways Christian teachers legitimized their teachings on page 340. What are some forms of authority people today use to legitimize their ideas, such as on the news or in books you've read? Are they the same as those of early Christians?
4. Why is Revelation so difficult to analyze? How best should it be approached when reading it from a scholar's perspective?

Bibliography

Barker, Margaret. *The Revelation of Jesus Christ*. Edinburgh: T & T Clark, 2000.

Barton, John. *Holy Writings, Sacred Text: The Canon in Early Christianity*. Louisville KY: Westminster John Knox, 1997.

Brown, Raymond E. "The Epistles of John." *Anchor Bible Commentary*. Vol. 30. Garden City NY: Doubleday, 1982.

Caird, George Bradford. *A Commentary on the Revelation of St. John the Divine*. San Francisco: Harper & Row, 1966.

Collins, Raymond F. *1 and 2 Timothy and Titus*. Louisville KY: Westminster John Knox, 2002.

Dibelius, Martin, and Heinrich Greeven. *A Commentary on the Epistle of James*. Hermeneia Commentary. Philadelphia: Fortress Press, 1976.

Fuller, Reginald H., et al. "The Letter to the Hebrews, James, 1 and 2 Peter, Jude, Revelation." *Proclamation Commentaries*. Philadelphia: Fortress Press, 1977.

Kovacs, Judith, and Christopher Rowland. *Revelation: The Apocalypse of Jesus Christ*. Hoboken NJ: Wiley-Blackwell, 2004.

Preston, Ronald, and Anthony Hanson. *The Revelation of St. John the Divine*. London: SCM Press, 1949.

Reicke, Bo. "The Epistles of James, Peter and Jude." *Anchor Bible Commentary*. Vol. 37. Garden City NY: Doubleday, 1964.

Trotter, Andrew, *Interpreting the Epistle to the Hebrews*. Grand Rapids MI: Baker, 1997.

ANALYTICAL ASSESSMENT

Tasks and Exercises

Chapter 1: Introduction

1. Select an interesting passage from one of the four gospels. Write an essay on the context and meaning of that passage.
2. A gospel is a document written to explain the importance of Jesus which takes the general form of a biography. Write a gospel of at least five pages. You may glance at the New Testament gospels to refresh your memory, but do not copy out passages word for word. You may invent stories and sayings if you wish. If you believe Jesus had no particular importance, your gospel should reflect that point of view.
3. Analyze one of the gospels written for the exercise above—your own or another's. What features are absent? What is stressed most strongly? For example, is the birth story stressed? Does Jesus appear to his followers after his resurrection? Are his sayings prominent? Is the Jewish Law mentioned? What view of the disciples do you find? Compare at least one saying or story in the gospel you read with a corresponding version in a New Testament gospel. What do you now know about the kinds of choices and decisions a gospel writer

must make? What sources does a gospel writer have? How much freedom of interpretation does a gospel writer have?

4. To show the changes that can result from oral transmissions of sayings, several people should be asked to write down the parable of the prodigal son (or some other commonly known parable) as best they can remember it. At the outset those people who declare they know nothing of the parable should be given the opportunity to read it, while those who declare they have some knowledge of it (however slight) should not read it. Compare the versions written with the original. What expansions, deletions, explanatory comments, or additional material appear in the various versions?

5. Take a map of your region and a map of Palestine at the time of Jesus. If possible, try and obtain maps where the "scale of miles" is about the same. Take a compass and draw circles around your location and around Nazareth (or Jerusalem) at, say, twenty-mile intervals. There's no better way to get a feel for the distances involved in the stories of Jesus.

Chapter 2: Judaism and the Roman Empire

1. Assume you have chosen to follow all Torah laws. Read Leviticus 11:1–47. Write a two-page letter to inform people what should no longer be prepared for your meals. Do not mention foods you would not eat anyway. Include specific citations from Leviticus (e.g. Leviticus 11:34–35).

2. Read Luke 5:1–6:11. Identify the social groups mentioned or implied in that section of the gospel. What arguments about Torah Law take place? What positions does Jesus take regarding the Law?

3. A wide variety of accusations are made against Pharisees in chapter 23 of the Gospel of Matthew. From the perspective of a Pharisee, write a defense of Pharisees against some of the accusations. Use common sense.

Chapter 3: Paul's Letters

1. Carefully read Galatians 3:1–18. Paul's argument repeatedly refers to the Hebrew Scriptures. Look up each reference below:

Galatians 3:6	Genesis 15:6
Galatians 3:8	Genesis 12:3 and 18:18
Galatians 3:10	Deuteronomy 27:26
Galatians 3:11	Habakkuk 2:4
Galatians 3:12	Leviticus 18:5
Galatians 3:13	Deuteronomy 21:23
Galatians 3:16	Genesis 12:7, 13:15, 17:7, 24:7
Galatians 3:17	Exodus 12:40

    How does Paul use the passages given above to construct his argument?

2. Either through careful reading or the use of a concordance, locate the passages in Galatians speaking of Jesus as the Son of God or of Christians as Sons or children of God. Using these passages, and referring to their context, write an essay on the concept of the Son of God in Galatians.

3. Read 1 Corinthians from chapter 11 to the end. This section contains many crucial and interesting passages, including Paul's version of the Lord's Supper. Write a description of a communion meeting of the church in Corinth featuring some of the difficulties Paul wrote to correct.

4. Read 1 Thessalonians and compare the eschatological ideas you find there with those in Mark's chapter 13. To what extent are they saying the same thing? Are there

significant differences? Read 2 Thessalonians and compare the ideas there to those in 1 Thessalonians. Would you conclude Paul wrote 2 Thessalonians?

Chapter 4: Gospel Sources

Miracles Sources

1. Read 2 Kings 4:1–44, especially the end, 4:42–44, and compare the story there with Mark 6:30–44, Mark 8:1–9, and John 6:1–13. Some scholars believe the miracle of the loaves and fishes is derived from the account of Elisha's similar miracle. Do you agree? Or do you find there are such substantial differences that the two are only coincidentally similar?
2. Read each of the miracles stories contained in the sources and make careful note of what actions Jesus performs. What does he do? What words does he use? Do you think the more detailed stories are original, or that details were added? Justify your answer with examples from the text.

The Q Source

1. Read the book of Jonah in the Hebrew Scriptures and references to it in Luke 11:29–32. Then read the parallel, Matthew 12:38–42. Determine as best you can the basic message the book of Jonah seeks to communicate. The Q passage refers to the book of Jonah; what do you believe the passage means by "the sign of Jonah"? Does the version of the saying in Luke or the version in Matthew seem most likely to be original? (The reference to the Queen of the South is to the Queen of Sheba mentioned in 1 Kings 10:1–10).
2. Read Proverbs 22:1–23:29. These are sayings written down before the time of Jesus but well-known in his

time. What similarities of style and content exist between these sayings and Jesus' sayings in Q? What differences are there?
3. Find references in Q to the "Son of Man," and, from those references, describe the Q people's view of the Son of Man. Is Jesus Son of Man in the sense of God's agent in the final days? Is the future son of man in Q something Jesus only talks about or is it Jesus himsefl? Use as evidence only the Q sayings you have located and not other New Testament passages.
4. There are three ancient versions of the parable of the wedding feast. Two come from Q, one from the Gospel of Thomas. Those in Q are found in Luke 14:16–24 and Matthew 22:1–14. The version in Thomas is saying 64 (consult a translation from the internet). Possibly one or more of these stories refers to a passage in Deuteronomy (20:5–8) allowing certain excuses. Which version of the parable has a superior claim to being the original version? What kinds of decision did you make in selecting one (e.g. shorter is better, longer is better, ones with explanations are better, and/or the one that most closely resembles the Deuteronomy passage is better)?

Chapter 5: The Gospel of Mark

1. Read Daniel 7:1–8:27 in the Hebrew Bible. Chapter 13 of Mark is probably influenced by a passage in the book of Daniel (7:13) referring to "one like a son of man," which is also translated "one like a man." Many early Christians believed this being who is "like a son of man" was Jesus, the Son of Man. Reread Mark's chapter 13. How might it be argued that the statements about the Son of Man in Mark 13:26 and 14:62 are derived from the passage in Daniel?

2. Compare Mark 10:1–12 with Matthew 5:31–32, 19:3–12, Luke 16:18, and Paul's 1 Corinthians 7:10–11. Is divorce permitted according to these passages? If so, under what circumstances? Is remarriage after divorce permitted? Why or why not?
3. It is possible that the story in Mark 5:1–20 is not a miracle story at all but an allegory. In the allegory the man possessed by demons could signify the nation of Israel occupied by Romans. Pigs might signify Gentiles, for Gentiles ate pork while Jews regarded it as forbidden. The word *Legion* is a Latin word for an army division. Does this make sense in the context of the Roman occupation of Israel, or is it reading too much into the story? Locate Gerasa on a map of ancient Palestine. What does its location on the map and its implied location in the story tell us of Mark's knowledge of Palestinian geography? Why do you suppose here, as almost nowhere else, Jesus forbids a person to follow him, does not order silence, and commands the person to go and announce what happened?
4. Reread Mark 12:38–44. Write an argument either that the poor widow is an example of proper piety in giving her money to the temple treasury, or that she is an example of someone misled by the "doctors of the law" who "eat up the property of widows."

Chapter 6: The Gospel of Matthew

1. The following are passages from the birth story and the prophecies to which they apparently refer:

Matthew 1:22	Isaiah 7:14
Matthew 2:6	Micah 5:2 and 2 Samuel 5:2
Matthew 2:15	Hosea 11:1
Matthew 2:18	Jeremiah 31:15

| Matthew 2:23 | Isaiah 11:1 |
| Matthew 3:3 | Isaiah 40:3 |

Read these passages in their own context in the Hebrew Scriptures and refer to standard commentaries on the Hebrew Scriptures for information about their historical settings. Prepare arguments for or against the idea that Matthew's interpretations are justified.

2. Use a copy of *Gospel Parallels* and locate a passage or set of passages showing changes made by Matthew when he revised the Gospel of Mark. Make reasoned guesses as to Matthew's motivations in making such changes and discuss these motivations in an essay, giving your reasons for ascribing them to Matthew. Your guesses should reflect your understanding of Matthew's overall perspective as given in his gospel.

3. You have read Paul's letter to the Galatians. Assume that Matthew, passing through Galatia on a vacation trip to the Black Sea, stops in the home serving as the Christian church in Galatia and is shown a copy of Paul's letter. Write a response, in the form of a letter, from Matthew to Paul.

Chapter 7: The Gospel of Luke and the Acts of the Apostles

1. In the book of Acts, several passages refer to the psalms of the Hebrew scriptures. The psalms are traditionally said to have been written by King David (ca. 1000 BCE), and Luke accepts that attribution, although no analytical scholars do so today. Read the Psalms 2, 16, 69, 109, 110, and 132. To what extent do you believe they are interpreted correctly in Acts 1:16–22, 2:22–36, 4:25–27, 13:32–41, and why?

2. Read the accounts of the women who came to Jesus' tomb and discover it to be empty. These are found in

Matthew 27:55–28:10, Mark 15:40–16:8, Luke 23:49–24:11, and John 19:38–20:18. Make a list of common features and of the features you think are significantly different. Write an essay giving your opinion as to why certain of these differences exist.

3. Use *Gospel Parallels* and locate a passage or set of passages showing changes made by Luke when he revised the Gospel of Mark. Make reasoned guesses as to Luke's motivations in making such changes and discuss these motivations in an essay, giving your reasons for ascribing them to Luke. Your guesses should reflect your understanding of Luke's overall perspective as given in his gospel.

4. Read the "we passages" in the book of Acts: 16:10–18, 20:4–21:18, and 27:1–28:16. Write an essay defending either the point of view that (1) these were invented by Luke to add interest to the book of Acts, (2) they were eyewitness accounts Luke used in the writing of Acts, or, (3) indeed, that they are evidence that Luke traveled with Paul.

Chapter 8: The Gospel of John

1. John refers to Exodus 16:1–17:7, where "bread from heaven" and miraculous water are given by God. Read these passages in the Hebrew scriptures and compare them to John's chapter 4, where "living water" is mentioned, and his chapter 3, where "bread from heaven" is discussed. What interpretations of the Exodus passage does John make?

2. Read Proverbs, chapter 8 and 9. Write an essay comparing the concepts of Wisdom in those chapters with the concept of Logos in the opening poem of the Gospel of John. Specify elements of difference as well as similarity.

3. Six versions of the miraculous multiplication of loaves and fishes appear in the New Testament: John 6:1–44; Mark 6:30–44, Mark 8:1–10; Matthew 14:13–21, Matthew 15:32–39; and Luke 9:10–17. Matthew's and Luke's versions are revised versions of Mark's. List the differences in the six stories. Assume there once was a single version of the story and write an account you think might have been the original, using elements from any or all of the six. What decisions did you make in order to complete the exercise?
4. Locate the stories of Jesus' resurrection appearances to his followers in the Gospels of Matthew, Mark (use the passages following 16:8), Luke, and John. They are different. What common features can you discover? What conclusions can be drawn from these common features? What differences to the stories contain? What conclusions can be drawn from the stories' differences?

Chapter 9: Apostolic Letters and the Revelation to John

1. Reread Jude and compare it carefully to 2 Peter. Note the changes or deletions made in Jude by the author of 2 Peter. What motivated the author to make these alterations?
2. Reread the letter of James. Write an essay to defend the position that this letter resembles *either* Matthew's perspective on Law more than Paul's *or* Paul's perspective on Law more than Matthew's. Be sure carefully to read Galatians from chapter 5:13 to the end before making a judgment, for the answer is not obvious.
3. Study the Letter to Hebrews and write a list of the ways in which Christ is said to be the exalted equivalent of an aspect of the Jerusalem Temple, citing chapter

and verse. Construct an argument that the Letter to Hebrews was, or was not, written while the Temple was still standing, i.e. before or after 70 CE.

4. Write a commentary in which you decode as best you can one section of the Revelation to John chosen from chapter 4 to the end in terms of events that took place in the last century. Don't take your results too seriously. Conclude your summary with a discussion of the kinds of decisions you had to make in the process of decoding.

APPENDIX

The Gospel of Thomas

In 1945, a collection of Coptic language manuscripts was found in Nag Hammadi, Egypt, that constitutes the most important discovery of ancient Christian writings in all of history. All of those manuscripts were originally written in Greek, but they were translated in ancient times into the Coptic language of Egypt for the convenience of Egyptian Christians. The collection was buried around 360 CE and may have been part of a monastery library hidden when the monastery was ordered to destroy all questionable or possibly heretical books. Many of those books represented the Christian heresy called Gnosticism, but not all of them did.

In this newly discovered collection of ancient texts, scholars discovered a complete manuscript of a text that had been unearthed in fragments of the original Greek language version in 1898. That Greek text was a list of sayings called the *Gospel of Thomas*. Now, thanks to the Nag Hammadi Coptic translation, scholars have the entirety of the Gospel of Thomas. It has recently been translated into many languages and is widely available.

The Gospel of Thomas is a list of sayings attributed to Jesus of Nazareth. Roughly half of those sayings are recognizably similar to sayings found in the synoptic gospels of Matthew, Mark, and Luke. However, the other half are new, unfamiliar, challenging sayings of Jesus that have never been heard by modern ears before. Some of those sayings really do come from Jesus himself, but many do not. Virtually no sayings in Thomas' gospel are also found in John's gospel.

Scholars separated and numbered the sayings in the Gospel of Thomas mainly at the occurrence of the words "Jesus said," and in doing so they isolated 114 sayings. In fact, there are many more individual sayings units for some of the 114 are two or three short sayings numbered together. While it is virtually certain that many of the previously unknown sayings were invented after Jesus' time and that he never said them, it is also virtually certain that he did indeed say some of them. Readers of the Gospel of Thomas must think about these new sayings and wonder which of them Jesus really said and which ones were conceived by early Christian people and mistakenly attributed to him.

The Gospel of Thomas begins by declaring that "Didymus Judas Thomas" wrote down these sayings of the living Jesus. That name is the nickname "twin" in Greek (Didymus) and in Aramaic (Thomas) with a common proper name "Judas" in the middle. In John's gospel, the apostle Thomas is called "Didymus Thomas." Despite the text's name, the apostle Thomas plays a very minor role in the Gospel of Thomas, being mentioned only at the outset and in saying 13.

At the beginning of the gospel we are told that the sayings of Jesus are so difficult and enigmatic that they are like riddles, or a code that must be deciphered by interested readers. If the readers are successful, we hear the scribe say, they will never die.

Thomas' first sayings, numbers 1, 2, and 3, are something of an introductory statement declaring the Gospel of Thomas' principal theme, which is that the Kingdom of Heaven is already here on earth, both within people and in the world outside of them. People who look for the Kingdom across the sea or up into heaven will not find it there. This principal theme is echoed in what was probably the original ending of the Gospel of Thomas, saying 113, where again we hear that the Kingdom is presently in the world and that people must try to find it for themselves.

The concept of a Kingdom that is already here and now contradicts several New Testament writings, such as Q and Paul's letters, which declare that the Kingdom is coming in the near future but is not here yet. Mark 13 discusses the events that will accompany the future coming of the Kingdom. The idea found in saying 113 that the Kingdom is present throughout this world now also contradicts Gnostic Christianity, which regarded this world as a place entirely alienated from the true heavenly Kingdom of the God beyond the creator of the earth. Saying 114, where Jesus defends women's right to be full Christians, but which is worded in a way that modern Christians find offensive, was probably added later to an original list that concluded with saying 113.

The question of Thomas' relationship to the New Testament is an extremely important one. It may be that about half of the sayings in the Gospel of Thomas originate from the New Testament's sayings and so Thomas' gospel is dependent on the New Testament gospels. However, beyond the framework provided by the first three sayings and the next-to-last one, there is no organization at all in the Gospel of Thomas and no relationship between the order of sayings in Thomas and the order of sayings in any New Testament gospel, or in Q. Since the order of sayings in the Gospel of Thomas is completely unrelated to the order of sayings in the New Testament gospels, and since the wording of the Gospel of Thomas' version of sayings is quite different than the wording of the New Testament versions, it is impossible to think that somebody just copied sayings out of a set of written Biblical books onto a new Thomas list.

It is possible, however, to imagine that the Biblical version of the sayings found in the Gospel of Thomas were learned from the canonical gospels and then repeated by word of mouth over a period of years, and that eventually those derivative versions were written down onto a list. If that was the case, then many of the Gospel of Thomas' sayings could have been indirectly derived from sayings that first appeared in the gospels of Matthew, Mark, and Luke. If so, then the Gospel of Thomas would be a text dependent upon the New Testament's synoptic gospels, which would mean that it probably originated at some time in the middle of the second century. According to that point of view, while the Gospel of Thomas might be an interesting example of what happened in the course of the transmission of New Testament sayings, it would be only a secondary and unreliable source for knowledge of Jesus' teachings.

It is more likely, however, that the sayings in the Gospel of Thomas were all taken directly from oral tradition, and that the canonical biblical gospels had nothing to do with Thomas' sayings traditions. Just as some of the sayings found in the gospels of Matthew and Mark and Luke, and all of the sayings in the Q list, were written into those texts from oral tradition, so sayings were written into the Gospel of Thomas from oral tradition. It seems very unlikely, in a second-century Christian religion increasingly based on a canon of narrative gospels, that people would decide to make a sayings list of materials from the synoptic gospels combined with materials found nowhere in the canonical traditions, and that they would do so while deliberately ignoring everything in the Gospel of John. Furthermore, it is unlikely that the major themes of second century Gnostic Christianity (having to do with the devolution of God into entrapment on the earth through the fall of God's wisdom) and the major themes of Orthodox Christianity (having to do with Jesus as the Christ who was crucified and resurrected) would be completely absent in a mid-second century Christian text. Those themes appear nowhere at all in the Gospel of Thomas.

Simple lists are about the most primitive possible form of the Christian tradition. Thomas may have come into being on a single occasion when a small number of Christians in a room discovered that one of them was literate and, seizing the opportunity, they all recited sayings they believed to come from Jesus while their literate friend wrote them down. It appears that there were lists of miracle stories before gospels were written, and most scholars are confident that there was a sayings list they call Q that existed before Matthew and Luke incorporated it into their books. Thomas probably originated at that same time, somewhere in the middle part of the first century. If so, then the Gospel of Thomas is by far the most important text about Jesus' teachings ever discovered outside of the Bible because it is from a line of Christian tradition separate from the traditions that are included in the Biblical gospels.

The Gospel of Thomas is a witness to a brand of Christianity critical of Jesus' disciples (as Mark's gospel also is). When the disciples ask questions in Thomas' gospel, Jesus' answers correct the implications of the questions. The disciples' questions generally imply that people should look to the future to find the Kingdom of Heaven and that they should look to Jesus himself to find salvation. Those are positions held by the Christians of the New Testament and by virtually all Christian churches today. But in the Gospel of Thomas, Jesus' replies indicate that looking to the future (and also, in saying 3, looking to the heavens) is the wrong approach, for, according to the Jesus portrayed in the Gospel of Thomas, the Kingdom is here now and has been here from the very beginning of creation. Thomas' gospel (sayings 18, 19) indicates that the Kingdom in the world today came into being in Genesis 1, but the fall of Adam, in Genesis 2 onward, led people to lose awareness of the Kingdom. The Kingdom did not go anywhere; it stayed on the earth, but people lost sight of it. Jesus came to bring people back to an awareness of what has been true since Genesis 1. Furthermore, in the Gospel of Thomas it is not Jesus himself who brings salvation. Rather, people are saved through their own efforts, through their seeking and their finding (saying 2), through the light within themselves (saying 24), and their discovery of the Kingdom now (saying 113).

The Gospel of Thomas is critical of principal points of view found in Q and the synoptic gospels. It doesn't simply supplement New Testament accounts of Jesus' teachings but portrays those teachings in a very different and, actually, a very modern light, for it is important to modern ways of thinking that people find divinity within this world now and find it by themselves and within themselves.

Sometimes we can be confident that a new authentic saying of Jesus has appeared in Thomas' gospel. Two examples of such sayings are the parable-sayings numbered 96 and 97. While sayings 24, 70, and 77 may or may not come from Jesus, they represent a fascinating early Christian view of humanity and of Jesus. There are many other interesting sayings to be found in the Gospel of Thomas, and the best way to encounter them is to read the text carefully so as to seek and find what valuable insights it might contain.

The Gospel of Thomas has been translated into many languages and there are several good English translations of it available on the internet. One internet site that you may find useful is The Gospel of Thomas Homepage that can be found at http://users.misericordia.edu/davies/thomas/Thomas.htm. There you can obtain several different translations of the Gospel of Thomas, as well as translations of other ancient Christian texts.

Bibliography

Davies, Stevan. *The Gospel of Thomas Annotated and Explained*. Woodstock VT: Skylight Paths, 2002.

DeConick, April. *Recovering the Original Gospel of Thomas: A History of the Gospel and Its Growth*. London/New York: T & T Clark, 2005.

Hedrick, Charles W. *Unlocking the Secrets of the Gospel According to Thomas: A Radical Faith for a New Age*. Eugene OR: Cascade Books, 2010.

Uro, Risto. *Thomas: Seeking the Historical Context of the Gospel of Thomas*. London/NY: T&T Clark, 2003.

Index

Aaron, 24
Abraham and the covenant, 24, 71–74
Acts of the Apostles, 3, 21, 57–59, **233–75**
    Analytical Assessment Tasks and Exercises, 363–64
    Apostles' speeches in, 240–43
    Author of, 234, 255–56
    Bibliography, 274–75
    Christian community, 267–68
    Compromises in, 259–63
    Controversies in, 268
    Conversion of Jews and Gentiles in, 259–63
    Date of, 234, 241
    Eschatology, 266–67
    Holy Spirit in, 243–44
    Jerusalem Elders and Paul, 260–61
    Jesus' life in, 151, 242, 266
    Jesus' death in, 242
    Peter, vision, 261–62
    Place of Origin, 234
    Relationship to the Gospel of Luke, 241
    Sources, 264–65
    Summaries within, 242–43
    Torah Law, 260–63, 267
    Travel patterns, 256–57
    We passages, 264–65
Adam and Eve, 27, 333
Adonai, 24
Advocate, 291, 299–300
Ahaz, king, 218
Alexandria Egypt, 31, 265
Alexandrian text, 156
Analytical Study, 4–9
Andrew, disciple, 150, 173, 285, 311
Angels, 139, 142, 158, 178, 234, 348
Anna, Prophetess, 248–49
Anno Domini, 10
Anti-Semitic writing, 154, 268
Antioch, Syria, 25, 80, 98
Antitheses, 209–14
Apocalyptic, in Revelation, 344, 346, 355
    In Second Thessalonians, 330
    Mark's Apocalypse, 173–74
    Sayings, 135
Apocrypha, 1–2

Apostolic Letters and Revelation, Growth Chart, 315
Aramaic language
    In Early Christianity 10–13, 105, 115, 129
    In John's Gospel, 282
    Jesus' Use of, 136–38, 182
Asia Minor, 44, 234, 333 – 334, 344
Assumption of Moses, 337
Assyrian Empire, 52, 218
Attis, 44
Augustus Caesar, 20, 44–45
Autograph Manuscript, 158
Baptism, 65, 296, 335
Barabbas, 38
Basic Tools for Research, 15–17
Beatitudes, 128, 206, 223–24
BC—Before Christ, 10
BCE—Before the Common Era, 10
Beloved Disciple, 15, 281
Bethlehem, 49–50, 52, 193, 234, 285
Bible dictionaries, 16
Bishop, 332–33, 340, 343
Bishop of Rome, 202
Books of Moses, 27, 31–32, 47
Byzantine text, 156
Caesar, 20, 44–45, 270, 287, 388–89
Caesarean text, 157
Canon, Christian, 324–25, 336–37, 339, 341–43
    Apostolic authority, 336, 340, 341
    Institutional authority, 340
    Irenaeus' evidence, 343
    Marcion's influence, 343
    Personal authority, 340
    Spiritual authority, 332, 340
Carpenter, 12, 50–51, 104, 161
Centurion, 172–73, 182, 222
Cephas, disciple, 70, 78, 80, 340
Christology, 86, 169, 184, 303, 312–13
Church ministers, 8
Circumcision, 46, 49, 68, 70–71, 74, 383
Citation method, 9
Civil war, 38–40
Colossae, 91
Colossians, Letter to, **91–93**
    Authorship, 60–63, 92
    Christ and Creation, 92–93
    Role of Timothy, 92
    Scribal Dictation, 92
Comforter, see Paraclete
Commentaries on the New Testament, 16
Common Era, 10
Communion meal, 25, 29, 87, 296–97

Concordances, 16–17
Conversion to Christianity, 76, 256–58
Conversion to Judaism, 46
Coptic, 367
Corinth, 59
Corinthians, First Letter to, 61, **86–89**, 90, 96, 324
    Loving unity, 88–89
    Spiritual Gifts, 88–89
    Structure of, 86–87
    Wisdom in, 87
    Women's role, 87
    Worship Practices, 87–89
Corinthians, Second Letter to, 57, 86, **89–90**
    Biographical information, 89–90
    Opponents of Paul, 89
    Paul's ascension experience, 89–90
    Separate sections, 89
    Weakness and power, 90
Covenant, 24, 72–74, 174–75, 320
Crucifixion
    Absence of in Q, 138–39, 144
    In the Gospel of John, 304–5, 335–36
    In the Gospel of Luke, 250, 252, 267, 269
    In the Gospel of Mark, 159, 162, 172, 182
    Paul's understanding of, 64–65, 87, 95–96
Cybele, 44
David, King, 33, 39, 51
Daniel, prophet, 138, 344
Deacon, 326, 332, 340
Dead Sea scrolls, 35–37, 72
Decapolis, 258
Demeter, 42–43
Deutero-Canonical, 1
Deuteronomy, 27, 75, 180
Diakonos, 332
Didymus Judas Thomas, 368
Divine inspiration, 6–9, 310, 332–33, 336
Domitian Caesar, 352
Edomites, 34
Elders, Christian, 257, 332–33
Elder, the, in the Letters of John, 325–27
Eleusis, 42–44, 46
Elijah, prophet, 115, 164–65, 286
Elisha, prophet, 116
Elizabeth, mother of John the Baptist, 247–48, 253
Emperor worship, 44–46, 153
Enoch, 337
Ephesians, Letter to the, **327–30**
    Authorship of, 60, 327
    Social teachings in, 328–30
    Theological ideas in, 327

Ephesus, 59
Episkopos, 332
Eschatology, 93, 96
   In the Gospel of John, 305, 308–10
   In the Gospel of Luke, 266–67
   In the Gospel of Mark, 178–79
   In the Gospel of Matthew, 222–23
   In the Q Source, 139–40
Essenes, 35–37, 40
Evangelion, 11
Evangelical, 70
Evangelists
   Luke as Historian 239
   Mark's perspective 150–54, 175–76
   Redaction criticism used by Matthew, 199, 202–3, 215
   Sources used by, 103–4, 111
   Symbols for Adapted from Revelation, 349
Exodus, 27, 38, 297, 306
Exorcisms, 104, 107, 115, 118, 160, 183
Eyewitnesses
   Biblical Authors as, 7
   John's Use of 15, 281, 299
   Paul as, 262
   Luke's Discussion of, 10–13
Ezekiel, prophet, 344, 348–49
Faith healing, 106
Farrer Hypothesis, 120
Form Criticism, 134–36
Gaius Caesar, 45
Galatians, Letter to the, 61, 68, **70–81**, 98–99
   Abraham allegory, 71–74, 80, 85
   Biographical information, 76–81, 94, 283
   Christ's death, 64–65, 71, 79
   Circumcision in, 70–71, 74, 76
   Date of origin, 61
   Faith in Christ, 71–77, 80
   Jewish People in, 70, 72–76, 79–80, 98–99
   Justification, 71
   Righteousness, 71–73, 75
   Torah Law, 71–81, 207, 261
Galilee
   Historical Background of, 51–52
   In the Gospel of Mark, 150–51, 158
   In the Gospel of Matthew, 177, 193, 195–97
   Jesus' Healings in, 104, 115
   Political Conditions in, 33–34, 49–52
   Signs Source Locations in, 109, 111
   Women Accompanying Jesus from, 252–53
Gamaliel, Rabbi, 58
Genesis, 27, 71–73, 319, 321
Gentiles

Christian Conversion of, 46–49, 185, 244, 257–62
In the Gospel of John, 306–7
In the Letter to the Ephesians, 328
Jewish Law and 29, 45–48, 66, 68, 266–68, 273
Matthew's Perspective on, 223, 226–25
Paul, Apostle to the, 58, 70–83, 98–99
Glory, Book of, 279
Glossolalia, 88
Gnostic Christianity, 367, 369–70
Gnosticism, 367
God's revelation
Of the Bible, 1–3, 6–9
Paul's Reception of, 93–94
Peter's Reception of, 261–62
God-fearer, 46
Gospel of Thomas, 13–14, 121–22, 139, 309, 367–73
Gospel parallels, 17, 123, 199–202, 259
Gospel Sources, Growth Chart, 101
Great Mother of life, 44
Greece, 12, 20–21, 41–42, 47
Greek language, 1, 3, 10–13, 16–17, 21, 118–21
Greek Translation of the Hebrew Bible, 192, 219, 255, 320
Griesbach Hypothesis, 119–20
Hagar, 72
Hearth religion, 41–42, 44
Heaven 35, 90–92, 132, 297
Hebrew Bible, 2, 51, 320–21, 323, 335–37, 342–44
Hebrews, letter to, 3, 9, 59–61, **319–22**, 345–50, 353
Christian Jewish comparison, 320–21
Heavenly temple, 321–22
Melchizedek priesthood, 321
Sacrifice, 321–22
Hedge for the Torah, 210–14
Hell, 35, 65, 223
Herod Antipas, 33–34, 49–50, 238, 270
Herod the Great, 33–34, 50, 52
Herodians, Men of Herod's party, 30, 33, 181
High Priest, 37, 39, 320–21
Iconium, 257
Idumeans, 34
Iesus Nazarenus Rex Iudaeorum, 288
Indo-European languages, 12
Inerrant, 158
Interlinear translations of the New Testament, 16
Ioudaios, Ioudaioi, 51
Isaiah, prophet, 36, 216–19, 251, 323
Isis, 43
James, Jesus' brother, 78–81, 99, 161–62, 164
James, letter of, 162, **317–19**
Authorship of, 162, 317–18
Jewish teachings in, 318–19

Sections of, 318
Wealth discussed in, 319
Jeremiah, prophet, 200, 202, 319, 323
Jerusalem temple
    Corban donations to, 211
    Destruction of, 24–25, 39–40, 173
    Essenes and, 35
    Letter to the Hebrews and, 320–22
    Priests of, 26, 37
    Purity Requirements of, 29–31
    Sacrifices in, 23–24, 28, 37–38
    Taxes for, 23, 26
Jesus
    Baptism of, 103–4, 129, 150–52, 194, 236
    Baptism by, 295–96
    Historical, 79, 94
    King of Israel, 285
    Physician, 104, 107–8, 163, 234
    Prophet, 108, 111–12, 115–16, 162–67
    Rabbi, 285
    Sacrificial death of, 40, 321
    Son of David, 166, 217, 220
    Son of God, 44, 85, 167, 172–73, 220–22, 321
    Son of Man, 138–43, 164–79, 221–22, 265–69, 304
    Virgin birth of, 217–19, 235
    Wisdom of God, 14, 285–85, 303, 309
    Word of God, 282–83, 292–93
Jewish creed, 23
Jewish Law, see Torah Law
Joanna, wife of Chuza, 252, 254
John, disciple, 4, 78–80, 94, 99
John, First Letter of, 3, 291, 282, 309, **322–25**, 340
    Conflict over Jesus' nature, 322–23
    Doctrinal definition in, 323–25
    Spirit inspiration, 309, 322–24, 340
John, Gospel of, 3, 14, 109–18, 134, 166, **279–313**
    Analytical Assessment Tasks and Exercises, 364–65
    Author, 280–82
    Beginning of the Gospel, 283–85
    Bibliography, 313–14
    Book of Signs in, 279
    Book of Glory in, 279
    Bread of Life in, 297, 306
    Christian Community in, 291–93, 306–7
    Controversies in, 307
    Date of Composition, 282–83
    Death of Jesus in, 295, 304–5, 310–12
    Discourses of Jesus in, 282–83, 298–303
    Duality in, 289–90
    Ending of the Gospel, 286–87
    Eschatology, 305

About the Author

Stevan L. Davies, a graduate of Duke University (B.A.) and Temple University (M.A., Ph.D.), is Professor of Religious Studies at Misericordia University, Dallas, Pennsylvania. He is the author of numerous articles and books about the origins of Christianity including *The Gospel of Thomas and Christian Wisdom, The Secret Book of John: The Gnostic Gospel Annotated and Explained, The Revolt of the Widows: The Social World of the Apocryphal Acts, The Infancy Gospels of Jesus,* and *Jesus the Healer: Possession, Trance and the Origins of Christianity.* Dr. Davies has appeared in documentary television programs for the British Broadcasting Corporation, the History Channel, the National Geographic Channel and the Arts and Entertainment Network.

www.ingramcontent.com/pod-product-compliance
Lightning Source LLC
Chambersburg PA
CBHW071225230426
43668CB00011B/1304

Source Criticism, 155
Speaking in tongues, 64, 88
Standard citation format, 9
Synagogue, 32–33, 39–41, 45–49, 196, 307
Synoptic Gospels, 118, 199, 279, 303–4, 370
Syria, 58, 78, 104, 192, 282
Talmud, 31
Tax collectors, 23, 38, 191–92
Ten Commandments, the, 28, 179, 262
Tenant farmers, 25–26, 38, 127, 130
Text Criticism, 155–58
Theophilus, 9–10, 14, 241, 247
Thessalonians, First Letter to the, **69–70**
    Date of origin, 61
    Rapture event, 70
    Return of the Lord, 69, 96
Thessalonians, Second Letter to the, 60–61, **330–31**
    Apocalypticism, 330–31
    Authorship of, 330
Tiberius Caesar, 20, 44
Timothy, First Letter to (see Pastoral Epistles)
Timothy, Second Letter to (see Pastoral Epistles)
Titus, General, 25
Titus, Letter to (see Pastoral Epistles)
Torah, 2, 27–35
Torah Law, Jewish Law, Law of Moses
    In Relation to Roman Society, 45–49
    In the Gospel of John, 294–95, 305–6
    In the Gospel of Luke and Acts, 257–73
    In the Gospel of Mark, 25–35, 179–80
    In the Gospel of Matthew, 191–92, 206–13, 215
    In the Letter of James, 318–19
Jewish interpreters of, 39–40
Paul's Views of, 66–87, 93, 95–99
Transjordan, 104, 196
Translations, 16–17, 85, 158, 280, 344
Twelve, the, 160, 252–54
Two Document Hypothesis, the, 118–20, 198
Tyre, 128, 258
Western Text, 157
Widows, 251, 253, 333
Wisdom of God, 14, 87, 284–85, 303, 309
Zealots, 38–40
Zechariah, father of John the Baptist, 37, 235, 248
Zechariah, prophet, 344
Zeus, 43

Heavenly Jerusalem, 350
Interpretations of, 348, 352–55
Organization of, 344–47
Persecutions by Rome, 344, 348, 350–52
Sevenfold Patterns in 346–47
Spiritual Letters, 344–45
Symbolism in, 345–55
Ritual categories, 28
Roman Catholic Church, 1
Roman
    Coin, 21–22, 44–45, 251–52
    Commerce, 21, 25–26
    Empire, 19–23, 32–33, 41, 44–47, 49–50
    Law, 21–23, 26, 45, 49, 142, 153–54, 288
    Religion, 41–47
    Roads, 21, 48
    Society, 19–23, 44–53
    Taxation, 22–26, 34, 38
Romans, Letter to the, 62, **81–86**
    Date of origin, 62
    Faith in, 83–84, 86
    Gentiles and the Law, 81–83
    Holy Spirit, 83–86
    Judaism in, 83
    Justification, 81, 84
    Righteousness, 82–86
    Sacrifice for expiation, 84
    Salvation of Israel, 83
Sadducees, 34–40, 288
Salome, 252, 384
Samaria, 33–34, 51–52, 257
Sanhedrin, 152–53, 288
Sarah, 72
Scribes, 30, 32, 40
Scripture, Inspiration of, 6–9, 332–33
Semitic languages, 12, 282
Sepphoris, 12, 50, 52
Septuagint, 219, 320
Sermon, Contemporary, 1, 32
Sermon on the Mount, 205–15
Servants of the Gospel, 10–13
Shema, 23
Sheol, 35
Shepherd of Hermas, 343
Sidon, 128, 258
Signs Source, 109–12, 297, 303, 307–8
Simeon, 248–49
Simon the Zealot, disciple, 38
Slavery, 65, 85, 91, 256, 329
Solomon, king, 51, 218
Sophia, 284, 303

Christ hymn, the, 90–91
Eschatological reservation, 91
Return of the Lord, 91
Separate sections, 90
Phrygia, 44
Pontius Pilate, 34, 38, 152–53, 195, 238–39, 287–88
Presbyteros, 332
Promised Land, 24, 27
Prophets, Christian
In the Q Source, 122, 126–30, 137, 142
In the Gospel of Mark, 174
As a Source of the Sayings of Jesus, 302, 309–10, 323–24, 330–32
Protestant churches, 1, 8, 91
Proverbs, book of, 92–93, 284
Proverbs, of Jesus, 134, 279
Purity and Impurity, 28–31, 49, 66, 180
Q Sayings Source
Bibliography, 144–45
Christian community, 141–42
Controversies in, 142–42
Date of Origin, 121
Eschatology, 139–40
Holy Spirit, 128–29, 137, 141
Kingdom of God in, 126–28, 130–33, 137
Miracles Sources, Relationship to, 143
Mission, 128–29, 137
Moral Principles, 132–33, 136
Paul, Relationship to, 143–44
Prophets in, 122, 126–31, 137
Q hypothesis, 120–21
Q people described, 122–23, 126–28
Q sayings listed, 123–25
Quelle, 120
Son of Man in, 138–43
Sources of sayings, 128–29, 137
Torah Law in, 140–41
Way of Life
Qumran, 35
Rabbinic Judaism, 30–31, 41, 210
Rabbis, 23, 32, 72, 180
Redaction Criticism, 198–99, 202–3, 207, 214, 227
Resurrection, 34–35, 44, 95
In the Gospel of John, 286–87, 304–5, 311–12
In the Gospel of Luke, 155, 237, 243, 250, 253, 271–73
In the Gospel of Mark, 158–59, 168–69, 172, 177
In the Gospel of Matthew, 155, 194, 220, 222, 225
In the Second Letter of Peter, 338
Revelation to John, **343–55**
Apocalypticism in, 344, 351, 353
Authorship of, 344–45
Ezekiel imagery in, 344

Pastoral Epistles, **331–33**, 339
   Authorship of, 331
   Church leaders in, 332–33
   Faith in, 332
   Women in, 333
Patmos, 344, 348
Paul, Apostle, (See also individual Letters of Paul's)
   Analytical Assessment Tasks and Exercises, 359–60
   Authenticity of Letters, 59–61
   Bibliography, 99–100
   Biography, 22, 40, 57–59, 61–62, 77–79
   Christian community, 46, 49
   Covenant idea, 72–74, 80
   Eschatology, 91, 93, 96
   Gospel of, 62–69, 74, 76–79, 87–89, 94–95
   Judgment in, 82, 97
   Persecutor of Christians, 58, 78
   Physical Appearance of, 58
   Return of the Lord, 91, 96
   Revelation, 74–75, 78, 93–94
   Saul, name, 57
   Significance of Jesus' Death, 58, 64–65, 71, 84, 95–96
   Spirit, 63–65, 73, 76, 84–91
   Torah, 28–29, 46
   Traditions handed on to, 70, 94–95
   Views of Jesus' Life Story, 95
Paul's Letters, Growth Chart
Peasants, 27, 31, 38
Pentateuch, 27
Pericope, 134
Persia, 43, 52, 193
Peter, disciple
   Confession of, 164–70, 200–202
   In the Acts of the Apostles, 260–64, 267–68, 273
   Name of, 70
   Relations with Paul, 78–80
Peter, First Letter of, **333–35**
   Authorship of, 333–34
   Baptism in, 335
   Submissiveness theme, 334–35
Peter, Second Letter of, **337–39**
   Authorship of, 337
   Delay of Jesus' Return, 338–39
   Interpretation of Scripture in, 339
   Vision of the Lord in, 338
Pharisees, 30–33, 35, 39–41
   In the Gospel of Mark, 180–81
   In the Gospel of Matthew, 206–12, 214, 221–22, 224
   In the Q Source 140–42
Philemon, Letter to, 59, 62, **91**
Philippians, Letter to, 62, **90–91**

Prophetic fulfillment, 215–20
Q Source, Relationship to, 226–27
Redaction criticism in, 198–204
Sermon on the Mount in, 205–15
Sources of, 220–21
Special Matthew material, 204–5
Virgin Birth in, 193, 217–19
Matthew, Gospel of, Growth Chart, 189
Mediterranean world, 12
Melchizedek, 321
Messiahs for Essenes, 36
Messianic Age, 40
Miracles of Healing, 103–9, 113, 115, 117–18, 159–60
Miracles Sources, 102–18
    Bibliography, 144–45
    Nature and Healing Miracles, 105–8
    Signs Source in the Gospel of John, 109–12
    Miracle Stories in the Gospel of Mark, 112–14
Mishnah, 31, 211
Mithra, 43–45
Mithraic bull, 43–44
Moses, also see Law of Moses, 27–28, 31–32, 304–6
Mount Sinai, 27, 72, 83, 209
Mystery religion, 41–46
Nag Hammadi, Egypt, 367
Names of the Gospels, 15
Nature Miracles, 105–8, 115, 136
Nazareth in Galilee, 12, 49–52, 108–9, 193, 234
Nero Caesar, 351–52
Noah, 27, 131–32, 335
Numbers, 27, 304, 306–7
Number of the Beast, 352
Old Testament, see also Hebrew Bible, 1–2
Onesimus, 91
Oral Torah, 30–31, 34–35
Oral tradition, 11–12, 113, 134, 163, 198, 370
Orthodox Christianity, 370
Osiris, 43–44
Palestine, 23–26, 38, 45, 152–53, 218
Palestinian economy, 25–27
Parables of Jesus, 134–35
    In the Gospel of Luke, 246, 249, 251
    In the Gospel of Mark, 165, 167, 171–72
    In the Gospel of Matthew, 197, 216
Paraclete, 48, 291, 295, 303, 309
Parenesis, 87
Parthian Empire, 20, 26
Passover
    Festival, 28, 38, 104, 109, 197, 285
    Meal, 25
    Sacrifice, 25, 304

    Jesus' family in, 161–64, 170
    Jewish groups in, 19–41
    John the Baptist in, 150–52, 164
    Messianic secret, 159, 164, 171
    Miracles in, 112–14, 159, 170–72, 174, 176
    Miracles Sources, 112–14, 176, 183
    Misunderstandings in, 160–67
    Organization of, 159–60
    Parables in, 165, 167, 171–72, 176
    Paul, Relationship to, 160, 162, 171, 175, 179–80, 184–86
    Place of Origin, 150
    Pontius Pilate in, 152–54, 173
    Q Source, Relationship to, 183–84
    Sources of, 176–77
    Resurrection appearances, 155, 158, 177–78
    Those who understand Jesus, 172–73
    Torah Law in, 175, 179–80, 184
Mark, Gospel of, Growth Chart, 147
Mary and Martha, 252
Mary Magdalene, Mary of Magdala, 108, 155, 236, 252, 254
Mary, mother of James, 252
Mary, mother of Jesus, 161–62, 193, 217–20, 234–35, 247–48
Mary, mother of John Mark, 326
Matthew, Gospel of, 155, **191–229**, 244, 259, 282
    Analytical Assessment Tasks and Exercises, 362–63
    Antitheses in, 209–14
    Author of, 197–98
    Beginning of the Gospel, 192–94
    Bibliography, 228–29
    Christian community, 223–24
    Christian obedience, 215
    Christian rivals, 206–7
    Controversies in, 224–25
    Date of, 192
    Ending of the Gospel, 194–96
    Eschatology in, 222–23
    Hypocrisy discussed in, 207–8, 214–15, 222, 224
    Jesus as Messiah in, 193, 200–201, 208, 215–17, 219–20
    Jesus' birth in, 192–94
    Jesus' death in, 222
    Jesus' life in, 221–22
    Jewish rivals, 207–9
    John the Baptist in, 194
    Kosher practices, 210–11
    Mark, Gospel of, Relationship to, 227–28
    Miracles Sources, Relationship to, 225–26
    Organization of, 196–98
    Paul, Relationship to, 227
    Pharisees discussed, 206–14, 221–22, 224
    Place of Origin, 192
    Pontius Pilate in, 195.

Luke, Gospel of, 3, 9–15, 155, 120, **233–75,** 343
    Analytical Assessment Tasks and Exercises, 363–64
    Author of, 3, 234, 254–56
    Beginning of the Gospel, 9–15, 234–35
    Bibliography, 274–75
    Birth of Jesus in, 234–35, 244, 247–48
    Compromises in, 259–62
    Date of, 234
    Ending of the Gospel, 236–39
    Eschatology, 266–67
    Financial support discussed in, 254
    Holy Spirit in, 243–44
    Jesus' death in, 242–43
    Jesus' life in, 240–41
    John the Baptist in, 235–36
    Mark, Gospel of, Relationships to, 271–72
    Matthew, Gospel of, Relationships to, 272–74
    Miracles Sources, Relationship to, 269
    Mission to the Jews in, 258–59
    Passages featuring women in, 248–56
    Paul, Relationships to, 270–71
    Pontius Pilate in, 238–39
    Q Source, Relationships to, 269–70
    Responsibilities of Wealth, 246–47
    Resurrection in, 237, 243, 253, 263, 266
    Salvation history in, 239
    Special Luke materials, 244–45
    Travel theme, 256–58
    Women in, 247–56
Luke, Gospel of, and Acts, Growth Chart, 231
Lydia, 246, 255–56
Macedonia, 59
Magnificat, 235
Mandaeans, 235
Manuscripts, 85, 103, 155–58, 367
Map of Palestine, vi
Mark, Gospel of, 119–21, **149–87,** 283–86
    Alternative endings, 157–58
    Analytical Assessment Tasks and Exercises, 361–62
    Apocalyptic in, 159, 173–74
    Beginning of the Gospel, 150–51
    Bibliography, 186–87
    Central section of, 159, 165, 167–72
    Christian Community in, 173–74, 178–79, 181–83, 185
    Controversies in, 159, 181–82
    Date of Composition, 149–50
    Disciples in, 159–72, 175, 179, 181–82
    Ending of the Gospel, 152–55, 157–58
    Eschatology in, 178–79
    Identity of Jesus in, 164–73
    Jesus' death in, 152–55, 165–66, 172–75, 176–82

Holy Spirit in, 286, 291–92, 295–96, 298–303, 307, 309
Identity of Jesus in, 166, 280–81, 284–85, 288–97, 304–5
John the Baptist in, 286
Judgment in, 293–94, 300
Life of Jesus in, 288–98
Living Water, 296–97, 306
Luke, Gospel of, Relationships to, 312–13
Mark, Gospel of, Relationships to, 311–12
Matthew, Gospel of, Relationships to, 312
Messengers of Jesus in, 300
Paul, Relationships to, 310–11
Pontius Pilate in, 287–88
Q Source, Relationships to, 308–10
Resurrection of Jesus in, 286–87, 304–5, 311–12
Salvation in, 290–91
Sources of, 109–18, 307–8
Torah Law in, 305–6
Unity in, 289, 291–92
John, Gospel of, Growth Chart, 277
John, Second Letter of, **325–26**
John, Third Letter of, **326–27**
Joseph of Arimathaea, 172–73, 182
Joseph of Nazareth, 193, 217, 234, 247–48, 285
Judas, disciple, 162
Judas, brother, 162, 335
Jude, Letter of, 162, 199, **335–37**
  Authorship of, 162, 335
  Scriptures used in, 336–37
  Spirit inspiration in, 336
Judea, 28, 33–34, 38, 51–52, 256–57
Julius Caesar, 44–45
King James Version, 289
King of the Jews, 33, 154, 287–88, 336
Kingdom of God, 96, 126–33, 137–41, 173, 239, 309
Kore-Persephone, 42–44
Kykeon, 42
Kyrios, 24
Landlords, 25–26
Last Supper, 174, 281, 295–96
Latin language, 12, 21, 150, 288
Law of Moses, see Torah Law
Lawyers, 29, 33
Letters of Clement, 343
Levite Priests, 24, 321
Leviticus, 27–28, 180, 261
Lists of miracles, 13, 103–18
Lists of sayings, 13–14, 118–44, 367–73
Locusts, 36–37
Logos, 283–84, 303, 313
Lord's Prayer, 138, 141
Lord's Supper, 25, 64, 94